# Roots and Fruits of Scottish Culture

## Scottish identities, history and contemporary literature

Edited by
IAN BROWN
and JEAN BERTON

Occasional Papers: Number 19
Association for Scottish Literary Studies

Published by
**Scottish Literature International**
Scottish Literature
7 University Gardens
University of Glasgow
Glasgow G12 8QH

Scottish Literature International is an imprint of
the Association for Scottish Literary Studies

**www.asls.org.uk**

ASLS is a registered charity no. SC006535

First published 2014

A CIP catalogue for this title
is available from the British Library

ISBN 978-1-908980-07-6

ALBA | CHRUTHACHAIL
ASLS acknowledges the support of Creative Scotland
towards the publication of this book

# Contents

# Contents (continued)

# Introduction: The many versions of identity and history

IAN BROWN

In October 2011 the Société francaise d'études écossaises and the Association for Scottish Literary Studies held a joint conference in St Etienne with the theme 'Roots and fruits of contemporary Scotland: literature and society'. This conference included many lively and stimulating papers. Inspired by those, the editors of this volume proposed to the ASLS academic publishing wing, Scottish Literature International, that a book derived from some of the interrelated papers then presented might be produced. This would be based on this volume's theme, *Roots and Fruits of Scottish Culture: Scottish identities, history and contemporary literature*. The aim was to allow contributors to develop their papers, to rewrite and extend them in order that we might produce a coherent volume. This collection is the result.

Both the title of the original conference and of this book reflect the editors' concern with exploring varieties of ways in which roots embedded in contemporary Scottish life and letters bear fruit, often in surprising ways. Of course, it is to make no exceptionalist or arcane claim to say that the generation of ideas, themes and attitudes through the centuries is intrinsic to any society. What fascinated the editors was the particularities of the examples being offered by the individual authors collected in this volume, the ways in which they perceived a process by which at this particular moment in Scottish culture and history, earlier identities were being re-examined and re-presented in literature, and the ways in which both personal and cultural histories were being redefined and reconsidered in contemporary life and literature. It is these themes of re-examination, re-presentation, redefinition and reconsideration that this book explores. Taken together, its chapters offer a series of angles and perspectives from which the re-creation and reimagination of Scottish culture – its identities and its tropes – have been, and are being, developed by a range of leading Scottish writers.

This process is not confined, however, to literature, although that remains the central concern here. Chapters are included on the visual arts and the

iconography of tartan. Both these aspects of contemporary Scottish identities dynamically engage with the ways in which both scholars and members
of the general public see Scottish identities embedded in contemporary life.
In order to highlight the structure of this volume as it addresses its themes,
the editors have opted to provide three subheadings for chapter groupings.
These are 'Performing identities', 'Poetic roots and identities' and 'The fruits
of fiction, myth and history'. The first considers the ways in which different
aspects of Scottish identities can be seen as stagings or performances. The
second addresses the work of contemporary poets as they reflect on identities from both personal and national cultural perspectives. The third
considers ways in which twentieth-century and later novelists have questioned Scottish history and related myths of Scottish life and embedded
them in their work.

The first chapter of the 'Performing identities' section by Trish Reid is
'"Breid, barley-bree an paintit room": history, identity and utopianism in
Lyndsay's *Thrie Estaitis* and Greig's *Glasgow Girls*'. Its title quotes from
Hamish Henderson's great 'Freedom Come All Ye', a song of political aspir-
ation, searching for liberated identities in an international context. Reid
uses a close discussion of two highly popular plays separated by centuries,
David Lyndsay's *Ane Satyre of the Thrie Estaitis* (1552) and David Greig's
*Glasgow Girls* (2012) to explore, in her words, 'the implications of Henderson's
utopian rhetoric, and its emphasis on pleasure' (1). This she does as she
considers Scottish theatre's continuing active contribution to 'the reimagining and refashioning of Scotland' (1). She explores, drawing on a wide
range of thinkers including Richard Schechner and Michel Foucault – and
paying due attention to modern discussion of the nature of site-specific or
site-sympathetic dramatic production – a number of ways in which the
theatre she examines has 'performed' Scottish identities. Early in her chapter
she identifies three key aspects of this performance. One is theatre's role as
part of an oppositional tradition, allowing artists to articulate Scotland's
grievances. The second is the way that 'participation in the joyful is in large
part the means by which contemporary Scottish theatre practitioners have
conjured a vision of a better Scotland' (2). Thirdly, she argues that the
Scottish theatre tradition has emphasised politicised populism – and pleasure
– grounded in its historic dramatic roots. Her engaging and complex discussion examines how Scottish theatre has become so rich and dynamic as it

'conceptualises its own history, and [...] thinks about its relationship with Scottish culture in the broader context' (3).

Camille Manfredi's chapter considers other aspects of performed identities in her discussion of the work of Ross Sinclair, David Mach, Ross Gillespie, Tricia Malley and Calum Colvin. Her chapter examines recent interactions between performance, visual arts and literature as these artists 'use and abuse, figure or disfigure the nation's iconic literary past' (18). Manfredi analyses a range of their work, opening up intriguing questions about the relationship of the fruits of their art to that art's underlying roots. In some cases, too, she draws attention to the ways in which visual arts categories are blurred by the engagement of some of her exemplars with performance. She discusses in detail, for instance, Ross Sinclair's *Real Life Rocky Mountain* (1996) in which the artist performed, with his back to the audience/exhibition attenders at the CCA in Glasgow, a variety of twentieth-century Scottish songs – from sentimental or comic music hall to punk and post-punk music songs – amid a constructed scenery of kitsch Scottish icons, his body tattooed 'Real Life' across his upper back. She argues that Sinclair and others probe in their work 'Scotland's difficult handling of its historicity/contemporaneity dialogic' (17). For Sinclair, as for other artists Manfredi discusses, there is an alienating distance or perhaps a Brechtian *Verfremdungseffekt* between modern Scotland in its many manifestations and the icons that reflect so many different, sometimes kitsch, varieties of 'Scotland'. As Manfredi shows, there are continuing 'tensions between the ancient and the new, absence and presence, reality and artifice, Romanticism and the (to many, necessary) deromanticising of the national imagination [...] where intertextual playfulness often comes to blur the frontiers between homage and self-mockery' (18). One such example she cites – in which not only literature, but the body of the writer engages in performance – is that of Janice Galloway in Malley and Gillespie's 2009 exhibition of lexiconographic collages, *As Others See Us*, at the Scottish Parliament. Galloway sits, two sheep at her feet, facing the camera wrapped in a tartan plaid, illustrating her chosen text, 'Ca' the yowes to the knowes', both paying homage to and ironising her relationship to her literary history and creative roots. This exhibition was part of the 2009 Homecoming Scotland programme of events which also included David Mach's *Robert Burns Match Heads*, a set of two life-size match-head sculptures, one of which was later burned at the opening of the St Andrews poetry festival StAnza, a performance literalising the relationship between the poet's surname and one of its meanings. Calum Colvin's three-dimensional digital collages, Manfredi goes on to argue, similarly defy 'the laws of official art only to revalidate them and finally offer new visual and mental patterns for Scotland's greatest literary and identity myths' (21). Her chapter discusses in a stimulating manner the creative interaction of contemporary visual/performance arts with their past literature and history and the ways in which the interaction of different perceptions of identities, iconographies and intentionalities may be contradictory, constantly questioning and renegotiating versions of Scotland's past.

While the first two chapters in the first section relate to performance within more or less conventional performance contexts – theatres, playfields or galleries – Ian Brown's chapter addresses the ways in which varieties of Scottish identities have been performed through the wearing of tartan. His chapter draws on the research he and others have published in his 2010 collection *From Tartan to Tartanry: Scottish Culture, History and Myth* and makes the point that – in parallel with the theatrical, literary and visual performances discussed in the previous two chapters – to wear tartan is to perform versions, often theatricalised, of 'Scottishness'. Brown draws on a wide range of historical sources to illustrate that, far from being a kitsch nineteenth-century addition to Scottish iconography with simple inauthentic Romantic implications, tartan has been and is multivalent. He exposes the attacks on tartan and its meanings by Hugh Trevor-Roper, Tom Nairn and the *Scotch Reels* group as themselves deeply flawed, historically inaccurate and mythical in content. Rather than being simple-minded iconography, Brown suggests that tartan and the wearing of the kilt is a continuing, vibrant and vitally alive 'rich resource for the expression of varied perceptions of Scottish identities' (27). His chapter makes the case that both the historical inaccuracy and limiting attitudinising of negative critics of tartan's meanings fail 'to grasp the positive energy and vitality of tartan and the kilt – both in the past and currently – in expressing, indeed performing, significant positive aspects of Scottish culture' (27). His argument concludes that twenty-first-century uses and meanings mark tartan and the kilt's 'continuing relevance and modernity, even postmodernity' (27). Just as the previous two chapters argue for the variousness of the ways in which theatre and the visual arts perform Scottish identities, Brown's chapter considers the case that in daily life and in many different social and cultural contexts, the tartan continues, with its strict but flexible grid patterns and infinite range of colours, to reflect and embody a wide range of Scottish identities, some paradoxical, but all evolving, all engaging with aspects of Scotland's past and contemporary life and, directly or indirectly, its literature and history.

The second section of this volume – 'Poetic roots and identities' – is more directly focused on the roots and fruits of Scottish literature; indeed it largely, though not exclusively, focuses on the fruits of recent work by poets. It opens with Karyn Wilson Costa's *'New Poems, Chiefly in the Scottish Dialect*: "A sly wink to the master"'. Here, Costa analyses in detail a number of poems included in Robert Crawford's *New Poems, Chiefly in the Scottish Dialect* (2009), the anthology of twelve contemporary Scottish poets marking the two hundred and fiftieth anniversary of Robert Burns's birth. She discusses the implications of her analysis, considering the ways in which the collection reflects both an anxiety of influence – and resistance to that anxiety – and the creative and politico-cultural implications of the language choices made by the poets under discussion. As she observes, Crawford himself 'justifies the allusion to the title of the 1786 Kilmarnock edition of Robert Burns's poetry as "a way of keeping faith with a persistent sense of poetic language, with Scottish accents, and with the art of verse. It is, if you like, a sly wink to the master"' (40). She argues that each poet, while finding her or his own creative path and appropriate linguistic registers, also expresses continuity with Burns and, behind him, of course, Robert Fergusson. In their engagement with language(s), she identifies the poets as participating 'in an ideological debate on the status of Scots and its "legitimacy" and the "authority" to voice Scottishness and Scotland' (41). Each poet she sees as rejecting the view once held that Burns's English poetry was inadequate as she or he engages a linguistic range that includes, and extends in some ways beyond, Scots and English. Costa makes the point that

> Underpinning Crawford's collection is the idea that choosing to write, or not to write, in Scots is much less of a nationalist or a political statement and more of an aesthetic one, one which continues the conversation with other poets in which Burns actively engaged in his poetry; by looking outward, Scots is employed as a resource to

> address other fundamental issues, thereby raising the profile of Scots
> in an international context. (41)

At the heart of her chapter is Costa's conception that 'Scotland has arguably always been a demotically energised place to write, where poets express themselves in a vivid, direct, colloquial style' (45). Just as Burns revelled in both the high-flown and debunking irreverence, so the poets she discusses, in her view, demonstrate a capacity to address topics of serious import and yet often do so in an ironic and humorous manner. As for language usage, Costa contrasts, for example, Douglas Dunn's poetic choices as 'a Scot who writes in the English-language-with-a-Scottish-accent, that is, in my mother tongue' (43), with Liz Lochhead's raising of the issue of language ownership. As Costa says, 'Mixing high and low language and high- and lowbrow cultural references, Lochhead rejoices in the debunking tradition in Scottish literature, and irreverently makes a case for the use of colloquial Scots in literary texts' (48). Costa makes clear that, while Burns is now a historical figure, her chosen poets – whichever form of Scotland's languages they employ, whether literary, urban demotic, Scottish-accented English, 'dictionary Scots' or Scottish Standard English – make confident use, as cultural roots for their own work, of what his aesthetic and linguistic choices embody for them now.

Two of the leading poets included in Crawford's anthology, Liz Lochhead and Jackie Kay, are the focus of Margery Palmer McCulloch's chapter, 'Bards and radicals in contemporary Scottish poetry: Liz Lochhead, Jackie Kay, and an evolving tradition'. McCulloch reminds us that these poets are also dramatists of high distinction. The initial discussion in her chapter addresses what McCulloch sees as a distinctive tradition among the many traditions of Scottish literature. She discusses what she sees as a particular approach in Scottish poetry, one she identifies as both 'a "bardic" and a "radical" approach to the role of poet' (54). She goes on to discuss the nature of this approach, making the case that

> in the poetry of the generation of writers who came after Morgan,
> this bardic, radical (both ideologically and aesthetically) and historic-
> ally male approach to the poet's role has to a significant extent been
> taken over by female poets such as Liz Lochhead and Jackie Kay.
> (54–55)

After briefly discussing aspects of Lochhead's poetry, McCulloch engages in a detailed discussion of her linguistic and dramatic achievement represented in her exploration of Scottish history in *Mary Queen of Scots Got Her Head Chopped Off* (1987). McCulloch notes that Lochhead's 'play is itself very different from what one might call an endorsement-of-historical-reality drama' (57). She might have added, of course, that such a quizzical approach to historical 'truth' was common with the work of many other dramatists after the pioneering production of Stewart Conn's *The Burning* (1971). McCulloch points to Lochhead's eclectic approach, employing varied presentational styles among which she identifies music, dance, pictorial detail, anachronistic costuming and interchangeability of characters. Of course, we are aware that such presentational styles are to be found elsewhere in Scottish drama of the decade and a half before the writing of *Mary Queen of Scots* ... They are found not least in the work of Communicado, the company that produced the play, and its director, Gerry Mulgrew, and, pre-eminently, in the dramaturgy of John McGrath, but also in the dramaturgy of Conn, C. P. Taylor and Ian Brown, in such individual plays as, for example, Taylor's *Columba* (1973), Conn's *Thistlewood* (1975) and Brown's *Mary* (1977), problematising, interrogating and having the audience question any concept of a single historical 'truth' through presentational experimentation and variety. McCulloch, nonetheless, rightly pays tribute to Lochhead's great achievement in *Mary Queen of Scots* ..., employing what McCulloch sees as Brechtian dramaturgy. In then moving on to discuss Jackie Kay's work, McCulloch reminds us of Kay's 'unusual upbringing and identity situation' (60). She celebrates the confidence Kay has derived from these and her bardic and radical non-conformity, which, McCulloch argues, 'has enabled her to speak so powerfully, and yet so lyrically as well as humorously of less happy instances of being "off colour", of not fitting into what another Scottish poet Angela McSeveney called the "pre-arranged pigeonholes" of society' (60). In Kay's case, as with Lochhead's, while McCulloch briefly mentions the poetry – and Kay's novel- and memoir-writing – she focuses on one of her plays, in this case Kay's BBC Radio Three play, *Lamplighter* (2007). Written to commemorate the abolition of slavery, this explores in a number of voices women's individual experiences of this iniquity. McCulloch's close discussion of the play and its re-exposure of what has often in Scottish culture been hidden history is illuminating and insightful. McCulloch's chapter reminds us of the depth and range of both Lochhead and Kay in writing across genre, gender and cultural boundaries, questioning history and the identities 'history' seems to underpin. McCulloch makes a clear case for our appreciation of both women's radical and bardic role as they represent a shift of authority in the tradition of which McCulloch reminds us. Where in an interview three years before she wrote *Mary Queen of Scots* ... Lochhead could, while expressing her admiration for the work of Hugh MacDiarmid, distance herself from it, saying 'I think it's because it is so male and bardic in the old priestly kind of didactic tradition',[1] McCulloch makes a convincing case for Lochhead and Kay's having adopted, adapted, subverted, refreshed and regendered that tradition.

The third chapter in this section, Matthew Pateman's 'Adopting cultures and embodying myths in Jackie Kay's *The Adoption Papers* and *Red Dust Road*', is focused on Kay's poetry and her important 2010 memoir. Pateman begins by discussing his own sense of identity as an adopted child to illuminate the ways in which Kay in the work he discusses, as well as other of her plays, poems and prose, problematises any simple conception of identity or indeed roots. He repudiates his initial response on meeting Kay to constitute himself, with her, as part of a community of adopted people. Rather he explores the ways in which through her writing Kay

> refuses to simplify either herself or her self's relation to history [...] by highlighting the inevitable differences which seeming sameness seeks to occlude, and by gesturing towards the dangers of mythologised histories and communities whose 'truths' also hide the violence of creation inherent in the myth structure. (65–66)

Pateman explores issues of roots and identities to question the conception that hybridity is bound up in an individual like Kay, arguing it is embedded instead in 'the cultures and communities, nations and histories from which she comes, to which she belongs and with which she engages' (67). As he points out, Kay's great skill as a performer of her poetry already creates a crossing of genre boundaries, a form of hybridity, in which she is 'part poet, part performer, part dramatist, part essayist, part novelist, part memoir writer' (68), a professional hybrid. The ways in which Kay crosses boundaries, Pateman implies, not only challenge the nature of those boundaries and the identities and histories those boundaries seek to define, but also combine in new syntheses – as in her poem *The Adoption Papers* – the political and the domestic, the bureaucratic and the personal in a way that makes clear freshly and immediately the political nature of the personal. Both works considered by Pateman are based on biography, which, as he says, is anyway complicated. Kay's biographical complications and her creative reflection on them 'manifest many of the difficulties associated with many of the most seemingly simple assumptions about identity – and biography is only ever the location of identities into meaningful narratives' (70). Kay's living in and between cultures, narratives and performed identities, her adoption of cultures as much as her being adopted, and the directness with which she refuses easy categorisations of what 'history' or 'identity' are, all reflect her creative transgression of genre borders. In this she interrogates and rejects national myths derived, as Pateman puts it, 'from commodified versions of a supposed "real" country and the specific attempts to create a physically "true" version of that country' (74). Pateman concludes:

> Endings, like identity, are not just one kind of thing – identity, nationality, belonging, adoption all are unstable, complicated, contradictory things and Kay's work refuses to simplify itself or her, or her reflections on Scotland, or England (to say nothing of sexuality, motherhood, class and so on). It is hard to make it real. Jackie Kay is an exceptional Scottish writer, and she challenges us to not know what that means. (81)

Pateman's ending of his chapter might serve, in its insistence on identities' instabilities, complications, contradictions and refusals of simplicity, as a summary of the underlying themes explored in the three chapters which comprise this volume's second section. If it is challenging to know what it means to be a 'Scottish writer', it is just as challenging to define the roots of contemporary Scottish poetry and the identities it embodies, expresses and explores – and, as Pateman shows, just as enriching.

The final section of this volume, 'The fruits of fiction, myth and history', is very much focused on the novel. Each chapter constituting it explores in one way or another the ways in which recent Scottish fiction is imbued with history or myth – or both – complicating, and in some sense celebrating, the multiple identities embedded and expressed in the modern Scottish novel. Scott Lyall's chapter, with its thought-provoking title 'The Kailyard's ghost', introduces this section, offering a survey and critique of several of the most important twentieth-century Scottish novels. He focuses on the concept of 'community', which he argues 'is important in twentieth-century Scottish fiction' (82), sometimes by the aporia of community's noticed absence or, more often, by its apparent failure. As part of that exploration of 'community' Lyall addresses ways in which Kailyard has been a recurrent theme in these novels, whether, as in George Douglas Brown's *The House with the Green Shutters* (1901), represented as a demonic dystopia or, as in Jackie Kay's *Trumpet* (1998), as, in a dilute form, a home to which to return. As Lyall acutely observes,

> Community is a contentious, heavily debated term, perhaps wishy-washy, and certainly not easily definable. The influential nature of Benedict Anderson's highly evocative phrase 'imagined communities' has meant that, if previously we were not, we are now highly attuned to seeing community as a narrative, a work of the imagination, every bit as much as, and also influenced by, narratives of the literary imagination. (85)

Within that literary imagination Lyall sees twentieth-century cultural production, including, of course, the novels he explores, as 'plug[ging] the holes in an absent national community, and preced[ing] and inform[ing] politics, in the broadest sense of that term, on what the practice of that community might actually look like' (85). In many of the novels he discusses he also identifies education, so often seen as having a central role in the mythologies of Scotland's cultural identities, as central to community's functioning or failure to function. He provides a historical perspective to his presentation of the ways the mythopoeia of community has developed by identifying three key periods: pre-1979 devolution referendum, post-1979 and the devolutionary 1990s. This framework allows him to relate his insights to the politico-cultural contexts in which the novels he discusses were written. In doing so, he reminds us that 'community' as a singular term is deceptive. Just as this volume insists that Scottishness is not expressed in any single essentialist identity, but is a result of many interrelated performed identities, so Lyall identifies a range of communities, some under threat and some developing, which may be seen as Scottish. Not least among these is community between women. Given this, it is appropriate that he concludes his discussion with Jackie Kay's *Trumpet*, published only two years from the end of the century whose first year saw the appearance of Douglas Brown's great dystopic novel. As Lyall puts it, in some sense echoing themes addressed in Margery Palmer McCulloch's and Matthew Pateman's chapters,

> As the twentieth century turned into a new century, Kay gave us a novel that is a story of diaspora, the exile of identity and the merging of identities; a novel, too, that, without forgetting the ghosts of the past, may allow us to view community in Scotland in the twenty-first century in a more open, diverse light. (94)

His concluding sentence reflects a recurrent and central theme of this volume when he argues 'that the concept of "community" became more and more varied, complex and problematic in Scottish fiction as the twenty-first century and its new political settlement approached' (94).

Where Lyall critically surveys several key twentieth-century novels, Philippe Laplace adopts a different approach, focusing on a single novel, published in the current decade – Karin Altenberg's *Island of Wings* (2011), set in nineteenth-century St Kilda – to explore the interaction of historicity, narration and myths. He begins by observing that

> One of the most conspicuous features when researching Scottish literature […] is the collusion of history and myths. Mythopoeia is indeed a classic occurrence throughout the literature of Scotland. After all, as many scholars have convincingly argued before, history and myths are natural constituents of sentiments of nationhood. (97)

He goes on to note that history and myths have often been used to express feelings of identity or belonging, not least in work set in the Scottish Highlands and islands. His analysis of the novel is illuminating as he explores the way Altenberg has crafted her novel by drawing together what he calls 'a mosaic of accounts' (101), historical, mythical and fictional. His chapter establishes a context of earlier accounts of life on St Kilda before the arrival of Neil Mackenzie to be minister on the island, accompanied by his wife, Elizabeth. Her inability to speak Gaelic means that she remains isolated in that community, having only her husband and the occasional visitor with whom to speak. In Altenberg's use of archival and documentary material about Mackenzie's work and St Kildan life, Laplace suggests 'she keeps confusing the reader and, in a way, clouding the issue: is this a fictional work based on Rev. Mackenzie's life or a very detailed – quasi-historical – document about life on the island and Rev. Mackenzie's achievements?' (102). The effect is that the novelist, by adding entirely fictional material, problematises history, fiction and myth. Further, the novel seems to present Elizabeth Mackenzie's perceptions of her husband's inner turmoils so that its complexity is deepened by questions about the nature of what is perceived as 'reality' and the conditionality of point of view. The novel's title and its imagery emphasise the importance of birds to life on St Kilda at the time the novel is set, the exploitative and often fragile quality of the interaction there of nature and humankind. The conditional fragility Laplace addresses is not only of viewpoint, but of the tenuousness, and sometimes mythopoeia, of understanding of identity, community, history and memory. Laplace's focus on the detail of an individual novel, and the problematics of what 'community', 'identity', ' history' and 'myth' may be, offers a highly specific example to complement those of Lyall as the latter questioned perceptions of the nature of identities and communities in twentieth-century Scottish fictional narratives.

Just as Philippe Laplace's chapter focuses on a single novel to address this volume's themes, so do the next two chapters, those of Morag Munro-Landi and Jean Berton. Munro-Landi, in a witty wordplay, talks of *And the Land Lay Still* (2010) as 'James Robertson's angle' on Scottish society and politics, picking up her cue from the novel. There, in one of the central elements of its narrative, the preparation of an exhibition of the photographs of the father of the leading character, Michael Pendreich, we learn that the exhibition's title will be the 'Angus Angle'. This is the name given to Angus Pendreich's technique, which is represented as taking a photographic perspective on life in Scotland somewhat like that of Cartier-Bresson, focusing on 'bystanders or onlookers rather than on central figures or objects, creating off-centre and sometimes asymmetrical visual narratives' (112). Munro-Landi demonstrates with insight, clarity and helpful detail the ways in which Robertson, through a similar apparent indirection, focuses not on leading politicians and social figures of the years his novel covers, but on those whose life stands by, contributing to public life only in their private ways of living, loving and believing. Thus, like the fictional artist Angus, the novelist Robertson reveals much about the changes, compulsions and developments over the last half-century in Scottish society and politics. Munro-Landi's chapter does this by addressing three main areas. The first 'considers the overall configuration and the multi-level, multi-voiced inter-connected narratives as a challenge for writer and reader' (112); the second, 'representations of social and political identities and their evolution over the decades' (112); the third, 'Robertson's approach to gender issues' (112) and sexuality, particularly homosexuality. Munro-Landi in her chapter achieves a kind of 'Morag's Angle', one which illustrates and illuminates the ways in which Robertson's landmark novel explores the history of contemporary Scotland and the myths of community, identity and nationhood with which that living history and contemporary politics engage. Her chapter in a masterly way demonstrates the range and depth of Robertson's engagement with everyday life and the larger and deeper issues of political and cultural identities that the everyday embodies.

Jean Berton's chapter, like Munro-Landi's, focuses on a single novel with a particular way of seeing Scottish history imbued in and perceived through the everyday. Whereas, however, Robertson's novel is very much concerned with contemporary history, Berton shows that Andrew Greig's *Romanno Bridge* (2008) echoes, re-echoes and modifies 'Scotland', literature and history over a longer time scale, even in some respects from Roman times. The novel itself is a follow-up to Greig's revisiting in *The Return of John Macnab* (1996) of John Buchan's *John Macnab* (1925) and his adventures, but Berton makes the point with great clarity that Greig is not simply chan-nelling or making intertextual cross-reference to one author. The novel is, as Berton shows, intertextual in a variety of ways. For example, Greig presents us with an ornamental garden entitled 'Little Delphi', a clear evocation of Ian Hamilton Finlay's garden, Little Sparta, itself full of intertextual refer-ences, including a kailyard which is, indeed, a cabbage patch. Berton also outlines Greig's debt to, or rather *hommage* to, the work of Walter Scott in using Scotland's history to feed 'the roots of fruitful Scottish literature' (131). He argues that *Romanno Bridge* is a 'narrative of a quest for the essence of Scotland, metaphorically represented by the search for the real Stone of Destiny' (131). To do this, Berton suggests that

> Greig shapes his novel not on a particular historical background, but on the whole of the history of Scotland from Roman days up to the day before the Stone was given back to Scotland by John Major in 1996. More precisely, the Macnab gang's narrative is set in 1995, but the group of heroes are sent to travel through history as far back as the days of the Celts, on the trail of the Stone of Destiny. (132)

The novel's intertextuality – Berton entitles the second section of his chapter 'A narrative encompassing Scottish literature' – is complemented by its vision of history embedded transhistorically in the present. References are made to and action takes place at such immanent sites as Dunstaffnage with its great castle, Dunadd, the place of appointment of the kings of the early-medieval proto-Scottish kingdom of Dalriata, and Finlaggan, the seat from the thirteenth to the fifteenth centuries of the Lords of the Isles. Greig names the place where the stone is found 'Dunsinnan', the modern spelling of Dunsinane, Shakespeare's location for Macbeth's deposition and death. As the fluidity over the centuries of what is history, what is myth, and what are Scottish identities engage Greig, so the idea of 'home' is fluid. As Berton argues, Greig's novel seems to leave a definition of Scotland as

> an unattainable achievement, which accounts for endless questioning. Home is where roots grow: Leo asks, 'Where do you feel at home?', and Kirsty the wanderer answers 'Home doesn't figure big with me, Leo. On good days it's wherever I happen to be'. (140)

Berton implies there are no simple answers in this novel, only layer upon layer of complexity – of historical reference, of intertextuality, of identities.

The final chapter in the third section of this volume – 'The fruits of fiction, myth and history' – by David Clark approaches intertextuality and the transhistorical in a manner different from the last. In considering Paul

Johnston's Quintilian Dalrymple novels, Clark reflects upon the way in which Johnston employs dystopian fiction's motifs and tropes to satirise the present, inlaying that present, offered as the near-future, with transmuted references to both Scotland's present-day and its past. The central myth deconstructed in these novels is embedded in the name of the regime that controls its Edinburgh, the 'Enlightenment'. Arguing that 'James Hogg's *The Confessions of a Justified Sinner* can be seen as a forerunner of the Scottish form of [the dystopian] novel' (146), Clark suggests that the

> dystopian state, in such narratives, generally reinvents or embellishes its own history, especially with regard to supposed foundational myths and the perceived 'duty' of the dystopian government in righting the alleged wrongs of a pre-dystopian past. [...] Thus, the ruling elite in dystopian fiction inevitably sees itself as being a saviour of sorts, and this role is believed to have been forced onto the governing class by the misgovernment of a past regime or a past political or social system. (147)

Clark goes on to link the appearance of these novels between 1997 and 2001 to renewed examination in fiction – and one might add drama – of the nature of Scottish identities as its parliament was in the process of being re-established. Johnston's dystopian novels are set in Edinburgh in the 2020s but Clark sees them as 'fine examples of political satire based on the Edinburgh of the immediate pre- and post-devolution period' (149). Here, Johnston explores a conception of community in which Scotland no longer has a coherent identity and indeed the conception of community has collapsed into those who oppress and those who are oppressed, subjected to what is represented as an Enlightenment cult focused on the powers that be. Against the positive nature of much debate around the impact of the eighteenth-century Scottish Enlightenment and its enduring legacies, Johnston subverts the historical myth of 'Enlightenment'. Corruption of state and individuals marks his novels. While other chapters in this volume argue Scottish identities and histories are the result of performance and creative literary imagining about past roots and their modern fruits, Clark suggests that Johnston's novels represent a salutary alternative imagined possible future history. In this, identity myths are, as this volume's contributors would agree, entirely manipulable, and, in Johnston's case, clearly for no good ends. Clark observes that 'the vision of the UK, of Scotland and of Edinburgh in Paul Johnston's Quintilian Dalrymple novels is rooted as much in a sense of guilt and trepidation about the past as in a sense of uncertainty about the future' (154). The many versions of the past and present, of histories and identities, of roots and fruits, discussed in this volume and embedded in the work of the many authors discussed therein may in a positive way imply a pluralism and openness to the range and variety of possible 'Scotlands'. Clark reminds us that Johnston's Dalrymple novels suggest these possible Scotlands may include forms that, if they came to pass, would be deeply unattractive.

Contemporary Scottish literature continues to insist on the complexity of histories, myths, fictions and identities, and that these all include ambivalence rather than certainty, dark as well as light, and potential for corruption as well as genuine enlightenment. Each of the chapters of this volume explores, as the editors hoped in planning this volume, the varieties of ways in which roots embedded in contemporary Scottish life and letters bear fruit, often in surprising ways. They all remind the reader of the performative and plural nature of identities, histories and creative approaches in contemporary Scottish life and literature.

## Notes

1    Ian Brown, 'Cultural centrality and dominance: the creative writer's view – conversations between Scottish poet/playwrights and Ian Brown' [1984], *International Journal of Scottish Theatre and Screen*, Vol. 4, no. 1 (2011), p. 5

# 1: 'Breid, barley-bree an paintit room': history, identity and utopianism in Lyndsay's *Thrie Estaitis* and Greig's *Glasgow Girls*

TRISH REID

As many readers will recognise, the title quotation comes from Hamish Henderson's much admired lyric 'Freedom Come All Ye', written in 1960 for the peace campaigners at the Holy Loch. In it Henderson articulates his utopian vision for an internationalist Scotland, one that both rejects imperialism, racism and elitism and values pleasure as highly as it does food:

> Sae come a ye at hame wi freedom.
> Never heed whit the houdies croak for Doom.
> In yer hoose aw the bairns o Adam
> Will find breid, barley-bree an paintit room.[1]

This chapter explores the implications of Henderson's utopian rhetoric, and its emphasis on pleasure, specifically in relation to Scottish theatre and the contribution it continues to make to the reimagining and refashioning of Scotland. To borrow Jill Dolan's phrase, I am interested in those 'briefly transcendent moments' that 'spring from alchemy between performers and spectators and their mutual confrontation with a historical present that lets them imagine a different, putatively better future'.[2]

The Performance Studies equivalent of Henderson's 'breid' and 'paintit room' dichotomy is to be found in Richard Schechner's notion of 'the efficacy–entertainment braid'. Schechner, it might be recalled, places entertainment and efficacy at two ends of a continuum, arguing that at 'any historical moment there is movement from one pole to the other as the efficacy–entertainment braid tightens and loosens'.[3] For Schechner the high points of Western theatre occur when the braid is tightest: Classical Athens, Renaissance England, and somewhat conveniently for Schechner's own reputation, New York in the 1960s and 1970s. This idea of efficacy and entertainment operating in productive tension has since been developed and complicated by a number of theatre scholars. James Thompson in his study of the positive impact of applied theatre *Performance Affects* (2009), for instance, has argued persuasively that these functions are best understood not as dichotomous but as continually interweaving. Importantly, Thompson, like Henderson, is interested in mounting a robust defence of pleasure and in insisting that 'participation in the joyful' has the potential to become 'an inspirational force' and consequently can contribute to progressive change.[4] Henderson's insistence on the right to 'barley-bree an paintit room', like Thompson's conviction that performance can 'make visible a better world', are enabling in the context of this present chapter for several reasons.[5] Firstly, because in what follows I want to insist that Scottish theatre has an active role in the present, as part of an oppositional tradition that has allowed artists to articulate Scotland's grievances. Secondly, I want to suggest that participation in the joyful is in large part the means by which contemporary Scottish theatre practitioners have conjured a vision of a better Scotland and, lastly, I want to test the notion that an emphasis on pleasure is characteristic of the Scottish tradition and has its roots in historically distant practices.

Writing in the *Scotsman* at the beginning of 2013, the theatre critic and cultural commentator Joyce McMillan playfully speculated about the year ahead in Scottish theatre. Among other things she pretended to foresee the announcement of a 'long awaited' National Theatre of Scotland production, 'to be staged at the Edinburgh Festival of 2014 [...] of David Lindsay's great *Satyre of the Thrie Estaitis*'.[6] In McMillan's witty version of events the newly appointed artistic director of the NTS, Laurie Sansom, would read this early modern play and immediately recognise it as 'a great satire about how the common man finally makes his voice heard in government again, after a long period of venality, corruption, and vulgar deference to wealth'.[7] Rather splendidly, Sansom's production would be timed to coincide with the final weeks of campaigning before the independence referendum on 18 September 2014. This in itself would be evidence, if any were needed, of the relevance of theatre to contemporary cultural and political debates. Moreover, in August 'the ghosts of John McGrath and David Lindsay' would be 'glimpsed very briefly, somewhere over the Mound, sharing a glass of claret, and drinking to the spirit of popular theatre for all the people, rowdy, magnificent, and not quite dead yet'.[8]

McMillan's 'predictions' are amusing and entirely in keeping with the holiday spirit in which they were intended. They also articulate a number of important shared assumptions about Scottish theatre, some of which I have already hinted at. The notion of a politicised populism – and consequently of pleasure – as central to the Scottish tradition, for example, or of Lyndsay's play as a foundational text, or of the idea of the National Theatre of Scotland as the primary custodian of the national tradition. This volume concerns itself specifically with tradition and legacy – or, as the subtitle has it, 'history' – and with the relationship between these discourses and contemporary discourses of Scottish identities. Consequently, alongside Henderson's clear-sighted utopian vision, McMillan's assumptions about the essential character of Scottish theatre provide a good starting point because they raise pertinent questions about how Scottish theatre came to be the rich and dynamic phenomenon it is today, how it conceptualises its own history, and how it thinks about its relationship with Scottish culture in the broader context. In what follows I intend to explore these questions in more detail primarily through a discussion of two performances staged several centuries apart, Sir David Lyndsay's satirical morality play *Ane Satyre of the Thrie Estaitis* (1552/4) and David Greig and Cora Bissett's musical *Glasgow Girls* (National Theatre of Scotland 2012). This might seem a dangerous strategy since, as we are often at pains to point out to our students, performances are a product of very specific historical circumstances. Edinburgh in the 1550s was clearly a very different place from Glasgow in the 2010s. However, recent trends in theatre historiography have encouraged me to boldness. In his introduction to *The Cambridge Companion to Theatre History* (2012), David Wiles notes the extent to which 'theatre historians have retreated from big stories, stories that catch the imagination and connect to the public domain, out of fear that they will prove inherently elitist or nationalist, racist or masculinist'.[9] As Wiles points out, this reluctance is based on a shared, if arguably dubious, assumption that 'big stories are necessarily right-wing stories'.[10] Further, such reticence might have the unwelcome effect of damaging theatre historians' 'ability to point up the interconnectedness of past events'.[11] It is, of course, just as impossible to understand the past without reference to the present as it is to understand the present without reference to the past. As the election in 2011 of a majority Scottish National Party (SNP) government has shown, contemporary events can and do affect our understanding of history. Scotland suddenly seemed a different place and, consequently, accounts of its past seem in need of revision and reworking. Even if we retain, as I think we must, a mistrust of 'grand narratives', we should certainly require historians to produce a repertory of new stories to tell us how we got here.

One approach to the production of new stories about the past is to apply contemporary theoretical paradigms to our understanding of historically distant performance events. This is a useful approach when thinking about the possible effects of Lyndsay's *Thrie Estaitis*. In particular, as Susan Bennett and Julie Sanders have observed, paradigms 'of site-specificity have been deployed almost exclusively to inform interpretations of contemporary performances' although there is no obvious reason why these paradigms might not also be utilised 'to unlock the meanings of past theatrical events'.[12] In fact, we have evidence of two large-scale outdoor performances of *Thrie Estaitis,* one at Cupar in Fife in 1552 and another on the Greenside playfield in Edinburgh in 1554. Lyndsay is also assumed to be the author of an interlude, thought to be a precursor of *Thrie Estaitis,* which was performed at Linlithgow Palace on 6 January 1540 in the presence of James V. Since each of these performances was staged outside a conventional theatre space – indeed no such conventional spaces existed during this period – they can usefully be understood as site-specific. Before commenting on the performances in relation to place it is helpful to provide, by way of context, a brief account of the play and its author.

Sir David Lyndsay (*c.* 1486–1555) was the son of a nobleman from Fife who spent his career at the Stewart court where, serving variously as tutor, poet and diplomat, he eventually rose to the position of Lyon King of Arms, Scotland's principal herald.[13] In spite of his international credentials, however, as Sarah Carpenter has noted, and as his vibrant use of vernacular Scots in *Thrie Estaitis* demonstrates, 'Lyndsay was always recognised and prized as an especially Scots writer, interested in European affairs and culture but directly addressing himself to the people and problems of Scotland'.[14] The plot is straightforward enough. In the first half the callow King Humanitie is tempted into a sexual liaison with the Lady Sensuality. Predictably this affair distracts him from his regal duties and responsibilities and, while he is otherwise lasciviously engaged, his authority is usurped by three Vices: Falsehood, Flattery and Deceit. The Vices indulge themselves and the realm sinks into chaos. Eventually, God dispatches Divine Correction who instructs the king to reform the government and restore order to the kingdom. The second half moves to the public sphere. The king calls a Parliament of the Three Estates – the Clergy, Nobility and Burgesses. During the parliament John the Commonweal, a figure representing the 'people' of Scotland, emerges from the audience to protest with fierce colloquial intensity about the misgovernment of the nation. At the play's resolution the Vices are hanged, and the corruption of the Clergy fully exposed. In its full version, *Thrie Estaitis* is very substantial indeed. It is also a very confident play so that, in spite of the paucity of play texts from this period, its sophistication has been taken as evidence of both an experienced dramatist and an established theatrical culture. Dramaturgically it shifts very freely between performance modes and genres, engaging its audience variously by combining elements of slapstick, satire, instruction, sentimentality and moral seriousness. Thinking about the original performances in relation to place is, I would like to suggest, a potentially productive approach.

Broadly speaking there have been three main tropes employed in thinking about this relationship between performance and place. Firstly, a number of scholars have drawn on Michel Foucault's elaboration of the notion of heterotopia in their discussions of site-specific performance practices. In his 1967 article 'Des espaces autres', Foucault argued that places often have more layers of meaning than immediately meet the eye.[15] In particular he emphasised the simultaneous invocation of multiple spaces both real and imagined in the same location. This way of thinking allows theatre scholars such as David Wiles in *A Short History of Western Performance Space* (2003) to think of site-specific performance as heterotopic because it often intentionally brings real and imaginary spaces into play.[16] Secondly, scholars have figured the relationship between place and performance as dialogic. Susan Bennett, for instance, in her 2008 chapter 'Universal Experience: The City as Tourist Space', focuses on the ways in which elements of particular performances are brought into productive dialogue with existing space, typically spaces in which performance has not traditionally taken place.[17] Lastly, scholars and practitioners such as Mike Pearson have thought about site-specific work as palimpsistic by emphasising the ways in which a performance might engage with a site's past uses, producing various ghosting or spectral effects.[18] Importantly, while they differ in emphasis all three approaches have tended to privilege the idea that site-specific performance can refigure the relationship between theatre and place in ways that question traditional hierarchies and are, therefore, potentially subversive. In this regard Fiona Wilkie's assessment can stand for many:

> Simply put, site-specific theatre privileges place. It suggests that the act of dividing the activity labelled 'theatre' from the building labelled 'theatre' holds possibilities for responding to and interrogating a range of current spatial concerns, and for investigating the spatial dimension of contemporary identities (personal, communal, national and international).[19]

The 1540 interlude on which the full-length version of *Thrie Estaitis* is widely believed to have been based was performed at Linlithgow Palace in the presence of the King, his queen and 'the hoole counsaile, spirituall and temporall'.[20] An eyewitness account of this performance was enclosed in a letter sent by the English knight William Eure to Thomas Cromwell. Eure, who did not see the performance himself, used his Scottish contacts to solicit the description because the interlude concerned the Reformation of the Church, a matter of serious concern to Cromwell and his associates. According to this account the character of Solace begins the play singing ballads and assuring the audience that what follows is intended purely as an entertainment and is not designed to offend. There follows the entrance of 'a King, whoe passed to his throne, having noe speche to thende of the playe' accompanied by his courtiers 'Placebo, Pikthanke, and Flatterye'.[21]

The performance stages, therefore, a fictional royal court in precisely the space occupied by the real court. It is therefore usefully thought of as heterotopic. The site is a closed elite chamber at the centre of power. Presumably the performance generated remarkable doubling effects; two kings, two sets of nobility, burgesses and clergy. The main action centres on a pauper who enters the elite chamber to complain to the king about widespread corruption at court, especially among the clergy. The poor man claims, for instance, that prelates are able to use large cash dowries to 'buy up' the sons of noblemen as husbands for their illegitimate daughters, thus 'polluting' noble bloodlines. For most of the interlude the player king appears to have been silent – along with the real King – only assenting to the pauper's demands after the nobility and burgesses within the interlude agreed, against the resistance of the clergy within the play, they were reasonable. Was the player king's silence intended as a direct comment on James's failure to exert his authority on behalf of his subjects? Was the silence of the player king intended to provoke the real King to action? Lyndsay had been James's mentor as he grew up fatherless. Was James somehow complicit in the shaping of the interlude? Unsurprisingly, even after their crimes have been catalogued the fictional clergy continue to object. Consequently, the real clergy became the focus of attention. According to Eure's letter, at the end of the interlude:

> The Kinge of Scots did call upon the Bushoppe of Glascoe being Chauncelour, and diverse other busshops, exorting thaym to reform thair facions and maners of lyving, saying that oneles thay soe did, he wold sende sex of the proudeste of thaym unto his uncle of England, and, as thoes wer ordoured, soe he wold ordour all the reste that wolde not a mende.[22]

James died in 1542 and it is impossible to predict how his attitude to church reform may have progressed had he survived. Lyndsay did survive, however, to develop his interlude into a spectacular and lengthy outdoor spectacle.

Unlike the one in attendance at Linlithgow, the 1554 Edinburgh audience for *Thrie Estaitis* was large and socially diverse. The printer Henry Charteris mentioned the Edinburgh performance in his introduction to Lyndsay's *Warkis* (1568), noting that the play was performed to: 'the Quene Regent and ane greit part of the Nobilitie, with ane exceding greit nowmer of pepill'.[23] Again the setting for the performance is of particular interest. In a charter of 1456, James II had granted the community of Edinburgh the valley and the low ground between Calton Hill and Greenside for the performance of tournaments and sports, so the audience that occupied the space on that day would have had some sense of ownership of it. The physical arrangement of the audience is also of interest. Edinburgh Burgh Council supported the 1554 performance by among other things hiring six carpenters to build a stage to seat the Queen Regent Mary of Guise, widow of James V and mother of Mary, Queen of Scots, and the French ambassador Henri Cleutin. Presumably, this structure would not only have improved sight lines for the Queen Regent and her closest ally but also made her response more visible to the crowd. We know from Charteris's summary that the performance was durational, effectively lasting all day 'fra 9 houris afoir none till 6 houris at evin', and that it was mixed in form, combining 'grave materis and merie trickis'.[24]

In both the interlude and the full-length version Lyndsay attacks the Catholic Church on numerous grounds including its overinvestment in ritual and ceremonial and its hypocrisy in relation to forced celibacy. He involves his audiences directly, in their own language, in questions of both religious and constitutional practice. By staging remarkably candid challenges to religious authority via the figure of John the Commonweal and by invoking a particular version of parliamentary government Lyndsay encourages his audience towards consideration of their own relationship with the body politic.[25] The vibrancy with which *Thrie Estaitis* was permitted to address contemporary and highly controversial issues to a very mixed audience is certainly striking. We might even productively think of the Edinburgh performance as dialogic since its focus on the well-being of the 'people' is played out publicly and on the common land. The play's utopian vision is crystallised in its resolution when John is dressed gorgeously and set down among the parliament, as if he were indeed entitled to a place there, as if the well-being of the common man were actually central to the health of the nation. At this moment in Scotland's history it seems that, to borrow Ruth Levitas's phrase, the 'reconstitution of the nation in imagination' was 'in reality a pressing need'.[26] Importantly, Lyndsay's utopianism, his vision of a better Scotland, is defined in terms of desire and is consequently best thought of as analytic rather than descriptive. Although he uses a wide range of performance modes and effects, he repeatedly returns his audience to the social and political domain. In the event his play was not to be revived for almost four centuries and then as part of another event that might be considered utopian.

From one perspective we can certainly regard the Edinburgh International Festival as a utopian project. Jen Harvie, in her article 'Cultural Effects of the Edinburgh International Festival', describes the circumstances in which the EIF was established in the immediate aftermath of World War Two, emphasising the extent to which the Festival made a 'meaningful material contribution to the post-war re-articulation and potential regeneration of European culture' at a time when much of central Europe was in ruins.[27] During the war, the great artistic cities of continental Europe suffered considerably more physical devastation than the Scottish capital; although Edinburgh did not emerge unscathed, it was well placed to provide the necessary spaces – theatres, concert halls, hotels and restaurants – for an international event of considerable scale. To its credit, Edinburgh City Council demonstrated the will as well as having the means to host the event. It was in this context that the first, and arguably most significant, revival of Lyndsay's play was staged. Tyrone Guthrie's widely admired production of an adaptation by Robert Kemp was performed at the second Edinburgh International Festival in 1948 in the General Assembly Hall of the Church of Scotland. Guthrie's production achieved a number of effects. For instance, it offered a very welcome demonstration of the power and versatility of vernacular Scots as a stage language. In addition, its eclectic range of theatrical modes and styles provided a working example of the deliberate combining of popular forms with political ambition that is increasingly recognised as a key signature of Scottish theatre practice over the centuries.[28] It is this connection that allows Joyce McMillan to imagine Lyndsay sharing a glass with John McGrath. Like much of the work of McGrath's 7:84 Scotland – Lyndsay's play actually inspired McGrath's *A Satire of the Four Estaites* presented by the 7:84 offshoot company Wildcat at the Edinburgh International Festival in 1996 – or indeed the National Theatre of Scotland in the new millennium, *Thrie Estaitis* shifts confidently between performance registers and genres, combining elements of slapstick, biting satire, didacticism, sentimentality and moral seriousness to explicitly political and often provocative ends. In June 2013, a version of the 1540 interlude and the unedited full-length play were staged at Linlithgow as part of an ongoing research project on staging the Scottish Renaissance Court.[29] The interest in the play itself continues as part of a wider preoccupation in Scottish culture with the nation's past.

For several decades Scottish playwrights have engaged with contemporary economic, social and political issues often by interrogating the ways in which Scotland's understanding of its own past impinges on its present. This has been a fairly constant theme and it is an emphasis that distinguishes Scottish practice from that of its southern neighbour. Since Osborne's *Look Back in Anger* in 1956, new writing for the theatre in England has been largely contemporary in its subject matter. This is part of the way in which it has defined itself. By contrast, of the twelve plays listed by the National Library of Scotland's website under the banner '12 Key Scottish Plays 1970–2010', nine are history plays: John McGrath's *The Cheviot, the Stag and the Black, Black Oil* (1973), Donald Campbell's *The Jesuit* (1976), John Byrne's *The Slab Boys* (1978), Chris Hannan's *Elizabeth Gordon Quinn* (1985), Liz Lochhead's *Mary Queen of Scots Got Her Head Chopped Off* (1987), Tony Roper's *The Steamie* (1987), Sue Glover's *Bondagers* (1991), David Harrower's *Knives in Hens* (1995) – which is admittedly more like a kind of pre-industrial fable than a traditional history play[30] – and Gregory Burke's *Black Watch* (2006), which also takes history and tradition as a major theme. This preoccupation might partly explain the continued interest in *Thrie Estaitis*. 'Scottish history', as Murray Pittock has observed, 'is a big subject in Scotland', so much so that 'Tom Devine's 1999 study *The Scottish Nation 1700–2000* briefly outsold J. K. Rowling in its home country'.[31]

A focus on history does not, of course, necessarily involve a turning away from the present. In 2011, David Archibald made the point that Scottish theatre practitioners in the 1970s, far from engaging in escapist flight, 'visited the past in an attempt to intervene politically in their present'.[32] This is a point well made, and it had been made before. In a chapter titled 'Plugged into History' (1996), Ian Brown argued persuasively that among 'the great achievements of the Scottish stage has been the variety and complexity of the ways in which it has dealt with history and the particular significance of this use of the past for the present stage of Scottish culture and history'.[33] As a public and communal art form, theatre has long been understood as a space for the exploration and performance of power, protest, intervention and identity. While debates about the relationship between theatre and politics are as old as theatre itself, both terms have been subject to continual historical change. The achievements of activist theatres of the 1960s and 1970s, for many epitomised by McGrath's *The Cheviot,* met significant challenges in the late twentieth and early twenty-first centuries. In *Political Theatre in Post-Thatcher Britain* (2008) Amelia Howe Kritzer points to one of the most pervasive of these challenges: that of postmodern detachment from the political. The fall of the Berlin Wall in 1989 triggered an era of neoliberal consensus, this argument goes. Consequently, we are presented with a complex and contradictory field of engagement, one in which community appears to have lost vigour and substance, and in which activism or intervention can seem naive or pointless. This had important implications for how political engagement was figured by Scottish theatre practitioners in the 1990s. In what remains of this chapter I consider this moment, but also and importantly I argue that Lyndsay's use of utopianism as a political method has made something of a comeback in post-devolutionary Scotland as the imperative to 'imagine' a new Scotland has increased in intensity. I do this via a brief account of the career of Scotland's most prolific and successful contemporary playwright, David Greig.

In terms of the 1990s we can certainly understand Greig's interest in identities that transcend national borders or boundaries as a response to the changing political landscape of Europe in the aftermath of the fall of the Berlin Wall. His sophisticated treatment of identity politics in plays such as *Europe* (1995) and *The Cosmonaut's Last Message to the Woman He Once Loved in the Former Soviet Union* (1999) or *San Diego* (2003) complicates reductive or essentialist conceptions of national identity at a moment when to do so seemed particularly prescient. As Janelle Reinelt has observed, 'landscapes that alternate between entrapment and transcendence' provide a consistent backdrop to Greig's narratives in this period of his work.[34] The twenty-first century has seen Greig return to a more direct kind of political engagement. In these years he emerged as an influential political commentator in Scotland, intervening in the debacle over Creative Scotland in 2012, for instance, and proving an effective advocate of Scottish independence in the run-up to the referendum in 2014. Clearly, devolution transformed Scotland's political and cultural scene in ways not intended by the New Labour administration that set it in motion with the referendum of 1997. Most significantly the devolved parliament has enabled the SNP to effect a rapid 'transition from being a small oppositional force, heavily dependent on voluntary activity, into a party of government'.[35] In May 2011 the SNP secured sixty-nine seats from a possible one hundred and twenty-nine, thus becoming the first to form a majority administration since the establishment of the new parliament in 1999. An agreement signed in Edinburgh in October 2012 by Scotland's First Minister Alex Salmond and the UK Prime Minister David Cameron paved the way for a referendum on Scottish independence scheduled for 18 September 2014. Although at the time of writing support for independence appears to hover around the forty per cent mark, few commentators would confidently predict the eventual outcome. What is clear, however, is that the SNP has been able to set the agenda in Scottish politics in ways few would have imagined in 1997.

Cora Bissett and David Greig's *Glasgow Girls* (2012) is a very different kind of play in terms of subject matter, setting and mode of political engagement than those produced by Greig in the earlier part of his career. I suggest the show is emblematic of a shift to, or perhaps it simply signals the re-emergence of, a more direct form of utopian political engagement in Scottish theatre. I am not suggesting that Scotland's future is necessarily or inevitably brighter than that of any other small nation in Europe. Rather I am suggesting that the 'possibility' of a better future has affected the vocabulary currently employed in Scottish theatre. What is striking about *Glasgow Girls* is its unfashionable emphasis on optimism, sincerity and affirmation. The show tells the story of seven Glaswegian schoolgirls and their teacher, who in 2005 conducted an award-winning campaign against dawn raids on asylum seekers in their local community. A motif that runs through this work is the moment of pure sincerity. Greig's dialogue uses the vernacular language of Glaswegian urban life – much as Lyndsay's play used vernacular modes several centuries earlier – often for comic effect, but at moments of extreme emotion the characters express themselves in unabashed and guileless tones. For instance, on discovering that a schoolmate has, in effect, been arrested by UK Border Agency action Emma responds: 'It's just not right. It's cruel. I can't believe this is happening in Scotland!'[36] Later in an attempt to explain her involvement in the campaign to her cynical father, Jennifer says:

> So one night I'm walking home – the sun's catching the top of the Scotstoun flats making them glow red. I can hear the traffic on Great Western Road, I can hear kids out playing in the street and I'm just thinking it seems – mad – that all this could be just taken away from you – as if a great big hand could reach down out of the sky and snatch you.[37]

There is a deliberate artlessness to the organisation of the sentences, here, that gestures beyond them in a manner that compels both emotionally and theatrically. The girls' ambitions for their campaign often appear decidedly unworldly – they are devastated when they fail to prevent the deportation of a mother and her young son, for instance. Importantly, however, although their campaign exemplifies the child's appetite for justice, sentimentality is offset in the show by the cruelty and brutality that surrounds them.

*Glasgow Girls* repeatedly, and clearly intentionally, exposes itself to sincerity and attempts to challenge cynicism in its moments – mostly musical – of breathtaking heart-stopping exuberance. Such tactics demand a corresponding openness from the audience. I attended three performances of *Glasgow Girls*, one at the Citizens' in Glasgow and two at the Theatre Royal, Stratford East, in London. On each occasion the evening culminated in an extended standing ovation. Such moments suggest, as Richard Dyer has argued, that 'utopianism is contained in the feelings it embodies [...] in what utopia would feel like rather than how it would be organised'.[38] In this sense, the utopianism of *Glasgow Girls* works substantially 'at the level of sensibility'.[39] Moreover, the structure of *Glasgow Girls* is not fiercely dialectical – like McGrath's *The Cheviot, the Stag and the Black, Black Oil* – nor is it intended to pull productively against the limitations of realism. Instead it privileges emotional space. Many significant events take place in between scenes: the arrest of Agnesa and her family, for instance, and the deportation of the mother and son. Consequently, rather than concretise these highly charged moments in a particular representation, Bissett and Greig open up spaces in the dramaturgy for the intense emotional responses of the young protagonists to inhabit, allowing their outrage and grief to situate itself beyond the precise world of the play, in the auditorium itself. Unlike much new writing of the 1990s, *Glasgow Girls* also examines the power of intergenerational relationships – principally between the teacher Mr Girvan and his pupils, but also between Noreen, a pensioner who becomes involved in the campaign, and the residents of the estate on which she has lived for many years. This span of experience gives a sense of life lived, and the perspective afforded by measuring memory in decades rather than years.

My reading of *Glasgow Girls* is of course unashamedly optimistic and aligns itself with Jill Dolan's arguments in *Utopia in Performance* in which she insists on

> the potential of different kinds of performance to inspire moments
> in which audiences feel themselves allied with each other, and with
> a broader more capacious idea of a public, in which social discourse

articulates the possible, rather than the insurmountable obstacles to human potential.[40]

In this chapter I have tried to think about Scottish theatre in these terms, in relation to how our playwrights past and present have tried to ensure the protective and resistant qualities of theatre without minimising or denying its capacity for pleasure and enjoyment. Rather more speculatively I have also attempted to argue that utopianism is an important aspect of Lyndsay's legacy. Among other things, *Thrie Estaitis* offers a tantalising glimpse of Scottish performance culture in its original glory, free from both the fear of pretension that has since haunted popular forms and the fear of vulgarity that has limited the classical tradition. Unsurprisingly, at various points in Scotland's history its theatre artists have been suspicious of this approach. In the 1990s, for instance, playwrights such as Greig, David Harrower and Anthony Neilson experimented with the vocabulary of postmodern theatre, consequently producing very fine work that nevertheless appeared suspicious of utopianism's claims about truth and about morality. This is not the case today. As well as *Glasgow Girls* we might cite Kieran Hurley, Julia Taudevin, Gav Prentice and Drew Wright's *Rantin* (2013) by way of example of the positive and playful reimagining of contemporary Scotland that is current on the nation's stages. Part gig, part storytelling, *Rantin* is comprised of a series of vignettes interspersed with song, in which we are reminded of the diversity of contemporary Scotland. Miriam, who long ago left her native Ramallah, trundles past on the way to a new cleaning job; Howard arrives at Prestwick airport from the States on a long-anticipated and largely misguided search for his Scottish roots; a young man leaves Stornoway for Glasgow University possibly never to return; Shona, a supermarket employee in Port Glasgow, applies Luddite tactics to the introduction of self-service checkouts. Most importantly, as Mary Brennan notes, 'this gorgeous piece of ceilidh-theatre, where music swirls engagingly, is taut, nuanced and illuminating, and refuses to be bleak.'[41] The show ends with Hamish Henderson's 'Freedom Come All Ye' set to a new tune.

# Notes

1    Hamish Henderson, *Collected Poems and Songs* (Edinburgh: Curly Snake Publishing, 2000), p. 143.
2    Jill Dolan, *Utopia in Performance: Finding Hope at the Theater* (Ann Arbor: University of Michigan Press, 2005), p. 168.
3    Richard Schechner, *Performance Theory*, 2nd edn (London: Routledge, 1988), p. 136.
4    James Thompson, *Performance Affects: Applied Theatre and the End of Effect* (Basingstoke: Palgrave, 2009), p. 2.
5    Ibid.
6    Joyce McMillan, 'Theatre in Scotland 2013: Mystic McMillan Peers Apprehensively into Her Crystal Ball', *Scotsman*, 3 January 2013.
7    Ibid.
8    Ibid.
9    David Wiles, 'Why Theatre History?', in David Wiles and Christine Dymkowski (eds), *The Cambridge Companion to Theatre History* (Cambridge: Cambridge University Press, 2013), pp. 3–6, p. 4.
10   Ibid.
11   Ibid.
12   Susan Bennett and Julie Sanders, 'Rehearsing Across Space and Place: Rethinking a *Masque Presented at Ludlow Castle*', in Anna Birch and Joanne Tompkins (eds), *Performing Site-Specific Theatre* (Basingstoke: Palgrave, 2012), pp. 37–53, p. 37.
13   Carol Edington, *Court and Culture in Renaissance Scotland: Sir David Lindsay of the Mount* (East Linton: Tuckwell Press, 1995).
14   Sarah Carpenter, 'David Lyndsay and George Buchanan: Contrasts in Reforming Theatre', *International Journal of Scottish Theatre and Screen*, 5:2 (2013), pp. 4–26.
15   Michel Foucault, 'Of Other Spaces, Heterotopias', *Architecture, Mouvement, Continuité*, 5 (1984), pp. 46–49.
16   David Wiles, *A Short History of Western Performance Space* (Cambridge: Cambridge University Press, 2003).
17   Susan Bennett, 'Universal Experience: The City as Tourist Space', in Tracy C. David (ed.), *The Cambridge Companion to Performance Studies* (Cambridge: Cambridge University Press, 2008), pp. 76–90.
18   See for example, Mike Pearson and Michael Shanks, *Theatre/Archaeology: Disciplinary Dialogues* (London: Routledge, 2001).
19   Fiona Wilkie, 'The Production of "Site": Site-Specific Theatre', in Nadine Holdsworth and Mary Luckhurst (eds), *The Concise Companion to Contemporary British and Irish Drama* (Oxford: Blackwell, 2008), pp. 87–106, p. 89.
20   'The Description of the 1540 Interlude' in Greg Walker (ed.), *Medieval Drama: An Anthology* (Oxford: Blackwell, 2000), pp. 338–40, p. 338.
21   Ibid., p. 339.
22   Ibid.
23   Douglas Hamer (ed.), *The Works of Sir David Lindsay*, Vol. 1 (Edinburgh: Scottish Text Society, 1931), p. 398.
24   Ibid.
25   See Sarah Carpenter, 'Monarch, State and People: dramatised ideologies in the 1550s', *Theta*, 9 (2011): *Ideologies in Debate: Spectacle and Representation in Tudor England* (umr6576.cesr.univ-tours.fr/publications/Theta9/).

26  Ruth Levitas, *Utopia as Method: The Imaginary Reconstitution of Society* (Basingstoke: Palgrave, 2013), p. xi.

27  Jen Harvie, 'Cultural Effects of the Edinburgh International Festival: Elitism, Identities, Industries', *Contemporary Theatre Review*, 13 (2003), pp. 12–24, p. 14.

28  See, for example, the diverse examples given in Ian Brown, *Scottish Theatre: Diversity, Language, Continuity* (Amsterdam: Rodopi, 2013).

29  www.stagingthescottishcourt.org

30  digital.nls.uk/scottish-theatre/index.html

31  Murray Pittock, *The Road to Independence?: Scotland Since the Sixties* (London: Reaktion Books, 2008), p. 7.

32  David Archibald, 'History in Contemporary Scottish Theatre', in Ian Brown (ed.), *The Edinburgh Companion to Scottish Drama* (Edinburgh: Edinburgh University Press, 2011), pp. 85–94, p. 85.

33  Ian Brown, 'Plugged into History', in Randall Stevenson and Gavin Wallace (eds), *Scottish Theatre since the Seventies* (Edinburgh: Edinburgh University Press, 1996), pp. 84–99, p. 85.

34  Janelle Reinelt, 'David Greig', in Martin Middeke, Peter Paul Schnierer and Aleks Sierz (eds), *The Methuen Drama Guide to Contemporary British Playwrights* (London: Methuen, 2012), pp. 203–22, p. 205.

35  James Mitchell, Lynn Bennie and Rob Johns, *The Scottish National Party: Transition to Power* (Oxford: Oxford University Press, 2012), p. 12.

36  Cora Bissett and David Greig, *Glasgow Girls*, unpublished rehearsal draft A14, p. 27.

37  Ibid., p. 41.

38  Richard Dyer, *Only Entertainment* (New York: Routledge, 1992), p. 18.

39  Ibid.

40  Jill Dolan, *Utopia in Performance: Finding Hope at the Theater* (Ann Arbor: University of Michigan Press, 2005), p. 2.

41  Mary Brennan, 'Rantin', Cottiers Theatre Glasgow', *Herald*, 19 April, 2013.

# 2: Figuring, disfiguring the literary past: the strange cases of Ross Sinclair and Calum Colvin

CAMILLE MANFREDI

In 1996 Ross Sinclair's monumental installation *Real Life Rocky Mountain* moved into the main exhibition hall of Glasgow's Centre for Contemporary Arts. As is the case with the vast majority of Sinclair's pieces, *Real Life Rocky Mountain* bore as a signature the artist's own body and the large telltale tattoo ('Real Life') that runs across his upper back. The piece recreated the side of a makeshift mountain covered with rolling Astroturf, scattered with stuffed Highland wildlife and kitsch nationalist paraphernalia. While mocking Scotland's versatile and fundamentally inauthentic myths of identity, the artist also sought to expose a form of social symbolism that to him remains stuck in early-twentieth-century Romantic kitsch, here epitomised by the accumulation of heterogeneous cultural items arbitrarily selected by the artist himself. Sinclair's piece was also a marathon musical performance: for several hours each day, Sinclair would grab an electric or acoustic guitar, sit on a fibreglass rock and, always facing away from the audience, perform a programme of popular Scottish songs of the eighteenth and twentieth centuries, starting with Robert Burns's and Lady Nairn's Jacobite songs. Sinclair then covered Scottish musical-hall hits by comedians and entertainers Will Fyffe and Harry Lauder, before finally moving on to 1980s and 1990s numbers by pop and post-punk Scottish bands Teenage Fanclub and Orange Juice, to name but two. Whereas the first and last parts of the gig-performance (or performance-gig) quite evidently aimed at probing Scotland's difficult handling of its historicity/contemporaneity dialogic, the part devoted to the 1920s and 1940s echoed more directly the actual installation. It is indeed widely acknowledged that the national stereotypes that were made (in)famous overseas by Fyffe and Lauder – of loud, joyful drunkards, kilted village fools and the like – took an active part in the reification of Scotland's self-image overseas and at home, as well as in the subjection of Scotland to a comedy broadly and freely inspired from an already largely mythicised past.

Sinclair's parodic staging of such cultural heritage is designed to exemplify the young artist's predicament: that there is no ignoring the constraints, that the Scottish contemporary scene has no choice but to confront the discordant clichés that ascribe Scotland to (in Sinclair's own caustic words) 'the sandpit of [national] imagination'.[1] 'Real life Scotland', presumably the one of the no-nonsense architecture and rarefied atmosphere of the CCA, then quite literally disappeared behind and under piles and piles of archaic paradigms, of Brigadoon-like simulacra characteristic of, to quote Baudrillard, a nation 'with neither origin nor reality'.[2] The feeling that we are presented with an authentic fake is made all the stronger by the artist's tattooed body that ironically contributes to enforce the aesthetics of fictitiousness from which it claims to be willing to break free. A few steps away from the installation, video monitors provided an endless sequence of popular songs again performed live by Ross Sinclair, only this time set in a variety of actual Highland locations. There again, Sinclair played on the geographical as well as psychological distance, enhanced by the fact that he quite literally turned his back on the audience, between the modern Scotland of the CCA and that 'other' Scotland, estranged in both time and space. Interestingly enough, the video was titled *The Sound of Young Scotland* after the motto of Postcard Records, an independent and rather ironically dubbed music label that happened to produce Orange Juice, a band whose successful compilation *The Heather's on Fire* (1993) borrowed its title from the very creator of historical novels, Sir Walter Scott.[3]

Shortly before the 1997 referendum, then, the three artistic media that Sinclair resorted to (music, literature, visual arts) re-enacted the somewhat hackneyed tensions between the ancient and the new, absence and presence, reality and artifice, Romanticism and the (to many, necessary) deromanticising of the national imagination. Such tensions are of course at the core of that new model of Scottishness that has appeared in recent literature, where intertextual playfulness often comes to blur the frontiers between homage and self-mockery. This chapter offers to explore that same blurring process in the field of visual arts by looking at how young Scottish visual artists and performers use and abuse, figure or disfigure the nation's iconic literary past. Particularly relevant to this approach will be those pieces that rely extensively on the word-and-image relationship, interpicturality and the new media; I shall argue that the virtually systematic ironical stance taken by these young artists continues to exemplify the ambiguity of their response to a literary culture that has become simply inescapable.

This ambiguity was best exemplified by Tricia Malley and Ross Gillespie's series of lexiconographic collages that were exhibited at the Scottish Parliament in 2009 to mark the 250th anniversary of the birth of Robert Burns. The project was simply put: 'each sitter', among whom were Janice Galloway and Edwin Morgan, 'was asked to produce a small body of text, response to a Burns quote communicating their own view of the relevance of Burns today'.[4] Janice Galloway's own homage and response to Malley and Gillespie's invitation was in itself thought-provoking: two sheep at her feet, she sat facing the camera wrapped in a Burns tartan plaid, the portrait a mimetic illustration of the text she had selected:

> Ca' the yowes to the knowes
> Ca' them whare the heather grows
> Ca' then whare the burnie rowes,
> My bonnie Dearie.
> As I gaed down the water-side,
> There I met my Shepherd-lad:
> He row'd me sweetly in his plaid,
> And he ca'd me his Dearie.

Let us consider the plaid as a metaphor for the tutelary figure's benevolence: Galloway is then expressing her gratitude to the poet who was kind enough to bequeath such a snug heritage to future generations of Scottish poets and writers. Yet on the other hand, Galloway's dressing up as Burns's 'bonnie Dearie', together with the copy-and-paste overall effect of the scripto-visual montage, hints at the fact that the literary past is once again, as in Sinclair's performance, tinged with irony and dealt with as counterpoint. The very title of the exhibition, *As Others See Us*, suggests that the latter may well be the photographers' own approach. The plaid turns into a burden as the sitter is made to enter a potentially grotesque role-play so as to mould herself according to the image that 'others' seek to impose on her. The gap thus widens between the real and the reproduction, as the two questions implied by the title, 'how do *we* see ourselves?' and 'how are we?', remain unanswered – exactly as those other questions, 'where is real life?'

and 'how can we tell right from wrong?', remained unanswered in Sinclair's *Real Life Rocky Mountain*.

Also part of the 2009 Homecoming Scotland programme of events were Scottish sculptor and installation artist David Mach's *Robert Burns Match Heads*, a set of two life-size match-head sculpture heads of Scotland's Bard. As their title suggests, the twin sculptures were made out of live matches, a technique that is usually associated with matchitecture, amateur crafts-manship and model building, all of which are more commonly interested in the reproduction of national monuments than in portraiture. But maybe this is exactly what Burns has become: a historic heritage monument, thus likely to be copied, miniaturised and trivialised. The parallel that Mach draws with a hobby about as obscure, potentially desocialising and 'anorak' as trainspotting (with all due respect for all matchitects and trainspotters who may come to read this) adds to the artist's pun on the poet's surname. Mach's point was quite evidently to counterbalance the nationwide eulogy that was expected from him, two centuries and fifty years after Burns's birth. The homage got even more ambiguous, if not verging on sheer irreverence, when one of the sculptures was spectacularly set alight to launch StAnza, Scotland's international poetry festival held annually in St Andrews. Blackened by fire, the head was then exhibited next to its unscathed twin in Parliament, thus creating a dramatic before/after contrast between the two sculptures. The performance of burning the head was significantly entitled 'Burning Burns' and was hailed as a metaphor for the inexhaustible creative energy that Robert Burns continues to evoke down the centuries, yet the very gesture of firing the sculpture allows several alternative inter-pretations. The performance may as well be interpreted as intentionally desecrating the literary canon as Burns's head is totemised, carried to a pike as in the times of the bloodiest revolutions or the cruellest forms of retribu-tive justice, then finally exposed to a rite of alchemical, purifying fire. Could it be that Mach thus seeks to parody the artist's Oedipus complex and urge to kill his father to liberate himself from the latter's overwhelming influence? Once again, the line is very thin between homage and transgression, between consecration and desecration: all four artists seem to rely extensively on irony to dismiss the figures that they may perceive as all the more imposed as they are conveniently brought to light in order to benefit commercial (touristic, for that matter) rather than cultural interest. But what such irony also demonstrates is the ongoing spread of the aesthetic of inconsistency from the literary realm to that of the visual arts: inconsistency between post-devolution Scotland ('*real* Scotland'?) and the partial image that it chooses to bring forward to the world; inconsistency, too, between modern modes of expression and more 'traditional' art forms.

These issues are at the core of Calum Colvin's art. Like David Mach, Colvin reworks portraits of and by prominent artists. He thus proves interested in both the who and the how of visual representation. From October 2002 to February 2003, Colvin's portraits were exhibited at the Scottish National Portrait Gallery, a venue where the great masters of Scottish high culture are not so much respected as worshipped. In order to repaint or subvert iconic pieces such as the portraits of Burns by Archibald Skirving and Alexander Nasmyth or the portrait bust of Sir Walter Scott by Bertel Thorvaldsen, Colvin relied on a complex digital photomontage technique that involved sculpting a three-dimensional background, projecting the portrait onto the construction, retracing the image as it fell across the sculpture, photographing the result and finally transferring the digital photograph back onto canvas. The *trompe l'œil* is striking: the projected disassembled portrait regains its original unity through digital recapture and subsequent restoration to the flat standardised surface of the canvas.

Calum Colvin's experiments with three-dimensional digital collage operate within a rather ambivalent form of anti-classicism, as Colvin defies the laws of official art only to revalidate them and finally offer new visual and mental patterns for Scotland's greatest literary and identity myths. Scott's portrait bust is thus displayed amongst the ruins of his own Edinburgh memorial littered with broken biscuits, a 'See you, Jimmy' hat and mock-Scottish items. These undermine the portrait's austerity and appear to blame Scott for the spread of the tartanry – an obvious reference to Scott's organisation of the plaided pageantry of George IV's 1822 visit to Edinburgh. In much the same way, Burns's portrait appears projected onto ruins (the Romantic setting par excellence) debris-strewn with tourists' trinkets (a miniature Saltire and, in a clever *mise en abyme*, Nasmyth's own portrait of Burns) and a few literary motifs that have somehow mutated into pictorial items: red red roses, green rushes, a heart-shaped anti-stress ball, all of them discarded as mere trash. The Bard is set against the ruins of a time long gone by, metaphorised into the ripped pages of a collection of poems, faded pressed flowers or the antlers of a once-majestic stuffed deer, a reminder of Edwin Landseer's *Monarch of the Glen* and other mounted portraits left to gather dust on a shelf.

Colvin's pieces draw a parallel between identity crisis and crisis of representation by playing on the proverbial ungraspable nature of reality: this is all an illusion, from the apparently flat image to the fabricated memories that clutter up Scotland's cultural landscape. It is, therefore, unsurprising that Colvin took a particular interest in that great figure in the hall of fame of alleged forgery: James Macpherson. The latter's portrait is inspired from Joshua Reynolds's controversial piece – controversial in the sense that it is claimed by detractors to be a copy by some unnamed artist. The irony is more than appropriate: this time, Colvin did not project the portrait onto the setting as he is used to doing, but Photoshopped the portrait instead onto a set recycled from earlier works. We are thus presented with a fake or rather the fake of a fake, as it is finally disclosed that Colvin is not the portrait's painter and that the portrait was made, at his request, by 'someone else'. Calum Colvin then re-enacts Scotland's most famous literary 'forgery' with modern technological tools and sets himself as the reincarnation of Scotland's most successful impostor.

After the creator comes the creature. Colvin's series of portraits of Ossian shows the Homer-, Christ-like face of the fictitious bard projected onto the same wasteland. Along the nine portraits that compose the piece, Ossian's face (clearly based on the controversial engraving attributed to Runciman, which makes the piece another fake of a fake) gradually fades away to reveal the ruins of some primordial Scotland strewn with symbolical artefacts: here a deer's antlers, there the embedded yet significantly torn portrait of a tattooed Maori, in an oblique reference to Macpherson's fascination with 'noble savages'. The tribal face tattoos meld into Ossian's beard, turn into intricate Celtic interlace patterns and finally into a large, mysterious finger-print – one that may well be Colvin's own. The artist's aesthetic ambition is to question the notion of evidential marks, as each of the identity markers (Pictish art, fingerprint) dissolve into elusive evidence of some long lost truth. Once digitised, the portraits are animated into a visual rhetoric that reproduces the progressive mutation of archaeology and anthropology into myth, and myth into folklore. Colvin thus sets himself as a mytho-photographer to demonstrate that digital photography as an art form is as able as literature to warp and distort history. Colvin hammers his point in his eight *Fragments*, in which the evolving portrait of the Maori warrior mutates into that of Harry Lauder, whose portrait set on a dust-coated viewing screen is further duplicated into a gradually disappearing portrait bust lying on an antique record player. Everything is pastiche, discarded and blasphemous: digital photographs of Macpherson's forged portrait lie on the ground, the Saltire is desecrated, anthropology turns into caricature. The animated portraits bear an obvious fatalistic tone as any trace of authenticity is bound to disintegrate, thus preventing both the viewer and the artist from identifying with the array of Scottishnesses offered to them.

This explains why Colvin chose to portray himself as a dejected fallen angel in his repainting of Dürer's allegorical self-portrait *Melencolia 1*. Calum Colvin's own version, entitled *Scota 01*, shows the artist despairing over the leftovers from his aborted pursuit of truth, dimly lit by the video-projector that is attached to his miner's helmet. We can but sympathise: the few identity markers that he has unearthed, the 'fruits' of his artistic quest, lie there, at his feet: in his cabinet of curiosities, media-reflexive objects such as a computer keyboard or discarded negatives lie next to a series of low-definition digital photographs of Macpherson's portrait. We find ourselves wondering whether these pictures get sharper or more blurry as they go, and consequently whether the process is one of inscription or of erasure. To the artist's left, a kitsch snowball contains the photograph of a derelict cottage, in a sad reminder of the Highland Clearances and of the reduction of Scotland to a miniaturised sunken civilisation, the bleak background to a mass-produced gadget bought by some nostalgic tourist somewhere in the rash of tacky souvenir shops along the Royal Mile. The symbol of an unravelling collective memory or, on a wider scale, of the human condition, *Scota 01* is also a sign of Colvin's embarrassment vis-à-vis the contemporary Scottish artists' predicament, that is to say the quest for a truth that may well never have been.

Art, whether digital or not – but especially when it is digital – thus continues to distort our perception of Scotland's cultural landscape. At the end of the day, the artist has no other option but to take his part in the shadow theatre that Scottish culture has become – and where we, too, have a crucial role to play. We viewers are indeed made to deconstruct Colvin's memento mori and, in so doing, to question the way we perceive and interpret images. Because we are invited to develop and formulate a critical discourse of the pieces, we in turn become actors in the assembly line that will eventually produce the national imagination. What is more, as there can be no guarantee that we shall not also partake in the distortion of 'reality', we are also liable for potential myth-making. If Scotland has indeed become a product, identifying its author becomes increasingly challenging; the risk is then to discover that it has no author, as Colvin and, before him, Ross Sinclair seem to imply.

Sinclair's installation art, Malley and Gillespie's photomontage, Mach's match-heads and Colvin's manipulated portraits all deal with the issues raised by the (mis)representation of Scottish history and identity in art. It appears that all five artists tackle these issues through a common process (montage), a common tone (bitter irony) and a common intention (ambivalence). The collage of apparently unrelated items to figure the cornucopia of national imagination is by no means specific to Scotland: after all, are not all cultures aggregates of textual and iconic signs gathered along the way? Of course, this is all consistent with the postmodern interest in recycling and rewriting: *Real Life Rocky Mountain* is quite literally built on the all-too-familiar kitsch inherited from *Brigadoon*, while Mach's *Robert Burns Match Heads* are clear reminders of Guy Fawkes bonfires. Likewise, Colvin's portraits were all the easier to identify as pictorial plagiarisms as the original paintings were and are still hanging in rooms directly adjacent to the one that hosted the exhibition at the Scottish National Portrait Gallery. Colvin's interpictorial practice nevertheless gets more complex with his pictorial translation of Burns's poem 'The Twa Dogs': there, the text–image relationship was entrusted to David Wilkie's 1807 painting entitled *The Rent Day* that acted as mediator and helped support the two different interpretations willed by the artist.

In the works of Sinclair, Mach, Gillespie, Malley and Colvin the core issues of the origin and the remains are dealt with in and around the pieces, in the sense that our identification of the hypoicons present within the works contributes to the creation of an interpretative community of informed viewers – or at least suggests that there exists such a community. The works then have two axiological functions as, whilst questioning the inherited literary canons (and thus entering the realm of metanarration), they also challenge the arbitrary divide between high art and popular culture. When these two intersect, the suspicious finger invariably points at the three usual suspects, namely Burns, Scott and above all Macpherson. It seems these writers have become scapegoats and are conveniently accused of having subjected the national imagination to a handful of debilitating stereotypes and surreptitiously turned Scotland into a kitsch and counterfeit nation.

The visual artists of the new Scottish generation have no doubt been influenced by the modern critics' idea that Scottish art has little to do with social reality – Tom Nairn's cultural 'sub-nationalism' naturally comes to mind. In much the same way, David MacCrone's *Scotland the Brand* (1995) found a sympathetic ear in Sinclair and Colvin. The latter's aptly titled painting *Anger* thus insists on the purely mercantile aspect of Scottish culture: here, kilted Action Men re-enact some inter-clan fighting, only adapted into the fierce competition between Campbell soups (we will not miss the interpictorial hint) and McDonald's. Colvin's game of mirrors and references to pop art both chastise cultural consumerism. They put the blame on the disposable forms of identity that are, according to him, the only ones that the nation has been offered for the past few decades, if not much longer.

But the necessarily multifaceted aesthetic of collage also highlights the contradictory intentionalities manifested in the selected pieces: between homage and blasphemy, between deconstruction and (re)montage, the works that boast a resolute post-colonial approach to Scottish art and identity reveal the inadequacy of post-devolution Scotland's constant renegotiation of the past. Such pieces then partake in the collective rethinking of what art can or cannot do, in a third millennium when any romantic form of nationalism would be dismissed as unconvincing and untimely. The idea that contemporary art does have a social function is confirmed by the fact that this problematic has succeeded in carving out a place for itself in the public sphere. It so happens that many of the works above mentioned were exhibited in the Scottish Parliament buildings, that is to say within an institution that, out of necessity, has to tackle issues of continuity and discontinuity. Let us consider art as an ideological barometer and assume that it still has 'the function of confirming the narratives which [the Scots] use to make sense of their lives'.[5] The only narrative that is confirmed by the new generation of Scottish visual artists is that of a self-loathing nation, still at odds with itself. The only thing that could prevent us from concluding that there remains an unbridgeable gap between

Scottish contemporary visual art and literature can be summed up in just a few points. First, the artists' quirky sense of humour that, come to think of it, is not that far from the one popularised by Harry Lauder; then, the collaboration of writers such as Janice Galloway whose interest in contemporary art is well known; finally, the many efforts made by the institutions to renew Scotland's visual imagination – however limited their subsidies. I shall, however, save the last word for what I consider a potentially redemptive piece: *The Kelvingrove Eight* was commissioned from Calum Colvin by the Scottish National Portrait Gallery in the year 2000 and includes Janice Galloway, Alasdair Gray, Tom Leonard, Bernard MacLaverty, Liz Lochhead, Alan Spence, Jeff Torrington and Agnes Owens. The painting updates Alexander Moffat's famous group portrait *Poet's Pub* (1980) and just manages to restore the idea that literature and visual arts can collaborate in the renewal of the national representation. The painting is all the more redemptive as three women writers are given an honourable place within Scotland's literary pantheon – some might add that it was about time. It remains to be seen if and how this particular painting will be parodied two or three centuries from now.

## Notes

1   Francis McKee, 'Ross Sinclair', *Frieze Magazine*, Issue 29, June–August 1996, www.frieze.com/issue/review/ross_sinclair1/
2   Jean Baudrillard, *Simulacres et Simulation* (Paris: Galilée, 1981), p. 10.
3   'Yet, into whatever deep and passive slumber our native country may have been lulled from habits of peaceful acquiescence, the Government have now found a way to awaken her. The knife has gone to the very quick, and the comatose patient is roused to most acute possession of his feelings and his intellect. The heather is on fire far and wide; and every man, woman, and child in the country, are bound by the duty they owe to their native land, to spread the alarm and increase the blaze.' Sir Walter Scott, letter of 28 February 1826.
4   See the artists' website: www.broaddaylightltd.co.uk/as-others-see-us/
5   The expression is borrowed from Kate Flint's *The Victorians and the Visual Imagination* (Cambridge: Cambridge University Press, 2000), p. 197: 'Art had the function of confirming the narratives which [the Victorians] used to make sense of their lives'.

# 3: History and tartan as enactment and performance of varieties of 'Scottishness'[1]

## IAN BROWN

This chapter explores ways in which Scottish identities have been performed through the wearing of tartan. Following on from Trish Reid's discussion of the use of heterotopic performance sites and their use in the expression of multiple identities and Camille Manfredi's on the revisualisation of icons, including tartan, it reviews ways in which the wearing, and design, of tartan have developed in different contexts over the last four centuries. It takes the position that, in parallel with literary and visual representations, the wearing of tartan is a performance, to an extent theatricalised, of versions of 'Scottishness'. In doing so, it addresses what it argues have been wrong-headed attacks on tartan as somehow reductive, rather than a rich resource for the expression of varied perceptions of Scottish identities. It therefore takes as a premise that a discourse influenced by Hugh Trevor-Roper's inaccurate historiography, the intellectually limiting attitudinising of Tom Nairn's concept of 'the tartan monster' and the *Scotch Reels* group's partial, and often flawed, insights lacks credibility. It will suggest that both this historical inaccuracy and the limiting attitudinising failed to grasp the positive energy and vitality of tartan and the kilt – both in the past and currently – in expressing, indeed performing, significant positive aspects of Scottish culture. It will consider the ways in which by the twenty-first century the uses and meanings of tartan and the varieties of ways in which the kilt is worn mark their continuing relevance and modernity, even post-modernity. It argues that tartan and kilt embody and represent diverse visions of what it is, in an international perspective, to be 'Scottish'.

The essence of tartan – and tartanry – is an absence of certainty. The very design of tartan embodies constant dynamic tension between the clarity, even rigidity, of its grid and the literally endless potential for colour and variety contained within, and visually threatening to break, the lock of that grid. Its impact visually has been compared to that of a flower garden. In 1723, the author of *A Journey through Scotland* described women's wearing it 'in the Middle of a Church, on a Sunday, look[ing] like a Parterre de Fleurs'.[2] A key element in this metaphor is that the flowers are not strewn wildly: they are contained, growing within, but also out of, a formal garden. Tartan embeds carefree design carefully, a celebration both of the vitality of nature and of the interaction of human intellect, aesthetics and dynamic growth. In a bon mot, John Laver has presented a parallel contemporary view. A senior academic, settled in Scotland for many years, he had planned to wear morning dress to his daughter's wedding. She persuaded him he should wear a kilt like the younger men. Afterwards he commented, 'I'm glad I did or I would have looked like a penguin in a flower garden'. The vitality, even vibrancy, of tartan – the ways its interaction of potential and rigorous vigour separate it from the frozen world of the penguin – are summed up by the designer and weaver Annie Stewart:

> Tartan is an ordered way of introducing a riot of colour in a very restrained manner because the design in the warp is the same as the design in the weft. The true colour that is created by the crossing of the warp with the weft is strong, but easier to look at because of the grid design. It remains organic instead of psychedelic even when vivid colours are used.[3]

Perceptions of tartan as a cultural phenomenon (and the developing concept of tartanry) raise issues of the relationship of historical evidence and myth-making in identity formation. This relationship develops in the historic context of the processes by which, in the eighteenth century, tartan, clan and regimentation interacted and of later perceptions of that interaction, particularly those of contemporary cultural commentators. In interrogating the assumptions underlying recent critical attitudes to tartan (and tartanry), this chapter draws on Mary Douglas's summary of Claude Lévi-Strauss's view of the nature of myth:

> the function of myth is to portray the contradictions in the basic premises of the culture. The same goes for the relation of the myth to social reality. The myth is a contemplation of the unsatisfactory compromises which, after all, compose social life. In the devious statements of the myth, people can recognise indirectly what it would

be difficult to admit openly and yet what is patently clear to all and
sundry, that the ideal is not attainable.[4]

The stance underlying this paper is that myths, including tartan mythologies, whether enacted or literary, are not false or inauthentic history,
although they may have historical roots. As thinkers like Roland Barthes
have suggested,[5] they are rather embodiments of, often rich, contradictions
that demand exploration, analysis and understanding, and cannot simply
be dismissed as 'backward' or substituted ingenuously by new 'progressivist'
mythologies.

One of the key tartan myths involves its role as an identifier of clan
or family membership. Colin McArthur has described the attachment
of tartan to clans or families as 'delusion', a 'grotesque act of mythmaking'.[6]
It may be worth considering the ways in which tartan appears to have
come to be linked to clans or families in order to see whether such an
assertion makes sense. Certainly it is common ground that the process
of linking specific tartan setts, or patterns, to specific families was system-
atised only in the early nineteenth century, particularly in the context of
George IV's 1822 royal visit to Edinburgh. It would be odd, however, if
such a process of linkage emerged from the ether without any precedent.
Of course, it did not. There is evidence, as we shall see, of earlier linking
of families and setts.

An incidental aspect of the mythology of the royal visit is that somehow
it imposed tartan on the Lowlands. It is clear from written, material and
portrait evidence since at least the sixteenth century that tartan, though
not what is now thought of as Highland dress, was worn throughout Scotland.
Based in Edinburgh, the Royal Company of Archers wore a tartan uniform
from 1713 at least. John Telfer Dunbar reports sixteenth-century ministerial
condemnation of women's wearing of colourful tartan in church.[7] He also
quotes Thomas Morer, an English clergyman who, in 1689, describes the
use of the plaid by Lowlanders:

> Their habit is mostly English, saving that the meaner sort of men
> wear bonnets instead of hats, and pladds instead of cloaks; and those
> pladds the women also use in their ordinary dress when they go
> abroad, either to market or church.[8]

In seeking to establish whether it is defensible to define tartan as somehow exclusively representing a Highland version of Scottish identity, the etymological history of 'tartan' offers interesting evidence. The *Dictionary of the Scots Language* (*DSL*) derives the term from Old French *tiretaine*, 'a sort of cloth half wool, half some other yarn; stuff of which the weft is wool and the warp linen or cotton'. This origin would identify it as the form of cloth now called linsey-woolsey. The earliest *DSL* entries, indeed, could suggest that it still meant simply a form of cloth: from 1532–1533, 'Ane uthir tartane galcoit gevin to the king be the Maister Forbes', and from 1538, 'For iij elnis of heland tertane to be hois to the kingis grace'. By 1561, however, an entry from Dundee suggests that colour is implied by 'tartan', not just a form of cloth, while the matter is entirely clear in an entry from 1616–1633: 'warm stuff of divers colours which they call tartane'. The emphasis on diversity – indeed hybridity – can be found, if the origin is in fact French, in the Breton use of *tiretaine* for cider made half of apples and half of pears. The complexity of the word, however, extends to debate as to its actual origin. Alan Bruford has made a case for Gaelic origin linking it with the Gaelic for 'across', 'tarsainn'.[9] Yet, the implication of a Franco-Scots derivation is that it would suggest a Lowland origin for tartan, for which clear evidence is lacking. Nonetheless, Richard Grange, perhaps boldly, has suggested 'It seems that tartan – and the tartan plaid – originated in the Lowland districts and its popularity spread to the Highlands'.[10] Meanwhile, for an argument for a Gaelic derivation from 'tarsainn', the difficulty is that the Gaelic word used historically is 'breacan', derived from 'breac', 'speckled' or 'spotted'. This complexity is compounded when James D. Scarlett suggests tartan design originates in Pictish society,[11] an ethnological speculation beyond possibility of proof. Whatever its derivation, one theme the etymology of the word foregrounds is that of hybridity or crossing, even contrariness. Meantime the related word 'plaid' seems also to emerge as a Scots term in the sixteenth century, firstly for cloth or a garment – a shawl for women or mantle for men – and its weave, and very quickly applied to its colouring. The Gaelic 'plaide' ('blanket') the *DSL* suggests is derived from Scots, though the journey may be in the opposite direction. Tartan's linguistic roots are intercultural and elusive, but intriguingly so. Their very complexity and elusiveness marks the way it offers diverse versions of 'Scottishness'.

It is striking that such an intriguing aspect of Scottish culture should at various times and in various ways have attracted the levels of hostility that it has, both from non-Scots and Scots. Sometimes the hostility has been based in political and military conflict. Daniel Defoe in his *Memoirs of a Cavalier* (1720), supposedly 'Written threescore years ago by an English gentleman', illustrates the typecasting of both the Highlander of the War of the Three Nations and his dress as beyond the exotic:

> I confess the soldiers made a very uncouth figure, especially the Highlanders: the oddness and barbarity of their garb and arms seems to have something in it remarkable. [...] their doublet, breeches and stockings, of a stuff they called plaid, striped across red and yellow, with short cloaks of the same. These fellows looked when drawn out like a regiment of Merry-Andrews ready for Bartholomew fair. [12]

The vocabulary here is of course coloured by hostility to the invading army of 1639. Key words like 'uncouth', 'odd' and 'barbarity' typify Highland dress as somehow outré, beyond civilisation, when, of course, it was an element in the Celtic civilisation of Scotland that was, and is, a source of art of considerable cultivation. The later-invented shibboleth that the kilt should not be worn south of the Highland line is, in a sense, another version of an attempt to corral the dress into some form of reservation for the eccentric. The very word 'barbarity', of course, arises from the ancient Greeks' fear of and contempt for those great civilisations around them that did not use Greek and so were beyond 'civilisation', at least so far as the Greeks, with their own special barbarisms, were concerned. Trevor Royle has referred to such perceptions, or rather typecasting, of the 'other' continuing when the Highland regiments were established:

> With the 'barbaric' allure of their uniforms Highland soldiers became an instantly recognised and widely feared element of the British Army and their service in Africa, India and north America helped to consolidate Britain's growing mercantile empire. [13]

Defoe's passage also includes a reading of the tartan as the patching of the costume of Merry-Andrews: buffoons or harlequins. A deal of recent resentment of tartan and tartanry has been focused on such twentieth-century comedic personae as those of Harry Lauder. Even a perceptive critic like Cairns Craig could at one time observe:

> No Scottish writer could have brought myth and history together, as Yeats did [...]. Such a conjunction was made impossible because the tartan myth was a myth of historical redundancy, and being redundant its images declined (as Yeats said the ancient gods of Ireland had declined to leprechauns) from the noble stature of Ossian and Scott's Jacobites to the parodic red-nosed, kilted, drunken, mean Scotsmen of music hall comedy and picture postcard jokes.[14]

In fact, as Paul Maloney, Margaret Munro and David Goldie have made clear, what is here presented as a degringolade is arguably more positive and certainly more complex.[15] As Jonathan Faiers has pointed out, reflecting – presumably unconsciously – Defoe's earlier text with regard to the comedic and subversive, not to say threatening and potentially anarchic impact of the tartan, an impact extending beyond Scottish artists:

> The great 'turns' of the nineteenth- and twentieth-century music halls, entertainers noted for their tartan costumes – for example Harry Lauder, Dan Leno, Marie Lloyd, or clowns such as Coco – donned their tartans as a masquerade that would allow them to become the transgressive characters beloved by their audiences. Their swaggering tartan costumes invested their performances with the spirit of rebellious and subversive clowning that can be traced back to the figure of Harlequin, British nineteenth-century pantomime's translation of Arlecchino from the original *commedia dell'arte*.[16]

Paul Maloney has pointed out to the present author that staged tartan in kilt, trews, bunnet, frock-coat and other items, seen often by some critics as demeaning, can equally – or perhaps even more – be seen as celebratory, joyously conspiratorial with the audience and full of ebullient life.[17]

Tartan and certain aspects of tartanry have been and are still a threat, at the very least, to critical convention and *amour propre* and often an element in direct challenge to established and even establishment values.

It could also, as Murray Pittock argues, be seen as embodying alternative traditions to those of the dominant hegemony. That it did so was, of course, a central reason for its prohibition in the 1746 Disarming Act. Tartan had, and retains within its polysemy, a capacity to bear meaning beyond many other sartorial designs. Domhnall Uilleam Stiùbhart recognises that, while the nexus of tartan and plaid might – indeed in the nature of things must – evolve, that evolution maintains and foregrounds the potential for tartan to represent an alterity that supports the unbuttoned, emotionally spirited and carnivalesque:

> by the late seventeenth century the plaid was increasingly becoming a male garment in the Gàidhealtachd, as women abandoned the traditional female plaid of *earasaid* in favour of contemporary Lowland fashions. In addition, the tartan, that clothing of brawn, vigour, and spectacular display *par excellence*, was more and more being compared to and distinguished from garments of 'renunciation' worn in the south, namely the black hat and cloak worn by Presbyterian ministers and, on a wider British stage, the rise of that most emblematic whig garment, the sober three-piece suit.[18]

Of course such potential for alterity carried a cost. One aspect of that cost was the recurrent process of stigmatisation, which in some critical discourses continues till the present day. Another is that of appropriation by the forces that regarded the tartan as 'other'. The dimension of tartanry called 'Balmorality' is a clear case, following on from the 1822 royal visit, of the winner apparently taking over the loser's tokens. In fact, of course, two things underlie that royal visit and the later development of Balmorality. One is the process by which tartanisation of public events and personae represents an attempt at reconciliation after conflict. This is hardly a shameful process and arguably a necessary one for the future of any body politic. The second is the way in which the appropriation of tartan iconography, within the context of the dominance of Scottish cultural tropes throughout the Western world after the impact of Ossian and Walter Scott, asserts the complex of values appropriation was intended to suppress. Victoria did not bring tartan to revival to Scotland. As John Telfer Dunbar points out, there was, as part of 1820s and 1830s Romantic Gothic revival, a continuing interest in tartan, including the Eglinton tournament of 1839,[19] which flowed into the spectacular 1842 welcome given Victoria and Albert at Taymouth Castle. Their Balmorality can be seen as an enthusiastic endorsement of and response to this. In short, it is an open question whether George IV in a kilt and Victoria and Albert at Balmoral are appropriating and subverting a set of values, or whether they are being appropriated and subverted.

Of course the 1822 royal visit is something of a *pons asinorum* for detractors from the tartan. Hugh Trevor-Roper in a notorious chapter uses it as a stick to attack the authenticity of tartan and its identification with clans and, so, somehow its historicity.[20] Trevor-Roper's assertion that the kilt in its modern form was 'invented' by an English Quaker, Thomas Rawlinson, is based on Dunbar's citation of a journalistic publication in 1785 of a private letter of 1768, written itself some fifty years after the 'invention'.[21] The evidence for 'English' invention is confused: Dunbar also quotes Sir John Sinclair as writing in 1795 (but not published until 1830), 'the phillibeg was invented by an Englishman in Lochaber about sixty years ago'.[22] Indeed, in tailoring terms, if the story of invention in about 1718 is taken as true, the conception may have been Rawlinson's, but the actual invention in this story was by an anonymous Inverness tailor. In any case, as Murray Pittock has noted,[23] there is evidence of the short kilt from the 1690s, while a costume drawing by Inigo Jones for Davenant's *Salmacida Spolia* in 1639–40 shows his perception of the 'ould habites of the 3 nationes' ('Inglish Irish Scottes'). In this drawing the 'Scotte' appears to wear a short kilt to halfway down his thighs and a separate plaid, certainly not a belted plaid, though it is impossible to discern what, if any, tartan is intended.[24] It is improbable that Jones would represent Scots in a short kilt for a stage presentation unless the garment were known. The alternative may, of course, be to backdate the 'English' invention of the short kilt to a stage designer in the first year of the War of the Three Nations.

Trevor-Roper's evidence in his *The Invention of Tradition* chapter, however, is notoriously shaky. William Ferguson analyses the weakness of Trevor-Roper's discussion in the same chapter of the so-called Ossian myth. He shows Trevor-Roper to have done little more than lazily appropriate Samuel Johnson's ignorant challenges to Macpherson, apparently failing to understand the working of oral tradition as it enters the written – and revising – record. Trevor-Roper asserts that

> Indeed, the whole concept of a distinct Highland culture and tradition
> is a retrospective invention. Before the later years of the seventeenth
> century, the Highlanders of Scotland did not form a distinct people.
> They were simply the overflow of Ireland. [...] Their literature, such
> as it was, was a crude echo of Irish literature.[25]

Ferguson points out in substantial detail that Trevor-Roper's 'account of
Highland illiteracy and cultural deprivation echoes, albeit without acknow-
ledgement, Samuel Johnson's views'.[26] Such appropriation of Johnson arguably
marks Trevor-Roper's apparent desire to roll logs rather than cast light. For
reasons that are unclear, he appears to want to twit the – in his own antique
phrase – 'Scotch' with the emptiness of their vaunted history, in a chapter
which, while at times witty, is, historically, often ludicrous.

Certainly one of the strong strands of Scottish nationalism in the nineteenth century expressed itself in a form of unionism that demanded the
defence and assertion of Scottish rights and institutions. And arguably that
process led eventually to the possibility – because sufficient specifically
Scottish civic structures survived and were active – of the re-establishment
of the Scottish Parliament in 1999. David McCrone makes such a case *passim*
in *Understanding Scotland* (2001).[27] Such structures were energised, even
embodied, by a variety of tartan identity tokens and Ian Maitland Hume's
ethnological research has highlighted the interaction of such tokens with
individuals' internalised sense of identity.[28] Indeed, as Michael Newton
has shown, the importance of such internalised tokens of identity for an
expatriate community cannot be overestimated.[29] However domestic Scots
may regard the resort to tartan and its symbols by expatriates, they have no
more right than any other home community with a large diaspora to pass
judgement on what their expatriate cousins evolve in response to their own
diasporic needs. The international dynamism of tartan and tartanry is not
to be restrained by attempts by the home community to police an iconography that is, whatever its roots and however Scottish-focused, international.
Indeed one of the debates Michael Newton has engaged in is whether the
word 'tartanry' can rightly be used of North American experience or whether
another word showing respect for expatriate developments such as 'tartanism'
might not better be used. In the end that debate remains open-ended.

The point about the discourse of tartan and tartanry is that it is not easily or simply defined. When Colin McArthur tries to do this, he produces a caricature, assimilating 'Tartanry' and 'Kailyard' into one linked phenomenon when they are quite distinct:

> The Tartanry/Kailyard ensemble permits and foregrounds only certain types of flora, fauna and humankind, the privileged icons being thistles, heather, stags, highland cattle, Scotch terriers, tartaned figures (often with military connotations) and a handful of historical figures of whom Burns and Scott are pre-eminent.[30]

In McArthur's *Scotch Reels* collection of essays, John Caughie observed in 1982:

> It is precisely the regressiveness of the frozen discourses of Tartanry and Kailyard that they provide just such a reservoir of Scottish 'characters', Scottish 'attitudes' and Scottish 'views' which can be drawn upon to give the 'flavour of Scotland', a petrified culture with a misty, mythic, and above all, static past.[31]

In fact, these discourses, as is shown by their continually developing and widespread presence, are far from frozen, rather being dynamic. As David McCrone, Angela Morris and Richard Kiely observed in 1995,

> A considerable literature has grown up to debunk heritage, to show that much of it is a modern fabrication with dubious commercial and political rationales. Being able to show that heritage is not 'authentic', that it is not 'real', however, is not the point. If we take the Scottish example of tartanry, the interesting issue is not why much of it is a 'forgery', but why it continues to have such cultural power. That is the point which critics like Hugh Trevor-Roper (1984) miss. As his fellow historians Raphael Samuel and Paul Thompson show, myths are no mere archaic relics but potent forces in everyday life. Myths are constantly reworked to make sense of memories and lives (Samuel and Thompson, 1990).[32]

Such an argument accords with the late Richard Prentice's concept in heritage tourism of 'endearment'. By this, he meant the ways in which memories, souvenirs and photographs become tokens by which tourists engage personally with the experience of visiting a site and authenticate their own experience of the act of visiting. In several ways Prentice's concept of 'endearment' applies to experiences outlined in Ian Maitland Hume. As Craig Beveridge and Ronald Turnbull remark,

> meanings are never passively consumed, but always subject to selection and adjustment to other discourses. [...] response to tartanry is not uncritical assimilation, but a complex negotiation dependent on the beliefs and values which are bound up with these other concerns.[33]

Jonathan Faiers observes: 'Apparently simple in construction, tartan is also capable of staggering complexity; it is multivalent and dichotomous' and, he goes on, globally consumed.[34] He is here making a point that applies not just to the material, but to the wide range of discourses that tartan inspires and with which it engages. Just as 'contradictory elements merged to make tartan a uniquely resilient textile',[35] so the contradictory elements of the discourses of tartan and tartanry and the interactions of the two create resilient discourses. These discourses may lie in the apparently superficial area of the implications of clothes themselves: whether in cultural transmission as the '[p]laid shirts of cowboys lead to US working class usage'[36] from the workwear of Scottish expatriate drovers – in some versions of history singing Burns's 'Green Grow the Rashes O' and becoming 'gringoes' to their Mexican auditors – to the working-class personae of late-twentieth-century American rock musicians and the remarkable creative working kilt products to be found on the utilikilts website,[37] or in modern high fashion:

> Talking about fashion and not mentioning tartan is like talking about fine dining and not bringing up wine. The fabric is an eclectic essential in high fashion, and Jean Paul Gaultier would agree.[38]

Beyond such international fashion-focused examples, however, the issues discourses of tartan and tartanry raise for Scottish culture, the interaction of history and myth and any concept of what is 'Scottish' proliferate and will remain unfrozen and lively for many years to come. As Jean Berton has suggested,[39] the complexity of tartan can be seen to reflect the complexity of a multilingual culture and literature like that of Scotland.

## Notes

1   This chapter draws on, conflates and extends arguments first set out by the author in his two chapters in Ian Brown (ed.), *From Tartan to Tartanry: Scottish Culture, History and Myth* (Edinburgh, Edinburgh University Press, 2010).

2   Quoted in John Telfer Dunbar, *History of Highland Dress* (Edinburgh: Oliver and Boyd, 1962), p. 97.

3   Quoted in Jeffrey Banks and Doria La Chapelle, *Tartan: Romancing the Plaid* (New York: Rizzoli, 2007), p. 241.

4   Mary Douglas, *Implicit Meanings* (London: Routledge and Kegan Paul, 1975), p. 156.

5   For example, *passim* in Roland Barthes, *Mythologies*, selected and translated from the French by Annette Lavers (London: Jonathan Cape, 1972).

6   Colin McArthur, *Brigadoon, Braveheart and the Scots: Distortions of Scotland in Hollywood Cinema* (London: I. B. Taurus, 2003), p. 49.

7   John Telfer Dunbar, *History of Highland Dress* (Edinburgh: Oliver and Boyd, 1962), pp. 91–92.

8   Quoted in Dunbar, *History*, p. 97.

9   Alan Burford, 'Is *Tartan* a Gaelic word?', in Derick S. Thomson (ed.), *Gaelic and Scots in Harmony: Proceedings of the Second International Conference on the Languages of Scotland* (Glasgow: Department of Celtic, University of Glasgow, 1990), pp. 57–71.

10  Richard M. D. Grange, *A Short History of the Scottish Dress* (London: Burke's Peerage, 1966), p. 4.

11  James D. Scarlett, *Tartan: The Highland Textile* (London: Shepheard-Walwyn, 1990), p. ix.

12  Quoted in Dunbar, pp. 38–39.

13  Trevor Royle, 'From David Stewart to Andy Stewart: the invention and re-invention of the Scottish Soldier', in Brown (ed.), *From Tartan to Tartanry*, p. 56.

14  Cairns Craig, 'Myths Against History: Tartanry and Kailyard in 19th-Century Scottish Literature', in Colin McArthur (ed.), *Scotch Reels: Scotland in Cinema and Television* (London: BFI Publishing, 1982), p. 10.

15  See, for example, their respective chapters in Brown (ed.), *From Tartan to Tartanry*.

16  Jonathan Faiers, *Tartan* (Oxford and New York: Berg, 2008), p. 166.

17  Private conversation, 29 March 2010.

18  Domhnall Uilleam Stiùbhart, 'Highland rogues and the roots of Highland Romanticism', in Christopher MacLachlan (ed.), *Crossing the Highland Line: Cross-Currents in Eighteenth-Century Scottish Writing* (Glasgow: ASLS, 2009), p. 173.

19  John Telfer Dunbar, *The Costume of Scotland* (London: Batsford, 1981), pp. 87–88.

20  Hugh Trevor-Roper, 'The Invention of Tradition: The Highland Tradition of Scotland', in Eric Hobsbawm and Terence Ranger (eds), *The Invention of Tradition* (Cambridge: Cambridge University Press, 1983), pp. 15–41.

21  See Dunbar, *History*, pp. 12–13.

22  Ibid., p. 13.

23  Murray Pittock, 'Plaiding the Invention of Scotland', in Brown (ed.), *From Tartan to Tartanry*, p. 33.

24  The drawing may be found reproduced opposite page 254 of J. O. Bartley, *Teague, Shenkin and Sawney* (Cork: Cork University Press, 1954).

25  Trevor-Roper, p. 15–16.

26  William Ferguson, 'Samuel Johnson's Views on Scottish Gaelic Culture', *Scottish Historical Review,* Vol. 77.2 (October 1998), pp. 183–98, p. 183.

27  David McCrone, *Understanding Scotland: The Sociology of a Nation* (London: Routledge, 2001).

28  See, for example, Ian Maitland Hume, 'Tartanry into tartan: heritage, tourism and material culture', in Brown (ed.), *From Tartan to Tartanry,* pp. 82–92.

29  Michael Newton, 'Paying for the plaid: Scottish Gaelic identity politics in nineteenth-century North America', in Brown (ed.), *From Tartan to Tartanry,* pp. 63–81.

30  Colin McArthur, 'Breaking the Signs', *Cencrastus* No. 7 (Winter, 1981–82), p. 23.

31  John Caughie, 'Scottish Television: What Would It Look Like?', in Colin McArthur (ed.), *Scotch Reels: Scotland in Cinema and Television* (London: BFI Publishing, 1982), p. 116.

32  David McCrone, Angela Morris and Richard Kiely, *Scotland – the Brand: The Making of Scottish Heritage* (Edinburgh: Edinburgh University Press, 1995), p. 207.

33  Craig Beveridge and Ronald Turnbull, *The Eclipse of Scottish Culture: Inferiorism and the Intellectuals* (Edinburgh: Polygon, 1989), p. 14.

34  Jonathan Faiers, *Tartan* (Oxford and New York: Berg, 2008), p. 1.

35  Faiers, p. 55.

36  Faiers, p. 124.

37  I am grateful to David Goldie for drawing my attention to this site.

38  www.fabsugar.com/Fab-Read-Tartan-Romancing-756417: accessed 8 February 2014.

39  Private communication, January 2014.

# 4: *New Poems, Chiefly in the Scottish Dialect*: 'A sly wink to the master'

## KARYN WILSON COSTA

In his introduction to *New Poems, Chiefly in the Scottish Dialect,* an anthology of poems composed by twelve of Scotland's leading contemporary poets, commissioned in 2009 to celebrate the two hundred and fiftieth anniversary of the birth of Robert Burns, Robert Crawford justifies the allusion to the title of the 1786 Kilmarnock edition of Robert Burns's poetry as:

> a way of keeping faith with a persistent sense of poetic language, with Scottish accents, and with the art of verse. It is, if you like, a sly wink to the master. [...] In title and linguistic flavour the book pays tribute to Burns and what he did with language [...] Poets have travelled with Burns's title in different directions [...] there remain important links between his work and some of today's Scottish poets.[1]

In title, Robert Crawford's anthology marks the affiliation of the contributing poets with Robert Burns and previous literary generations writing in Scots, in the same way as Burns used the title, in Alan Watson's words, 'to announce his continuity with Scots writers such as Allan Ramsay and Robert Fergusson'.[2] The contributors to Professor Crawford's anthology arguably highlight the interrelationship of Scots and English, rather than oppose it. They are as aware about linguistic nuances as Burns, delighting in the advantages of the *copia verborum*, literally 'abundance of words', that a masterly command of Scottish dialects and English, and also Gaelic in some cases, affords. Indeed, Scotland is, as Douglas Dunn reminds us, a country with 'three sound tongues / in which to utter poetry' ('English, a Scottish Essay', 73–74). My aim is to look at the way the poets in Crawford's anthology address the question of the linguistic authority of Scots, which is rooted in the Kilmarnock edition of Burns's poems, and the manner in which they fruitfully engage with the hybrid, dramatic, subversive, humorous and inherently sociable nature of his poetry, while clearing a creative space for themselves.

The vexed question of language provides the backdrop to this anthology, which arguably participates in an ideological debate on the status of Scots and its 'legitimacy' and the 'authority' to voice Scottishness and Scotland. For the best part of two centuries, critical wisdom held that Burns could not write good poetry in English, yet it is now widely recognised that his linguistic spectrum extends more widely than either Scots or English, absorbing both. The culture of enlightened anglocentric 'improvement' was part of the poet's horizon long before he left Ayrshire to be lionised in Edinburgh. Robert Burns's self-awareness of linguistic nuances allowed him to freely engage in code-mixing, choosing style, register and language to suit his subject matter and mood. Following in his wake, the poets in Robert Crawford's anthology confidently exploit their plural linguistic and cultural inheritance, acknowledging their freedom to legislate on linguistic and poetic choices. In his seven-part essay *The Curtain*, Milan Kundera posits: 'There are two basic contexts in which a work of art may be placed: either in the history of its nation (we can call it the small context), or else in the supranational history of its art (the large context).'[3] Robert Burns suffered for two centuries from being placed in the 'small context'; only recently have scholars and critics begun to recognise him as arguably the first of the Romantics, recognising that his *Poems, Chiefly in the Scottish Dialect* display features of style and sensibility that would be central to Wordsworth and many other subsequent Romantic poets.[4] Underpinning Crawford's collection is the idea that choosing to write, or not to write, in Scots is much less of a nationalist or a political statement and more of an aesthetic one, one which continues the conversation with other poets in which Burns actively engaged in his poetry; by looking outward, Scots is employed as a resource to address other fundamental issues, thereby raising the profile of Scots in an international context.

The ideological context was markedly different when Burns's poems were first published in 1786: in a bid to uphold the legitimacy of Scots as a literary medium, Robert Burns challenged the cultural authority of the Scottish literati who thought it necessary to write in English to be taken seriously in London, but who nonetheless spoke Scots in private.

Burns famously lampooned those social climbers in his epistle 'To William Simson, Ochiltree':

> In days when mankind were but callans;
> At *Grammar, Logic,* an' sic talents,
> They took nae pains their speech to balance,
> Or rules to gie;
> But spak their thoughts in plain, braid Lallans,
> Like you or me. ('Postscript', 7–12)

Liam McIlvanney suggests the espousal of linguistic propriety and the deliberate avoidance of Scotticisms in eighteenth-century Scotland were 'devolutionary' pressures operating on Scottish writers and intellectuals during the Scottish Enlightenment.[5] Arguably, the reverse has often been true in contemporary Scotland. In 'English, a Scottish Essay', Douglas Dunn revisits this centuries-old debate on the 'legitimacy' of Scots as a literary language, highlighting the 'plots and counterplots of history' that contributed to the imposition of first English, then Scots as the 'proper' tongue and refuting the idea that language should ever be a political choice. With ironic use of italics, he brushes aside the concept of a *national* poetry, written in Scots to defend a *patrie*; the choice of the French word is deliberate since Dunn often extends the boundaries of his poetry beyond Scotland. He is just as scathing about what he perceives as an unnatural choice as the Scottish literati were about Burns's refusal to heed their advice to write in English. The British Empire would arguably not have prospered as much without the numerous 'anglicised' Scots who occupied powerful positions at its head:

> Lists of neurotic Scotticisms; earnest
> Desires to write and speak like Englishmen;
> A wilful limpness in the national wrist –
> Heyday of Edinburgh elocution!
> [...]
> A foreign language for men on the make
> In London or Calcutta, Hudson's Bay,
> British regiments, enslaved plantations
> [...]

Legged up by legover. Intimate unions
Ran parallel before the paper Act
In Anglo-Scottish sexual communions
Where love and love of property, the fact
Embedded snugly in commercial chance,
Led straight to land, preferment, and finance.
(115–118; 144–155)

Dunn's poem is every bit as vehement and vigorous in style as the poems of Burns in the Kilmarnock edition. It is also a scathing attack on what he labels the 'Robert Burns Syndrome' and the literary navel-gazing it encouraged, pressurising twentieth-century Scottish writers into writing in Scots, about Scotland: 'Just write like him, and you'll be true / To Scotland when its good old self returns. / Then you'll be true to us, and true to you' (37–40). The belief that 'a long-deceased National Bard' is the 'forevermore "Authentic" measure of the way to write / Poetry grounded in archaic hindsight and retrospective fame' (33–37) is arguably an offshoot of Burns's mythic status and the skewed critical reception of his poetry which for a century and a half focused on his 'Scottishness' and ignored his poetic craftsmanship. Above all, it is the product of nostalgia for a long-lost bardic cult locked in the past when, as Dunn has it, 'we spoke / Each one of us as quintessential Jock' (62–63), thus spawning a parochial literature that stifled creativity and fuelled the myth of 'MacMinotaur [...] sectarian, preening his tammy, polishing his grin' (171–173).

Douglas Dunn defines himself as 'a Scot who writes in the English-language-with-a-Scottish-accent, that is, in my mother tongue':[6]

Is it instinctive only
To think and feel the language I write in
Selects me to be snapped at, and feel lonely
When it's the tongue I know, that I delight in?
English I'm not. As language, though, you're mine,
Disinterested, Scots, also benign,
Or so I try to make you, keeping time
On beats of Burns and Shakespeare, Pope and Frost,
Plundered affinities, rhythm and rhyme

> From any place or time and intercrossed,
> MacCaig with Milton, Stevenson with Keats,
> Byron, Browning, scanning the nationless beats.
> ('English, a Scottish Essay', 43–54)

Dunn's point is that in the nation called Poetry, 'policed by Muses, not by critics or theorists' (31), speaking in a particular 'tongue', a word repeated throughout the poem, underscoring its double meaning as both official language and basic means of human expression, is neither odd nor treacherous. Burns also 'plundered affinities, rhythm and rhyme': there are countless allusions to English writers in his epigraphs and echoes of them in his poems, and the Standard Habbie, his favourite measure, is one of the plants that 'have crossed / seas, seasons, different climates, to be here / Thriving in shaded Scottish horticulture' ('English, a Scottish Essay', 269–271). Scottish critics, says Dunn, should allow writers to be part of a bigger conversation. In his nation, poets have a choice:

> We've got three sound tongues
> In which to utter poetry, and three
> Good reasons, therefore, for our native songs
> To triplicate our nationality.
> My Muse is mine alone; but still, she's free
> To join her sisters in their choir of three. (73–82)

Ralph Waldo Emerson famously said of Robert Burns in 1859 that he had made Lowland Scots a Doric dialect of fame, 'the only example in history of a language made classic by the genius of a single man'. Yet, the poetic multi-vocality in his macaronic compositions arguably renders Burns's literary language more of an artefact, an artificial construct in which different vernacular strains of Scots encounter archaic English and formal Latinate and French terms, and where elements of 'low' culture and register rub shoulders with 'high'. David Kinloch, a founder member of the 'Informationism' movement in the 1990s, hints at the artificial nature of Burns's mixed tongue, in his contribution to Crawford's anthology, 'Atmospheres o' Montale an' wan postscript', in which he imagines an encounter between the Nobel Prize-winning Italian poet Eugenio Montale (1896–1981) and a Scots-speaking cuttlefish, a nod to Montale's collection *Cuttlefish Bones* (*Ossi di Seppia*):

> 'But careful
> noo', the dialeck repones,
> 'Ahm a kina speshul wan,
> ma heid's fae Ayr, ma bum's
> fae Banff, ma nether pairt's
> archaic.' 'Ye mean yer "artifeeshul".' (44–49)

Similarly, Kinloch's poem may be seen as 'a conflux of different languages', which, like 'Burns's collision of Scots and English, fuses disparate elements of different cultures to demonstrate the benefits of encounter and amalgamation'.[7] Kinloch, however, goes further than Burns: his 'dictionary Scots' is the product of his trawling of the word hoard in Jamieson's *Dictionary of the Scottish Language*, 'that particular boneyard of unexpectedly fertile words',[8] to create a self-conscious linguistic construction in a 'celebration of the very artificiality' of the Scots he uses.[9]

Scotland has arguably always been a demotically energised place to write, where poets express themselves in a vivid, direct, colloquial style. Burns revelled in lowering all that was high, debunking and degrading with inimitably irreverent frankness, more often than not in the Standard Habbie measure, the aristocratic origins of which have been traced back to the songs of eleventh-century Occitan troubadour William of Poitiers, Duke of Aquitaine (1071–1127), who used it in five of his eleven extant poems. With its phatic thrust, so well suited to apostrophising an interlocutor, its dramatic quality and the way it invites irony and encourages inventive rhyme and wordplay, this form was to become one of those best suited to the mockery and irony of eighteenth-century Scottish vernacular poets Allan Ramsay, Robert Fergusson and Robert Burns:

> It maks ye rax for far mair rhymes
> at a faster pace than the sad hauf-mimes
> o normal formal verse: its chimes

> can syncopate;
> it's bagpipe ragtime, bop's sublime
> Scots drinkin mate.
> (W. N. Herbert, 'A Habbie History', 31–36)

In Kinloch's poem, the poet Montale composes his 'Ode tae a Hose-fish' in Standard Habbie; it is, in fact, nothing less than a parody of 'To a Mouse', arguably Robert Burns's most quoted and most parodied poem. The opening lines of Montale's poem: 'Big, slochie, fliskie, braisant beastie, / Bluid fae three herts sturs thy breastie!' echo those of Burns: 'Wee, sleekit, cowrin, tim'rous beastie / O, what a panic's in thy breastie!' Yet Kinloch's cuttlefish is the exact opposite of Burns's mouse; it is big, slimy, skittish and brazen, whereas the mouse is small, sleek and frightened. The reference to the three 'herts' echoes Douglas Dunn's attempts to 'triplicate our nationality', although in his efforts to find rhymes to fit the Standard Habbie measure, Kinloch draws on Scots, English and – French, rather than Gaelic. French cultural and literary references and French words abound in Kinloch's work: *Paris–Forfar, Un Tour d'Ecosse*, and more recently *Finger of a Frenchman* point to the creation of a 'New Alliance' between French and Scottish literary traditions,[10] and the will to find a place for Scotland in a wider international context. Such rhymes as 'feisty'/'tasty'; 'IQ'/'Bung fu'; 'leid'/'screed'; 'trousseaux'/'low'; 'Bijouterie'/'charivari'; 'cephalopod'/'God' or 'scaup'/'talk' are so many ingredients of what may be called 'a stew of language', in which musicality is one of the main ingredients. With its linguistic hybridity and inventive rhymes, Kinloch's poem is a paean to Robert Burns, to the 'fizz' of the 'Burns Stanza':

> Gin it can mak 'rime riche' wi 'is'
> – there's anely five –
> Ye'll ken the standard habbie's fizz
> Is still alive! (91–94)

The postscript at the end of this poem, addressed to 'all the dialects of the world', is a reflection on the status of those 'words', that could not be called to witness, 'For all had vanished like frost in the November morning', and how each dialect had tried to save itself, 'how much it lived within the people's mouths, how dead it was, how raw and how poetic.' As elsewhere in his poetry, Kinloch is 'speaking for (and of) the strange revenge sometimes taken by secret or suppressed languages'.¹¹ While Kinloch sees the fate of Scots as part of a bigger linguistic picture, he demonstrates that a poem in Scots does not have to be about promoting Scottish national and cultural identity. Ironically, in the best Burnsian tradition, he hijacks the stanza most widely associated with the Scottish literary tradition in order to eschew the parochialism its detractors consider as its biggest flaw. Similarly, in a very sly wink to Burns's irreverent playfulness, W. N. Herbert hijacks what is arguably the most anthologised of poems in the English literary tradition with a nod to William Blake's 'The Tyger' in the title of one of his contributions to Crawford's anthology: 'Rabbie, Rabbie, Burning Bright'. In juxtaposition to this most English of literary references, he composes a lowbrow, tongue-in-cheek celebration of Burns Night in the most quintessentially Scottish stanza, in Scots.

Liz Lochhead, Scotland's Makar, follows in the wake of Kinloch and Herbert with her 'performance' poem 'Nick Dowp, Feeling Himself Miscast in a Very English Production, Rehearses Bottom's Dream', a cheerfully vulgar parody both of Shakespeare's *A Midsummer Night's Dream* and the Standard Habbie measure, joining in the debate on the 'legitimacy' of Scots as a literary language. Like Kinloch's poem, Lochhead stages, or rather performs, the writing of a poem, within a poem. Hers opens with Nick Dowp, alias Nick Bottom, engaging with the audience in a parody of a scene from the English bard's *A Midsummer Night's Dream*. The original,

> Feed him with apricocks and dewberries,
> With purple grapes, green figs, and mulberries.
> The honey-bags steal from the humble bees
> [...]
> Tie up my lover's tongue, bring him silently.
> (III. 1. 173–175; 210)

is transformed by Lochhead:

> 'Tie up my lover's tongue?' Yon's censorship!
> 'Hae anither English apricock and button your lip.'

> Neither dewberry nor honey bag from humble bee'll keep
> Me silent, I hate it! (1–4)

In this savvy staging of an ironic attack on the powers-that-were, who had for years decreed that speaking in Scots was only permissible in recitation competitions to celebrate Burns Night, Lochhead broaches the question of the ownership of language. Mixing high and low language and high- and lowbrow cultural references, Lochhead rejoices in the debunking tradition in Scottish literature, and irreverently makes a case for the use of colloquial Scots in literary texts. Her contribution to Crawford's anthology is another nod to Burns's deft handling of the Standard Habbie and to the way he plays with language, register and sound:

> Shakespeare (excuse me for being cynical)'s
> Attitude to Scotch verse is that it's kinna
> > Like McGonigal's
> And only guid enough for thae Rude-Mechanicals
> An Loss-the-Plots
> To tumpty-tum their numpty lyricals
> In accents Scots. (16–21)

There is also a nod to Burns's demotic treatment of the devil in his irreverent debunking of 'Auld Hornie, Satan, Nick, or Clootie' ('Address tae the Deil', 2) in the onomastics: for Nick Dowp, the miscast actor, one should read 'the devil's buttocks', or as he himself elegantly puts it: 'Whauras I get *mere prose* o which the bottom line is / That I'm an *erse*!' (10–12). Similarly, the Bard of Avon is 'Thon Shakespeare-felly', echoing the manner in which Burns was wont to deflate the political and literary movers and shakers of his day. Reductive impulses, Douglas Dunn reminds us, are common in Scottish literature and 'the Scots language is riddled with reductive terms and diminutives' (80). Arguably, the jocular form of playfulness inherent in the Standard Habbie suited Robert Burns's demotic humour and sense of daftness and thus extends an open invitation to the comedies of imitation, be it pastiche, parody or burlesque. As Liz Lochhead herself put it: 'Now none but a parodist dare essay the Burns stanza'.[12] Lochhead's poem ends, as it begins, in Standard Habbie, after the rewriting of a scene from Shakespeare's play in 'braid Glesca-patois', in Nick Dowp's 'ain wurds', not those put into his mouth by an English bard, nor even in 'the Doric', lauded by the snobbish critics, which is not low enough for Lochhead. Only the very vulgar will do, as she cocks a snook at the 'Speak properly' brigade, chastised elsewhere in the anthology in the poems of Douglas Dunn and Tom Leonard. Thus, with the slyest of winks to Burns, Liz Lochhead turns literary hierarchies on their heads, reversing high and low cultures, mapping the diabolical strand that runs through Scottish literature onto Shakespeare's English pastoral. Performing a subversive shift on English culture, as well as on its greatest writer, Lochhead transfers the Bard of Avon to the Glaswegian urban underworld. She refutes any linguistic hierarchy where Scots is concerned: a language should reflect its speakers.

Burns was a gifted inventor of personae and of voices, with whom Lochhead engages creatively in her performance poetry. Similarly, Jackie Kay employs the dramatic monologue Burns arguably invented in 'Holy Willie's Prayer' in 'A Drunk Woman Looks at Her Nipple (After MacDiarmid)', a playful appropriation in Scots dialect of Hugh MacDiarmid's epic harangue in synthetic Scots, following in the wake of Liz Niven's 'A Drunk Wumman Sittin oan a Thistle' (1997), although in Kay's poem, the nipple becomes an eco-friendly symbol of our endangered planet. 'Maw Broon Goes for Colonic Irrigation' is one of Kay's 'Maw Broon Monologues' written with performance in mind. The 'Broons', the characters of a popular comic strip created in 1936 by Dudley Dexter Watkins and arguably Scotland's first family, are iconic figures of the Scottish kitsch culture that conveys those consumerist manifestations of a national identity that came to be associated with the Burns Cult and which Douglas Dunn criticises so vehemently in his 'English, a Scottish Essay'. Jackie Kay embarks on a hilarious investigation of this vigorous, realistic popular culture by reinventing Maw Broon as 'a 21st-century woman on a quest for fulfilment'.[13] She creates a different poetic voice for Maw, whose atypical musings in an unexpected situation contrast ironically with the traditional representation of the family in the comic strip. When Maw Broon holds up a mirror to herself the Scots also see themselves in this oblique critique of Scottish society: 'Aw o' a sudden yer auld body is a hale new nation, / Rid o' the parasites, clean as a whistle, yer saying / Ho-ho, gone yersell!' (13–15). The outspoken apostrophising of Maw is rooted in the Scottish colloquial tradition and Jackie Kay juxtaposes vigorous speech idioms, clichés and snatches of Standard English that flow through the poem with the same energy and sense of urgency as the colonic irrigation itself. The association of the Scots language with humour has a long history, stretching back beyond Burns to the medieval Makars. Pawky humour of the 'Quintessential Jock' variety evoked by Douglas Dunn is central to the 'Broons' and arguably helps to create a powerful sense of a certain shared 'Scottishness' among readers of the *Sunday Post* comic strip. Kay exploits this shared bond in order to widen the identity debate and incorporate a feminist agenda. Women's voices are, indeed, often heard in Burns's poems and songs; women poets like Jackie Kay, much of whose poetry is concerned with a 'female revisioning of traditional, patriarchal Scottish culture',[14] assert female autonomy with unprecedented confidence and humour, debunking both high and low cultural icons, and in so doing, delineate a cultural and literary territory for women.

Just as Jackie Kay holds up a two-way mirror to Scottish culture and society, Kathleen Jamie and Robert Crawford, in their 'Eftir'/ 'After' poems, the reshaping in Scots of poems by two European poets, hold up a two-way mirror to the Scottish literary tradition. Jamie transposes two poems by German poet Friedrich Hölderlin (1770–1843), arguably one of Europe's greatest poets, into what David Constantine calls 'a feast of Scots', neatly sidestepping Standard English.[15] Relying on the word-for-word English translations of David Constantine and those of Michael Hamburger, Jamie's aim is to try to develop her Scots into a 'more tensile, robust and elegant medium':

> Robert Burns achieves a lovely intimate apostrophising in Scots – consider 'To a Mountain Daisy', Hölderlin has it too, but it's hard to carry off in English, so I thought it would go well into Scots. As well, I wanted the chance to risk bigger emotional and rhetorical gestures than are commonly allowed in English, which is a language easily embarrassed.[16]

In 'Hauf o Life' ('Hälfe des Lebens'), Jamie's apostrophising is indeed intimate, and unembarrassingly emotional: witness the graceful rhythm of 'But whaur, when winter's wi us / will ah fin flo'ers; / whaur the shadda / an sunlicht o the yard?' (8–11). She connects to the eco-poet in Hölderin: 'There's an anxious earth-love in Hölderlin, and I liked that' (*Metamorphoses*), and in her 'version', his landscapes take on a Scottish appearance: 'Bien wi yella pears, fu / o wild roses, the braes / fa intil the loch' (1–3). Jamie's poem thus includes Robert Burns, 'Scotia's Bard', who addressed daisies, mice and men in his concern for the effect of human progress on the natural environment, both in a wider, European community of poets and in the burgeoning art form that is eco-poetry.

Robert Crawford sets Burns beside Constantine P. Cavafy (1863–1933), one of the greatest poets of modern Greece and an opponent of all forms of fundamentalism. In 'Robert Burns and the Mind of Europe' Crawford foregrounds the democratic and European credentials of the Ayrshire Bard and explains why indeed he matters to the mind of Europe:

> In his tone and sometimes his content he articulates European democracy before any other major European poet [...] Burns matters because he is a great exemplar of the art form of poetry. We need to see this Ayrshire Orpheus as deserving and claiming a place among the historic and worldwide community of poets.[17]

Crawford includes both Scots and English versions of two of Cavafy's best-known poems: 'Waas' ('Walls') and 'The God Forleets Antony' ('The God Abandons Antony'). He transposes Alexandria to Edinburgh in the latter, and in another of his transpositions, 'Kirk' ('In Church'), a Greek church becomes 'a Scots kirk / wi' its bare wuid pews, / its metrical psalms, / the skinklin blak brogues o the meenisters / gaunt in their corbies' goons' (4–8), a sly wink not only to Burns, but also to the medieval ballad 'The Twa Corbies' and Liz Lochhead's play *Mary Queen of Scots Got Her Head Chopped Off*. In 'The God Forleets Antony' echoes of the poetry of Burns can be heard in the familiarity of diminutives, the use of colloquial, wry vocabulary and the sympathetic apostrophising: 'Mind an nae mak a daftie o yirsel, dinnae say / It wis aa a drame, jist a swick o the lugs: / Dinnae bemean yirsel wi tuim howps lik yon' (9–11). The tone is far more intimate than that of the version Crawford gives in English, arguably due to the simplicity and directness inherent in the Scots vernacular that 'avoids bathos and banality':[18] English being, as Jamie has it, 'easily embarrassed'.

The poems of Crawford and Jamie are 'versions' of other poems and responses to themes in those source texts that are transposable to existing strands in Scottish literature and are thus rewritten into a Scottish cultural context. They are not word-for-word translations, but, as Don Paterson says of his 'versions' of poems by German poet Rilke, they are 'trying to be poems in their own right; while they have the original to serve as a detailed ground-plan and elevation, they are trying to build themselves a robust home in a new country, in its vernacular architecture, with local words for its brick and local music for its mortar'.[19] Furthermore, by connecting with and transposing European poetry into Scots, Crawford and Jamie make it possible for the 'vernacular language' to contribute to the reinvigoration of the source culture while elevating its identity with that of the source language, here German and Modern Greek, arguably more prestigious languages: thus 'Translation becomes an act of reclaiming, of recentering of identity, a reterritorializating operation [...] it elevates a dialect to the status of a national and cultural language'.[20] The poets who have contributed to this anthology celebrate their cultural confidence in an inclusive use of literary Scots, the urban demotic, English-with-a-Scottish-accent, 'dictionary Scots' and Standard English. At the same time, they move Scottish poetry defini-tively out of the 'small context' of a confining national, sometimes parochial tradition and join the bigger conversation, taking Robert Burns with them. They keep faith with the skilful master of the tangy vernacular and the linguistically fluid poet, while managing to escape the anxiety of Burns's influence, and more importantly, rescuing the bard from his own bardolatry. These poets thus go some way towards ending the Robert Burns Syndrome: although 'Rabbie's star is still burning bright', to misquote W. N. Herbert, the page is perhaps less blinded by his after-image.

# Notes

1   Robert Crawford (ed.), *New Poems, Chiefly in the Scottish Dialect* (Edinburgh: Polygon, 2009), p. 11.

2   Alex Watson, 'Thirteen Ways of Glossing "To a Haggis": Disputing the Borders of Robert Burns's Paratexts', *International Journal of Scottish Literature*, Issue 6 (Spring/Summer 2010), p. 10.

3   Milan Kundera, *The Curtain*, trans. by Linda Asher (New York: Harper Perennial, 2005), pp. 39; 35.

4   Jerome McGann (ed.), *New Oxford Book of Romantic Verse* (Oxford: Oxford University Press, 1993), pp. xx–xxi.

5   Liam McIlvanney, 'Hugh Blair, Robert Burns, and the Invention of Scottish Literature', *Eighteenth Century Life*, 29, no. 2 (Spring 2005), pp. 25–46, 27–28.

6   Marco Fazzini, 'An Interview with Douglas Dunn', *Studies in Scottish Literature* 31, Issue 1 (1997), pp. 121–30, p. 125.

7   Alex Watson, p. 19.

8   Roderick Watson, 'Living with the Double Tongue: Modern Poetry in Scots', in Ian Brown et al. (eds), *The Edinburgh History of Scottish Literature* (Edinburgh: Edinburgh University Press, 2007), vol. 3, pp. 163–75, 173.

9   Ibid., p. 171.

10  David Kinloch with Richard Price (eds), *La Nouvelle Alliance* (Grenoble: Université Stendhal ELLUG, 2000), p. 14.

11  R. Watson, p. 173.

12  *Guardian*, 25 January 2013, www.theguardian.com/books/2013/jan/25/my-hero-robert-burns-lochhead, accessed 8 May 2013.

13  *Scotland on Sunday*, 25 October 2009, www.scotsman.com/news/interview-jackie-kay-poet-playwright-and-novelist-1-471761, accessed 8 May 2013.

14  Eleanor Bell, 'Old Country, New Dreams: Scottish Poetry Since the 1970s', in Ian Brown et al. (eds), *The Edinburgh History of Scottish Literature* (Edinburgh: Edinburgh University Press, 2007), vol. 3, pp. 185–97, 194.

15  David Constantine, *Modern Poetry in Translation*, Series 3 No. 3, 2005, www.mptmagazine.com/product/series-3-no3--metamorphoses-117/, accessed 15 April 2013.

16  Ibid.

17  Robert Crawford, 'Robert Burns and the Mind of Europe', in Murray Pittock (ed.), *Robert Burns in Global Culture* (Lewisburg: Bucknell University Press, 2011), pp. 47–62, 60.

18  John Corbett, *Written in the Language of the Scottish Nation: A History of Literary Translation into Scots* (Clevedon: Multilingual Matters, 1999), p. 111.

19  Don Paterson, *Orpheus* (London: Faber, 2006), p. 73.

20  Annie Brisset, 'The Search For a Native Language: Translation and Cultural Identity', trans. by Rosalind Gill and Roger Gannon in Lawrence Venuti (ed.), *The Translation Studies Reader*, 2nd edn (New York and London: Routledge, 2000, 2004), pp. 337–68, 340.

# 5: Bards and radicals in contemporary Scottish poetry: Liz Lochhead, Jackie Kay, and an evolving tradition

MARGERY PALMER McCULLOCH

In the early years of the twentieth century, literary scholars and critics felt able to define or argue over what they called *the* Scottish tradition in poetry. Today, after the literary revolution begun by MacDiarmid and his supporters in the post-World War One period, and with the evidence of its legacy in the outstanding number and diversity of Scottish writers in poetry, prose fiction and drama who have emerged over subsequent decades, we are more aware that literature, like language, is constantly evolving. We realise that there are, and historically always have been, several 'traditions' or 'tendencies' in Scottish writing, interacting with each other and with the influences from other cultures which they adopt and adapt for their own purposes.

On the other hand, it is possible to recognise a recurrence over the centuries of writers who seem to be drawn to a particular kind of subject matter or to a particular kind of literary role. In this present chapter my interest is in one such tendency or approach in Scottish poetry, and in how it has evolved in contemporary poetry from the later decades of the twentieth century to the present. I would identify this as both a 'bardic' and a 'radical' approach to the role of poet: 'bardic' in the sense that the poet takes on the ancient role of spokesperson for the tribe, the keeper of its history, the one who notices and publicly challenges what is unsatisfactory, who dares to say what others are unable or afraid to say; and 'radical' not only in an ideological or political sense, but also artistically, in an aesthetic sense: a poet who explores new ways of formal communication, who challenges outworn literary forms and traditions, as well as challenging received ideas and practices in a social or political context. We can identify such an approach to the poet's role in the work of Burns, of MacDiarmid, and in our own time, of Morgan (whose speaker in the poem 'At Central Station' acknowledges the role as being sometimes that of an 'accursed recorder').[1] What I find especially interesting in the contemporary period is that in the poetry of the generation of writers who came after Morgan, this bardic, radical (both ideologically and aesthetically) and historically male approach to the poet's role has to a significant extent been taken over by female poets such as Liz Lochhead and Jackie Kay. Both these poets have an extensive and varied oeuvre, but the discussion in this essay will focus predominantly on Lochhead's play *Mary Queen of Scots Got Her Head Chopped Off* (1987), Kay's 'Bessie Smith Blues' from *Other Lovers* (1993) and her radio play, *Lamplighter*, written to commemorate the abolition of slavery and broadcast by BBC Radio Three in March 2007.

Liz Lochhead's first collection of poems, *Memo for Spring*, published in 1972, immediately announced a new poetic agenda as she placed the lives and perspectives of her female speakers at the centre of the poetry's scenarios – a truly radical move in regard to Scottish poetry, perhaps in regard to poetry generally. She herself has said of her early poetry 'my country was woman',[2] and her explorations of this new territory not only replaced the dominant male perspectives and national identity themes of earlier Scottish poetry, but also anticipated and provided a creative equivalent for the later feminist academic interrogation of women's roles in society and the arts. Scottish female fiction writers in the interwar period such as Catherine Carswell and Willa Muir had transformed the themes and textures of Scottish fiction with their lively contemporary scene-setting and fluidity of dialogue, their imagistic language and psychological insights. Liz Lochhead brought a similar contemporaneity to her new poetry not only in the portrayal of the gender dilemmas of her principal characters, but also in the often unnoticed little dramas of everyday life which go on in the background of her scenes: for example, the warrant-sale which marks the end of a marriage (a social cruelty which accompanies the distress of lost love); the presence of 'Daft Annie' on the village main street, herself 'out of the mainstream' of life; 'the television showroom's window [which] / showed us cities burning in black and white' and the ambulance 'screaming past' in the otherwise ironically jaunty love poem 'Obituary' ('We two in W.2').[3] Edwin Morgan, of course, had from his male perspective also introduced such contemporary, topical contexts and conversational discourse into his poetry of the 1960s, especially in his outstanding collection *The Second Life* of 1968. Lochhead has never made any secret of the debt she feels she owes to Morgan, both as a friend and as a pioneer of a new way forward in poetry; and in her 'Five Berlin Poems' written after a visit to Berlin in 1990 shortly after the Wall came down, she wonders who could make sense of the impressions that are crowding in on her and answers: 'Morgan could, yes Eddie could, he would. And that makes me want to try'.[4]

Shortly before that memorable Berlin visit, however, Lochhead herself had explored the equally contradictory and confusing impressions of Scottish history in her play *Mary Queen of Scots Got Her Head Chopped Off*, commissioned by Communicado Theatre Company to mark the five hundredth anniversary of the Scottish Queen's beheading at the behest of Elizabeth of England in 1587. From the first, Lochhead's poetry had been marked by its dramatic quality, its capacity to communicate the voices and personalities of the speakers in her poems, to create dramatic scenes and episodes in the poetry. It is not surprising, therefore, that she soon began to write performance pieces, dramatic monologues and eventually works for the theatre, including an adaptation into Scots of Moliere's *Tartuffe* commissioned by the Royal Lyceum Theatre in Edinburgh and performed there in 1986. She commented in an interview in *Talking Verse* that *Tartuffe* was an especially important play for her since it was in this composition that she first found herself using the Scots language in a play: 'But to my great surprise it was in actual Scots, most of it. It wasn't a decision. It wasn't just English for Scottish speakers. It was Scots.' And then, having discovered 'this well that I didn't realise was there, of even vocabulary, and definitely thought and rhythm', she found that it 'was available for *Mary Queen of Scots Got Her Head Chopped Off*.'[5] She also found that in addition to using the Scots language in her play about Mary, she was able to bring together the gender concerns which had preoccupied her earlier with an exploration of issues relating to the nature of her country – and she found that these might even have something in common.

*Mary Queen of Scots Got Her Head Chopped Off* is a radical play, both formally and ideologically. Although one finds a dramatic quality in earlier Scottish poetry – in Burns, for example, and in MacDiarmid's long poem *A Drunk Man Looks at the Thistle* – in Scotland professional theatre drama, although not entirely absent, was slow to develop after the constraints put upon it by the Protestant Reformation. It is arguably only in the second half of the twentieth century that we can speak with any confidence of the development of a *tradition* or *traditions* of professional Scottish theatre drama. As might be expected as a result of its commissioning by

Communicado, a company that performed in a non-naturalistic, Brechtian mode, Lochhead's exploration of Scottish history in her *Mary Queen of Scots* play is itself very different from what one might call an endorsement-of-historical-reality drama. Her approach is eclectic in the sense that she makes use of a number of presentational styles such as music, dance, pictorial detail, anachronistic costuming and interchangeability of characters, all of which puncture any idea that this is an attempt to provide an illusion of historical reality; emphasising instead that it, as in Brechtian drama, is intended to provoke questioning, to involve the audience in reassessing and reinterpreting historical events as they have traditionally come down to us. From its very first words: 'Country: Scotland. Whit like is it?', spoken by what the stage directions call 'an interesting, ragged, ambiguous creature', La Corbie: 'the crow, the corbie, le corbeau, moi!', the audience is pulled into the drama, not to observe passively, but to question, to become involved in the action, to make unexpected connections.[6] Such a methodology also allows her to explore ideological positions in a way that defamiliarises them, thus enabling fresh insights and responses to be produced. For example, the traditional hero of the Protestant Reformation in Scotland, John Knox, is presented through the Brechtian method of *Verfremdungseffekt* – the 'making strange' effect – appearing on stage in Act 1 Scene IV wearing a bowler hat and behind him '*Two men, stamping, sway a big sheet like a blank banner*'. In addition to these physical attributes or 'Gests', there is a musical direction: '*Music and hoochs and ugly skirls*'. The audience member, without the aid of the written text's stage direction '*Knox is ranting*' (*MQS*, 19), might not initially recognise John Knox in this presentation, but will recognise an intolerant prejudiced stance too familiar from many sectarian parades of a religious or political nature. In a later presentation of a public parade in Act 2 Scene IV of the play, it is the musical Gest that dominates: a singing of one of the Lutheran *Gude and Godly Ballatis* popular in the sixteenth century, where the metaphor of the ballad is a hunting one and the hunter Jesus and his target the Roman Catholic fox are clearly identified. But here it is the dynamic of the sung ballad, the gradations of loudness and softness employed, that builds up the tension and ultimately its message of hatred. Here, Knox himself is identified only when, as the parade singing reaches its loud climax, he and the character playing the Earl of Bothwell peel off from the group and continue a previous private conversation, thus making it clear to the audience who they are. Yet in both these scenes, as a result of the method of their presentation, Knox and the rabble that surrounds him can themselves be seen as a metaphor for a wider intolerance in human society and relationships, for the certainty of rightness in a cause which closes the ears and mind to the possibility of other ways forward; for the idealism that can only too easily cross over the narrow line and become a destructive intolerance. Mary herself is presented, on the whole, sympathetically in Lochhead's characterisation and, in her interviews with Knox, his intemperate intolerance contrasts with her logical enquiry, a logic that the reader or listener recognises has much to support it. On the other hand, and in relation to the political power struggles going on in the play, both queens are shown to be attempting to deal with an impossible situation: that of being a female monarch in a period where the machinery of government is designed for a male ruler, and where the traditional role of the queen has been to act as intermediary between the king and his people through her beauty and virtue, thus allowing him to remain more distant. Public and personal roles are therefore critical in this story of the two queens, and both queens suffer for the decisions they make in their different ways: Mary's downfall is brought about largely by her attempting to personalise the role of monarch, and by her choice of an unsuitable husband to accompany her in her task; Elizabeth succeeds by refusing to countenance marriage and by ruling like a male monarch, but we see also through Lochhead's imagistic presentation of Elizabeth's nightmares, the psychological and emotional pain this decision brings with it.

There is no way in which the variety and complexity of Lochhead's *Mary Queen of Scots* can be conveyed satisfactorily in a short space of time. The play needs to be read as a whole, as well as being seen in performance if at all possible. And although Lochhead has continued to write poetry, and especially drama, that metaphorically explores ideological and social issues of continuing human interest – as for example her adaptation or reworking of plays such as *Medea, Antigone*, Chekhov's *Three Sisters – Mary Queen of Scots* remains in my view the most powerful demonstration of her role as bard and radical – intellectually, ideologically and aesthetically. In it, she has produced a text that is equally relevant to our present as to its historical past; and a text applicable beyond its Scottish contexts to worldwide contemporary and historical conflicts and cultures; a text that encourages us to interrogate the messages left for us by history, to question traditional interpretations of that history, but also to see the application of that questioning to the dilemmas that face us in the present. And what the play's methodology in particular does is encourage us to realise that we do have choices. Things do not need to be the way they seem to be. As Brecht told his actors:

> When you go on stage imply what doesn't take place as well as showing what does. Try to show that instead of moving down left – you could have moved up right. Instead of saying 'You'll pay for that' you could have said 'I forgive you'. [7]

The second poet under discussion, Jackie Kay, is in many ways similar to Lochhead in her willingness to introduce uncomfortable topics of public interest and in her inventiveness in her poetic discourse. Her poetry is notable for its imagistic language, its sounds and rhythmic movement, its humour and self-awareness, its dramatic speaking voices – and, like Lochhead, Kay has written plays as well as poetry, although she has added to these genres full-length fiction, short stories, and autobiography. The new formal approaches she brings to her writing are matched by her fresh exploration of themes which relate to the way we live with one another and organise our societies. On the other hand, Kay differs from Lochhead in that gender is not for her the primary structuring theme or metaphor that it has been for Lochhead – perhaps because the younger Kay began to publish in the years after gender studies had become a familiar presence in academia and the media, and social changes were providing more equality and opportunities for women. Gender is, however, not irrelevant to Kay's poetry. We notice that the speakers in her poems are most often women, whatever the poems' themes. Her first book of poems, *The Adoption Papers*, tells the story of an adoption through the voices of three women: the birth mother, the adoptive mother and the adopted daughter. In 'Gastarbeiter' from the collection *Other Lovers*, with its ironic title translating as 'Guest Worker', the immigrant who has to learn 'the new tongue' and to whom 'the trees were tall strangers' is a woman; a mother who sleeps with her children in the one bed, 'rolled tight' together for safety, 'a bandage on an open wound', and who jumps from the house with the children in her arms when an explosive device is put through her letterbox.[8] Jackie Kay might herself have grown up feeling something of an alien in Scotland, since, like the child in *The Adoption Papers*, she was a child of mixed race, the daughter of a Scottish Highland mother and a Nigerian father who abandoned his lover when he discovered she was pregnant. Kay, however, was brought up lovingly and intelligently by her Scottish adoptive parents, and seems secure with regard to national identity as well as gender. In her poem 'In My Country', a suspicious woman queries a girl's origins, but is quickly dispatched by the speaker's confident declaration that she comes from 'Here. These parts' (*OL*, 24). Kay herself has voiced her irritation that 'people can't contain both things, being Black and being Scottish, without thinking that there is an inherent contradiction there'. And it's not just the Scots who have difficulty with her dual identity. Black acquaintances also find her accent 'funny' and say 'they've never met such a person before'.[9] She made these comments about her identity in an interview in 2001, published in *Sleeping with Monsters*. Since then, she has visited her father's home in Nigeria and has written in her book *Red Dust Road* about this experience and how she discovered to her surprise how non-African she was perceived to be by the Nigerians she met, and how she herself discovered how different in identity she was from them. Yet it is perhaps her unusual upbringing and identity situation, and yet the confidence she derived from it and from its non-conformity, that has enabled her to speak so powerfully, and yet so lyrically as well as humorously of less happy instances of being 'off colour', of not fitting into what another Scottish poet Angela McSeveney called the 'pre-arranged pigeonholes' of society.[10]

Kay has explored many aspects of 'off-colour' identity in her writing, including in her novel *Trumpet* that of the star male trumpet player who was discovered after his death to have been a woman, despite his marriage and apparent fatherhood. What this chapter finishes with, however, is Kay's exploration of two individual situations relating to Africans who were victims of the slave trade, which, like her 'Gastarbeiter' poem, shows her taking her role as bard and radical beyond her immediate context into a wider history of human cruelty and suffering. The first of these instances occurs in *Other Lovers*, which opens with a series of poems derived from the singing life of the blues singer Bessie Smith. Here we have not the original African plantation slaves themselves, but their descendants, who still work the cotton and tobacco fields and have limited liberty and little self-determination or sense of personal identity. Bessie follows these workers on their tobacco and cotton work trails, entertaining and inspiring them: 'On she would come, the Empress, the Voodoo Queen. / Blast the blues into them so people remembered who they'd been' (*OL*, 11). There is a wonderful vitality and power in this poetry which patterns the story it tells of the blues singer's power over the people. Yet at the same time it can be tender and evocative, bringing to us through its rhythms and sounds the vulnerability of the people, and the importance to them of memory and music: 'Took them to the sad place. The place they were scared to go. / Took them to the mean place where they knew they'd been low' (*OL*, 11). Bessie herself is brought to us as a force of Nature:

> Every note she sang, she bent her voice to her will;
> her voice was a wood instrument or a wind one,
> her voice had the power to turn the sails of the windmill,
> or knock down a tree with the force of a hurricane.

Yet 'She could use it as a shelter, the roof of her mouth, / stopping the rain, stopping the rain soon as she sang' (*OL*, 12).

There was, unfortunately, no Bessie Smith to inspire or comfort the women who speak in Kay's radio play *The Lamplighter*, first broadcast by the BBC on Radio Three in March 2007. Apart from the voice of the man MacBean, who acts mostly as a narrator of the factual details of the sea journeys – the weather conditions, the number of slave deaths on board ship, description of the Jamaican landscape, description of how to beat the slaves – apart from his impersonal male voice, all the speakers are women: the voice of eleven-year-old Anniwaa who opens and closes the poem, whose subsequent story after her capture we never learn, but who keeps repeating the words she spoke immediately after capture: 'I am a girl. I am in the dark, I don't know how long I have been kept in the dark.'[11] The other women's voices weave in and out of each other, telling their individual tales which at the same time are tales of suffering which belong to them all: Mary, beaten and left for dead because she ran away; Constance, raped repeatedly by her owner, beaten by his wife, and whose three-year-old daughter was taken from her and sold; Black Harriot, taken to England, who discovers some self-determination in becoming a black high-class whore; Lamplighter, who finally manages to write down her story, to have it printed: 'It was printed and reprinted / And told. / And retold again' (*L*, 92). What is striking about this terrible narrative is in fact its vitality, the absence of self-negation in the midst of its horror. Listening to it and then reading it, one is reminded of the very different atmosphere of Elizabeth Barrett Browning's nineteenth-century poem 'The Runaway Slave at Pilgrim's Point', which tells a not dissimilar story of rape and beatings, of the denial to the slaves of identity other than that of slave, of the destruction of self-worth.[12] Barrett Browning's girl escapes her master, but only after her lover – another slave – has been killed by him and she herself raped and made pregnant by him. Having killed and buried the resulting baby because she could not bear to see the Master's look in the child's eyes (a comment made also by Black Harriot in Kay's epic), she is now at bay, ironically at Pilgrim's Point, where in an earlier century English pilgrims fleeing religious persecution had landed to make a new, free life. But for this girl, there is no freedom apart from death. Barrett Browning's poem was written during the nineteenth-century campaign to end slavery and its horror and pessimism is predominant. Jackie Kay does not allow us to forget Great Britain's complicity in this slave trade, with the cities of Liverpool, Bristol, London, Manchester, Lancaster and Glasgow creating a kind of litany of prosperity through exploitation throughout the narrative, especially in Scene XIII: 'British Cities'. The triumph of Kay's *Lamplighter*, on the other hand, lies not only in its artistic vitality, but in its optimism, an optimism on the part of its female speakers – and survivors. (And it is important to remember here that Kay has said that she does not speak up 'on behalf of' others in her work, but through her work she allows them to speak up for themselves – another radical reinterpretation of the bard's role which can be seen also to apply to Lochhead.)

The *Lamplighter* play ends with the announcement of the abolition of slavery: an event noted impersonally in MacBean's factual narration but also imagistically in the words of the former slave called Lamplighter, her words preceded and followed by music. This is not quite the end of the story, however, as Black Harriot reminds us. The final scene, 'Freedom', does not allow us to forget or bypass the past, but instead we participate in the women's celebration of their triumph over it: Lamplighter, who at long last and after many failed attempts has 'managed to tell my story'; Constance, who has lost all her children and who wonders if 'they'll ever / Try and come and find me', but who has become 'Aunty to all the children. / All children are my grandchildren'; Mary, who was raped and beaten continuously but who has survived her tormentors:

> You know the funny thing?
> Big Man is dead. Houselady is dead.
> The driver is dead. The overseer man passed
> Away last autumn. And me Mary
> Who hardly ate a thing
> And was beaten till
> An inch of my life.
> I survived! Trust in Jesus!
> I survived them all. (*L*, 92, 93–94, 94)

Yet, lest we become too triumphant, Kay leaves us also with Anniwaa, whose voice began the slave story, but whose own story is never fully told us. Her life seems to have stopped with her capture, and the narrative ends with her repeating yet again her memory of the life from which she was snatched: 'Once upon a time, I lived in a house with a cone-shaped roof ...' (*L*, 95).

Jackie Kay is an exceptionally vital storyteller, and like the 'Storyteller' in Lochhead's poem of that name – and like Lochhead also – 'to tell the stories was [and is] her *work*'.[13] Both Kay and Lochhead have taken the ancient role of the poet as recorder and challenger into new territory, bringing together past and present with a message relevant for all societies in our own time; and bringing it to us in wonderfully dramatic, revitalised poetic forms.

## Notes

1  Edwin Morgan, *Collected Poems* (Manchester: Carcanet, 1990), p. 405.
2  Liz Lochhead in interview with Colin Nicolson, 'Knucklebones of Irony', in *Poem, Purpose and Place* (Edinburgh: Polygon, 1992), p. 223.
3  Liz Lochhead, *Memo for Spring* (1972) in *Dreaming Frankenstein and Collected Poems* (Edinburgh; Polygon, 1984), pp. 132, 133.
4  Liz Lochhead, *Bagpipe Muzak* (Harmondsworth: Penguin Books, 1991), p. 79.
5  Liz Lochhead, *Talking Verse* 11.3–12.1 (1995), p. 126.
6  Liz Lochhead, *Mary Queen of Scots Got Her Head Chopped Off* (Harmondsworth: Penguin Books, 1989), p. 11. Page numbers for subsequent quotations will be given in the text prefaced by *MQS*.
7  Bertolt Brecht, *Brecht on Theatre*, trans. John Willett (London: Methuen, 1964), pp. 139–40.
8  Jackie Kay, 'Gastarbeiter', in *Other Lovers* (Newcastle-upon-Tyne: Bloodaxe, 1993), p. 22. Subsequent page numbers will be given in the text, prefaced by *OL*.
9  Jackie Kay in Gillean Somerville and Rebecca Wilson (eds), *Sleeping with Monsters* (Edinburgh: Polygon, 1990), pp. 121–22.
10 See the collection *Off Colour* by Jackie Kay, and 'I'm unemployed' in Angela McSeveney, *Coming Out with It* (Edinburgh: Polygon, 1992), p. 38.
11 Jackie Kay, *The Lamplighter* (Highgreen: Bloodaxe Books, 2008), p. 9. Subsequent page numbers will be given in the text prefaced by *L*.
12 See Elizabeth Barrett Browning, 'The Runaway Slave at Pilgrim's Point', in *The Poetical Works of Elizabeth Barrett Browning* (London: Henry Frowde, 1906), pp. 228–31.
13 Liz Lochhead, *Dreaming Frankenstein*, p. 70.

# 6: Adopting cultures and embodying myths in Jackie Kay's *The Adoption Papers* and *Red Dust Road*

## MATTHEW PATEMAN

I still have the copy of *The Adoption Papers*[1] that Jackie Kay signed for me in 1991 after a reading at Leeds University. It is signed to me and my then-girlfriend, and has the additional phrase 'from one to another'. This sentence was intended, I am sure, as a sincere expression of a kind of solidarity, of a shared experience or fact of being. As I am not black nor a woman, am not gay and am not a poet, the obvious point (arguably the only point worthy of note) of contact is our being adopted. This paper is about Kay, not me, but I do want to address briefly this notion of a shared experience between Kay and myself, an experience I know was shared by at least two other people in that single reading and, one would assume, multiplied vastly across the hundreds of readings Kay has given. There, additional points of shared experience – being gay, being black, being a single parent, being a poet, playwright, novelist – may also be inscribed on book flyleafs, and felt in hearts.

I had read Kay's collection precisely because it was about adoption. At the time, I was unaware of her work for Gay Sweatshop and felt writing about adoption, publicly declaring oneself to be adopted, to be a brave act. And indeed it was, for Kay, and I felt very moved and personally affected by her reading, and by my subsequent readings of her poems. And I think I felt, briefly, part of a community of adoptees, of an adopted community.

However, my response was sentimental and naive. It did a certain injustice to Kay's collection, and to her later writing, as well as succumbing to a simplified and historically evacuated notion of identity. I was attempting to build myself into a community that does not exist by mythologising its coherence. The remainder of this chapter will seek to illustrate how Kay refuses to simplify either herself or her self's relation to history. She does this, I will suggest, by highlighting the inevitable differences which seeming sameness seeks to occlude, and by gesturing towards the dangers of mytholo-gised histories and communities whose 'truths' also hide the violence of creation inherent in the myth structure.

One final mention of myself will offer an example of what I mean. I invented an adopted community of which both Kay and I were members. This cosy coterie could recount experience, share stories and celebrate our 'solidarity'. But the community could only exist as a meaningful group (however imagined) if the differences of experience were subsumed within the sameness in the violence of a dialectic: the annihilation of the black/white, man/woman, straight/gay in the dialectic of the adoptee. But this, rather dramatic, description presents untenable equivalences between categories whose experiences have histories of wild variance. My birth-mother was Irish, my birth-father English; my parents (the lack of a pre-modifier is here equivalent to an assertion of 'real': my adoptive parents are my real parents, but real parents need no descriptor as such so my adoptive parents are, simply, my parents), my parents are English. All of us (birth-parents, parents and myself) are white so the fact of my nation-hood (Irish/British by birth) can be occluded in the fact of my adopted nation (English); and the fact of my birth and of my adoption does not highlight my colour. Kay's parents, as we shall be reminded below, and her birth-parents do not share such easy similarities. Her adoption cannot subsume the other aspects of identification because they exaggerate them; my own tend to diminution. My biological paternity is mirrored in my adopted nationality; my biological maternity is occluded with ease (a useful state of affairs in the 1970s and 1980s in England where Irish Catholics were regarded with a certain distrust). Kay's biological maternity is also largely occluded, even though it is this which is mirrored in her adopted nationality; and it is occluded because the biological paternity is seen to be so marked, so immediate a fact of her being. We are both hybrid creatures, Kay and I, but the nature of hybridity could not be more different. Indeed, in a pre-emptive rebuke of the kind of analysis it may appear I am embarking on, Kay wrote in 1985 a poem which seems to assert a very simple view of her identity, to recoil from being seen as an object of study, and to decry a form of academicism that arguably overcomplicates issues of identity. In 'So You Think I'm a Mule?' she wrote:

If you Dare mutter mulatto
hover around hybrid
hobble on half-caste
and intellectualize on the
'Mixed race problem',
I have to tell you:
take your beady eyes offa my skin;
don't concern yourself with
the 'dialectics of mixtures';
don't pull that strange blood crap
on me Great White Mother.
Say I'm no mating of a she-ass and a stallion
no half of this and half of that
to put it plainly purely
I am black.[2]

The affirmation of a singular blackness is asserted against a hybrid identity, or at least against the 'you' hovering around 'hybridity', intellectualising her being, engaging in what is phrased as a theft or plundering ('take your beady eyes offa my skin'). The poems in *The Adoption Papers* seem less resistant to the notion of the hybrid, but one must be attentive to the claim of theft, of stealing her skin to create one's own new cloak of discourse, a gaudy display of appropriation and arrogance. Hovering around the hybrid, Peter Clandfield makes the following observation in respect of Kay's work wherein the hybrid is not so much Kay herself as the cultures and communities, nations and histories from which she comes, to which she belongs and with which she engages. He concludes that 'there is no definitive way to write about this hybridity [...] and no one correct way to talk about Kay's writing'.[3] Clandfield offers a plural Kay which is convincing and which provides interesting ways of figuring her many voices. In fact, one of the ways of reading Kay, as identified also by Alastair Niven and Sean O'Brien, is the quality of her own performances of her work, of the theatricality of her poetry and prose, as well as, more obviously, her drama.[4] Indeed, as Anne Varty points out, *The Adoption Papers* was dramatised by BBC Radio Three in 1990, and this demonstrates the poem's 'performative quality'.[5]

The alliterative power at the beginning of 'So You Think I'm a Mule?' is one method of drawing out the performativity, the many-voiced form; *The Adoption Papers* is another. Back in 1991, the reading I attended in Leeds certainly affirmed, if it needed affirming, the dramatic power of the performance of her words, not least because of the richness of her voice. Clandfield reads O'Brien's discussion of Kay's work to suggest that the power of her performances (the aural event) has somewhat obscured the power of the poetry as a textual event, and he offers a very interesting reading of the poetry text.

Half seen, half heard, the poetry is itself a hybrid form; and Kay, part poet, part performer, part dramatist, part essayist, part novelist, part memoir writer is, professionally at least, hybrid as well. Her status as one of the most well known, widely read and much loved Scottish writers of the last twenty years is beyond question. Her list of publications is a formidable combination of poetry, prose and drama; her list of awards and honours an astounding index of her position in contemporary literature. Among the specifically literary awards, there is an MBE. This award was met with scepticism by her parents. Her mother asserted, 'I'm not going to the bloody palace to sook up to the Queen' (*Red Dust Road*,[6] 85; Kay's 2010 memoirs are hereafter referred to as *RDR* in references). Her father felt she should reject the award, but conceded that it was Kay's own decision. Her parents' response is an unequivocal expression of their politics, which is expressed throughout *Red Dust Road* as a politics committed to communist rather than nationalist pursuits. In some ways, it is her parents' communism, a commitment to a global community of shared wealth as opposed to a commitment to a national identity, which meant they adopted Kay at all, as the colour of any potential child was unimportant: the markers of race and ethnicity, the claims to a shared national community, mattered less than a proposed universal humanity. The disclosure of her parents' motivations occurs in Kay's writing mainly in *Red Dust Road*. The engagement with adoption begins, of course, twenty years earlier with *The Adoption Papers*.

This collection begins with the sequence of poems which gives the volume its title. These poems present the first-person voices of three characters who can be glossed as Jackie Kay at various stages of childhood and young adulthood; her mother; and the woman who gave birth to her. These characters, as well as brothers, fathers, grandparents, ancestral aunts and uncles and various other friends, lovers, children and colleagues populate the 2010 memoir which, while not presented as a continuation of *The Adoption Papers,* is nevertheless concerned with many of the same people and themes. Kay's mother's communism finds ventriloquised expression in *The Adoption Papers* in a section where Kay imagines her mother preparing for the visitation of a social worker who is coming to ensure that the Kay household is a suitable venue for an adopted child to be brought up:

> I put Marx Engels Lenin (no Trotsky)
> In the airing cupboard – she'll no be
> Checking out the towels surely.

The express combination of the political and the domestic, the bureaucratic visitation and the intensely personal act of adopting a child (and the intensely political act of adopting a child) are here made clear. In Kay's work the well-worn maxim that the personal is also political is always given immediacy, clarity, purpose. Adopting Jackie is a political act, even if the political theory that informs it has to be hidden from the social worker (who will, therefore, not know the specific non-Troskyite form of communism that the parents follow). While the global communism of her parents' politics is being asserted, so too is their national identity. The use of Scots-language 'no' instead of the Standard English 'not' is simply one among a multitude of markers that asserts her parents, and Kay herself, as part of a speech community which is also a section of a national community: Scotland. Despite this, C. L. Innes seeks to claim that somehow 'Kay's distinctive Scots accent and idiom paradoxically identify her as British'.[7]

But I need to backtrack. The brief biography of Kay at the front of *The Adoption Papers* states that she 'was born in 1961 in Edinburgh and brought up in Glasgow'. It then provides information about her writing career. The biography in *Red Dust Road* says she 'was born in Edinburgh' and then gives information about her writing and her teaching. Her biography as provided by the British Council's website begins its, obviously longer, digest by saying:

> Jackie Kay was born in Edinburgh, Scotland, in 1961 to a Scottish mother and a Nigerian father.

It is not unusual for a writer to have slightly differing biographical notices, but there are some striking points in these three that are worthy of note, and which directly challenge my earlier descriptions of Kay. An obvious first question about my description is the status of the phrase 'Scottish writer'. First, why even locate her as a Scottish writer at all? The sentence makes as much sense by simply calling her a writer. Second, whatever the motivation for insisting on her Scottishness, what does it mean to call Jackie Kay 'Scottish'. If 'Scottish', then what is at stake for her (or her *Red Dust Road* publishers) is the specificity of place of birth (Edinburgh) and in *The Adoption Papers* also her place of upbringing (Glasgow), but not her nationality. Or does the statement asserting city of birth act synecdochically for nationality? The British Council version helpfully tells the reader where Edinburgh is (Scotland) but is equally hesitant to assert nationality (or else, is equally assured of the correspondence between city/nation and nationality). Instead, the Council extends the biography from place of birth to … to what, exactly? To 'a Scottish mother and a Nigerian father'. The spatial precision of Kay's birth with its attendant non-naming of nationality (whether from certainty or ambiguity) is added to by a seemingly uncomplicated nation- and relation-giving to the woman and man so easily figured as 'Scottish mother' and 'Nigerian father'. The privileging of the terms 'mother' and 'father' in discourses of belonging makes their use here especially problematic: the next sentence continues 'She was adopted by a white couple at birth'. What is of interest here is the way in which the specificity of the 'Scottish mother' and 'Nigerian father' is replaced by the effacement of nationhood by colour (white), and the individuated roles by an assumptive homogenising 'couple'.

All of this makes clear an obvious point: biography is complicated. Kay's biography is an exemplary expression of this complication because her own reflections on it make manifest many of the difficulties associated with many of the most seemingly simple assumptions about identity – and biography is only ever the location of identities into meaningful narratives. The rest of this chapter is an effort to complicate some of the assumptions about these narratives. It will not directly address (or answer) the question, what is it that makes Jackie Kay Scottish, rather it will use the multivalenced concept of adoption as a mechanism to displace some of the terms that underpin claims about identity and their relationship with ideas of nationhood and belonging.

Kay's parents' globally inclusive communism and their equally pronounced Scottishness in *The Adoption Papers* serve to ground a significant aspect of Kay's work more generally. As Matthew Brown asserts, Kay's view of Scottishness (or more precisely, Scottish citizenship) 'is motivated by a cosmopolitan world view, informed not by motifs of dispossession or rootlessness but by the ability to map international spaces onto local environs in order to make diasporic citizens feel welcome and "at home" in Scotland'[8]. This 'at home'-ness, is, however, tempered by Kay insofar as her belonging 'in' Scotland comes at the cost of occasionally feeling 'outside' Scotland. She writes in an interview, 'I do think that sense of being outside with being inside Scotland – with being very proud of the country and very proud of being Scottish, and also being outside in terms of receiving a lot of racism from other Scottish people – is what fuels my sense of how and what I write.'[9]

For Kay, at least in the two texts under discussion, the discovery–construction of identity asserts its pressure forcibly (though not exclusively) through the question of her adoption. This Brown very neatly describes as 'a condition that is as much an evocation of the author's "sense of being outside with being inside Scotland" as it is a bold challenge to racialised conceptions of national belonging'.[10] This chapter has begun by using the term 'adoption' in a fairly well developed and understood sense, relating to legally bringing a child into a family to which it does not belong by birth. Presently, this familial–legal definition will be extended, but it is not so much on parents and children that this chapter now focuses. Rather, it is on the extended investigation of what adoption means in terms of other identities with which it here engages. In a long passage from *The Adoption Papers*, the character that we might take to be the young Jackie is trying to make sense of the claim from her mother that she is 'no really ma mammy'. She writes:

> After mammy telt me she wisnae my real mammy
> I was scared to death she was gonnie melt
> Or something or mibbe disappear in the dead

Of night and somebody would say she wis a fairy
Godmother. So the next morning I felt her skin
To check it was flesh, but mibbe it was just
A good imitation. How could I tell if my mammy
Was a dummy with a voice spoken by someone else?

While this is clearly about a mother and a daughter, the aspect that is most compelling is the sense of simulation, of falseness, or, more positively, of magic. To ventriloquise (as Kay does repeatedly in *The Adoption Papers*, of course) is a kind of magic, is a way of making the dummy speak. So the daughter gives birth to the mother through giving her a voice. But more tellingly, the child imagines a different way of belonging with or to her mother. She renarrativises her relationship so that her mother is in fact a fairy/godmother, a creature of stories and fantasy. In a slightly different context, Brown insists on the ways in which Kay moves from an identity based in or derived from biological descent, but rather 'sets out to discover an identity-bearing narrative'.[11] The new narrative created by the young Jackie, this new imagining, is scary – with the corporeal body melting, disappearing – yet it offers new possibilities, new futures. The reality of her adoption is framed by her mother in such a way that the mother becomes unreal, an unreality that compels (or allows) Jackie to invent (or experience) a new real, situated in the discursive boundaries of fairytale and myth. These are wonderfully, and materially, expunged by the announcement at the end of the passage that 'Anyhow a day after / I got my guinea pig and forgot all about it'. Here, the structures of identity are absolutely bound up with experiencing the real in different ways, and experiencing different reals (I am neologising to avoid a too-easy ontology: Jackie does not experience her identity in different realities, but in different epistemic affects). The conceptual difficulty of one's parent not being one's parent is at once a cause for psychic pain, ontological doubt, epistemological inventiveness and, ultimately, here at least, a materially more significant intervention – a pet.

Young Jackie's doubts have come about because of a common linguistic choice that is central to an idea of adoption, and this is the notion of 'real'. Here, the importance of the privileging of the biological in terms of parenting is unambiguous. The 'real' parent is the one who either gave birth or impregnated; the lifelong carers are merely 'adoptive'. Various strategies are used to navigate this difficulty: as noted above, I would always use 'birth-parent'; Kay in *Red Dust Road* offers a common alternative in the context of a section detailing her annoyance at examples of unwitting racism (where the question of the relation between ancestry and nationality is vital). She writes, 'And when somebody asked me if I would ever trace my original parents, I always said no, that I had good parents and that I wasn't interested in tracing my original parents' (*RDR*, 193). 'Real', 'original', even 'birth': all are phrases that seem to promote biology (in all its guises) over other ways of perceiving relations.

Three moments in her work will stand as examples (however reductively) of thinking about belonging differently, and in asserting their relationship to notions of adoption. The first involves Kay's grandmother and her emigration to New Zealand. Already this needs qualification. Kay's grandmother in this context is both legal-familial and ancestral in as much as Kay's relationship with this woman is the consequence of her adoption by her parents such that she has a legal-familial tie to the person, but her mother has a direct ancestry. (Kay's ties to the relatives of her 'birth parents', the 'Scottish mother' and 'Nigerian father', are only ancestral, and have neither legal nor necessarily familial aspects – though in actuality the familial aspects do certainly appear in *Red Dust Road*.)

Kay's grandmother and grandfather both moved to New Zealand to join Kay's mother just before she was married. Kay's mother and father 'both ended up on the other side of the world, in the southern hemisphere, enticed by the completely free fare, in the days when Australia and New Zealand were determined to increase their working population' (*RDR*, 14). This globetrotting couple relatively quickly moved back to Scotland, but the grandparents stayed on (though not, as yet, of course, grandparents). Having made the journey, they stayed in New Zealand for a further twenty-six years. This absence allowed a particular version of national belonging to develop: a version of belonging that asserts nationhood via myth and exaggeration. Kay describes the time spent as 'intensifying' themselves, and in a stunning moment of description, offers us her grandmother's voice, her Fife accent as 'such a mixture of Lochgelly and nostalgia, that her friends had difficulty understanding *her*' (*RDR*, 19). Nostalgia is a species of myth-making, tainted more by 'quaintness and kitschness' (*RDR*, 19) than violence, but the violence of myth-making is its close cousin. New Zealand does not afford the grandmother a new adoptive culture, rather it is the location from which a home culture (Scotland, and its associated notion of Scottishness) can be mythologised into an originary force, the thing, according to Kay, that her grandmother 'valued most about herself'. The notion of value is important here, as the grandmother 'invests' huge psychic effort in creating for herself an identity that is not simply based in a nation, but is essentially predicated upon it. The complex facts of national belonging (international law, national boundaries, treaties, place of birth and so on) are occluded in a process of simplification and conceptual narrowing. Kay's quaint description of this is that she was 'like a woman on a shortbread tin come to life'. The simplified signifiers of a commodified version of a nation become the animating and lived version of that nation.

The creation of national myths derived from commodified versions of a supposed 'real' country and the specific attempts to create a physically 'true' version of that country are engaged with by Paul Robbins and Alistair Fraser. They describe the reforestation and afforestation in Highlands Scotland. By examining the extent to which the new forest regions are the consequence of a strategy for tourism, and to what extent the forest regions are part of an agricultural restructuring, they are able to show the powerful and coercive voices behind Scottish myth-building. For example, the much-boasted wilderness of Scotland can be seen as a product of natural exploitation and if 'wilderness is produced, just like a city, no state of nature is necessarily any more natural than another, and pristine states become difficult to distinguish from degraded ones'.[12] The shifting ecology is located as a consequence of economic changes that include the movement from cattle-rearing (and the concomitant forest clearances) to the re-creation of deer-stalking landscapes to compensate for the decline in profit from sheep farming due to the growth in availability of sheep products from New Zealand and Australia. The, perhaps coincidental, mention of New Zealand in the text just quoted, nevertheless serves to illustrate how Kay's grandmother's nostalgic creation of a version of Scotland is itself part of a global economy wherein nationhood is largely a product of capital. This is especially so to the extent that the symbols and signs of nations are the products (either explicit in the case of shortbread tins, or implicit in the case of topography) of the processes and requirements of successive forms of industrial and post-industrial capitalism.

The landscape of red deer forests, in other words, is a cultural palimpsest on which the economic history of the Highlands is inscribed. Not just this, but the different modes of capital being deployed (the deer-stalking estates and the sheep farms alongside which these grew up, never entirely having been displaced) allows 'modern and postmodern capital to "coexist schizophrenically in the same geographical and cultural region" free from immediate contradiction (Escobar 1996:56)'.[13] While the modern remains, it is the postmodern that is dominant, it would appear: 'The re-emergence of native forests thus reflects an economy increasingly reliant on tourism – a branch of capitalist production in which "authentic" landscapes are demanded by the tourist gaze [...] which holds a preference for "authenticity" rather than "fact", for the believable over the actual' (McCrone, Morris and Kiely 1995:8)'.[14] The embodied landscape offers either authenticity (which is in fact simulacrum) or a supposed factuality (which is actually so multilayered as to be impossible). Kay's biography, her adopted body, her 'real' identity are similarly unreliable. The Scottish landscape is explicitly a political landscape; its hills and valleys, forests and farms are inscriptions and re-inscriptions of capital, commerce and a retrospective effort of will to mythologise and romanticise the landscape as 'natural', 'originary', 'real': in a word, Scottish. The landscape becomes Scotland; Scotland becomes the landscape. A myth-making set of discourses recedes into a supposed history and what is left are

> paper forests (Robbins 1998): an imaginary geography (Toogood 1995) for an imagined community (Anderson 1991) in an imagined Scotland (Gold and Gold 1995). The re-emergence of Scots pine reveals the discursive, as well as economic instrumentalities, of landscape change.[15]

The image of the tree (this time the African moringa planted in a Manchester street rather than the Scottish pine in an industrially farmed Highlands) will be returned to later in order to revive this sense of Kay's grandmother's interpellation into and expression of a mythologised Scottishness: a Scottishness that Kay seeks to interrogate through her investigation into her own body, her own sense of the 'real', the 'originary', the 'actual'.

This is, doubtless, to overstate Kay's position in relation to her grand-mother and to embroil the grandmother in a history of topographic myth-making that is absent from Kay's own account. It is, however, true that (for reasons that could easily be reduced to simple chronology, but which seem to necessarily exert political and thematic force) an idea of simplified notions of national belonging, and attendant myth-making potential, are offered early in her memoir. The opportunity to choose to adopt a new culture is spurned in favour of an almost desperate-seeming over-affirmation of origins, of birth, of 'the real' – but the real has of course become a simulacrum, like Jackie's mother in *The Adoption Papers*, and landscape of the nation itself. When the real is so devoutly sought, its imitative, reduced, myth-induced other (be it the politically catastrophic myth of Aryan ascendancy or the seemingly twee over-exaggerated accent of an imagined speech community) is a disturbing inevitability. The impor-tance of myth in developing forms of simplified national identity is clear; and these myths always demand exclusion. For some, like the French theorist Jean-François Lyotard, the mechanisms, institutions and systems of exclusion are arguably constitutive of a certain idea of Europeanness, a category already and inevitably inscribed with racism. But equally, and as importantly, the simplification process occurs in the defining of others. Kay is unflinching in her demonstration of these simplifying myths as they relate to 'Africa' in her experiences at school and after in Scotland and beyond in what she describes as 'a rather primitive racist society' (*RDR*, 76) – a phrase I take to apply to her experiences of Britain and Europe, rather than just Scotland.

The second moment in her work I refer to appears when Kay asks, 'What did we learn about Africa in School?' (*RDR*, 39). Beyond the answer being 'not a lot' the detail of this limited knowledge is disappointingly predictable – natural rhythm, big penises, heat, superstition. As Kay notes, the intervening forty years have changed some of these images, but there remains, she claims, the failure to accord to 'Africans' the 'same basic right as white people – to be seen as a whole person' (*RDR*, 78). This may well have been the animating principle behind her insistence that 'to put it plainly purely / I am black', where a simplified and totalised identity (plainly black) appears to be and feels more 'whole' than a 'hybrid' 'half and half' identity. With so much work having been undertaken in the last decades around the idea of hybrid identities, the temptation may be to claim that hybrid is somehow more whole than non-hybrid, or to assert that all identity is hybrid. Peter Clandfield is keen neither to reduce Kay to an emblem of the hybrid, nor to unduly extol hybridity's virtues. He states that his aim is to show how Kay's

> Socialist-feminist inflected British/Scottish blackness that [she] articulates [...] not only challenges Eurocentric forms of racism, but also represents an alternative to essentialist constructions of Black identity and, further, demonstrates that hybridity itself should not be conceived simply as a generic new global norm.[16]

Kay's desire for 'wholeness', then, can be articulated via a sense of community and belonging, and away from discourses of essentialism. While Kay does not locate it in quite this way, the possibility of being seen as whole person is related to the idea of belonging. One belongs to a community, a group, a nation exactly to the extent that that group, community or nation understands you as a whole person. Indeed, in the simplified rhetoric of exclusion, being 'whole' is the same as being one of 'us'. The very articulation of an 'us' at the political level (in the very many declarations of national belonging in republics such as the USA) presupposes a non-us who is not only not us, but is inevitably incomplete.

Developing an idea of Lyotard's, Bill Readings observes:

> The project of the Republican 'we' is to build a consensus that defines its community as that of humanity in its freedom. As Lyotard puts it, the Republic asks, What must we do to become ourselves, to become a freer, more American, more human society? Our community is established in the suppression of difference and the revelation of the common humanity that underlies our various cultural and racial 'clothes'. The achievement of tolerance will be a consensus, the community of a homogenous 'we', in which our association is grounded on our common humanity. But the question we don't ask, can't ask, is 'Who are we to speak?' We cannot enquire into that 'we' that grounds the possibility of our becoming 'ourselves'.[17]

The third of my moments from Kay's work illustrates in a different context the process of the creation of homogeneity, of a 'we', an 'us' and the political and personal violence that is attendant on this. Recounting a tale of her school days, she remembers the racist urge to 'send them home', 'them' being the non-British, non-white, non-we of simplified mythologisation. The general violence of this rhetoric found especial personal force when her best friend Sandra 'said she agreed that black people should all be sent home', but continued, 'not you, of course, Jackie. You're one of us' (*RDR*, 195). She has been adopted into the community, but this adoption by the community can only be at the expense of the effacement of her individuality, in this case, what makes her different will have to be ignored – not just by the community, but by herself (not unlike my brief flirtation with the adopted community I mentioned above). A little while later the force of this desire to be 'us', to welcome the simplifying urge, the effacement of difference, the celebration of homogeneity – to be adopted into a culture to which you should already belong, already be 'inside' – is made saddeningly clear. Kay tells of the day when the class was verbally insulting two new Chinese girls, and she joined in. The desire to belong superseded any other thought. Kay expresses 'shame' at this memory, 'more than [at] any other' (114). Yet, while the shame felt is certainly understandable, arguably so is the desire to be part of the 'us'. Not belonging is equivalent to being experienced as (and maybe even experiencing oneself as) partial, unfinished, incomplete. Nonetheless, as Kay's story shows, the emotional and psychic sacrifices that have to be made in order to be accepted, to be adopted into a group, can be so extreme that the assumed benefits of wholeness, or completeness, are entirely lost. Indeed, the dislocations of self required can be so devastating that 'shame' is the response.

Nevertheless, Kay's book is not a celebration of not-belonging. It is a text that strives to find ways of belonging that do not rely on totalising concepts of the 'original' or the 'real'. To that extent the question asked of Kay about her 'original' parents and the implication that without these people 'you weren't whole or complete' (*RDR*, 193) takes on added resonance. Adoption in this context is still perceived, and possibly felt, as incompleteness. The character of the older Jackie in *The Adoption Papers* berates an imagined interlocutor (possibly a doctor, possibly anyone) and says:

> I have my parents who are not of the same tree
> And you keep trying to make it matter,
> The blood, the tie, the passing down
> Generations.

Neither Scots pine nor moringa, Kay posits the tree as a generational marker, a sign of lineage, a symbol of both fertility and separation. While the tree will be returned to, for now it is the infuriating emphasis on the material, the biological, the originary, the ancestral that so annoys Jackie. 'And you keep trying to make it matter', she says, thereby expressing her disquiet at the insistence on blood and its supposed importance; but also she indicates the requirement to keep the metaphor of the tree as a metaphor, not to make it matter, tactile, physical. The 'matter', the physical, the real, all tell lies about her, about her relations, her being. Or, less dramatically, the physical matter of the real can only tell certain kinds of truth; and her adoption requires other kinds of truths, different ways into being, into self, into history.

The truths that this 'matter' hides (and the relations of belonging that are also hidden and exposed by this matter, this real) are described by Kay in a scene from 1981. Standing on a Tube platform with some friends who had come down from Scotland, Kay and her group are verbally assaulted by five drunken white racists. Calling her Wog and Darkie, they also break bottles and threaten her physically. She continues:

> Rowena, my friend, and the youngest of us, only sixteen, intervenes, and one of them smashes her face. Her face is pouring with blood. I shout to the people on the platform. 'Isn't anyone going to help us?' A businessman, well dressed in a smart raincoat and with a leather case, standing next to another businessman, turns to me and calmly says, 'No, we support them.' (*RDR*, 189)

The 'matter' of the businessman, his smart coat and case, proposes a certain kind of real. This real, of course, is its own myth, its own over-invested, over-determined simulacrum. The businessman's 'matter' – his raincoat and leather case – provides signs of security, sense, tradition, respectability,

Englishness of the fair play and stiff upper lip variety. This is a myth: indeed it is possible to imagine a section called 'Businessman with raincoat and case' in Roland Barthes's *Mythologies*. But the myths of respectability, virtue, civic pride that may be imagined are precisely what make his remark that 'we support them' 'all the more unnerving'. His real is unreal, his myth itself a mask for a more chilling truth: he and the fascists are an 'us'. The brutal violence of a drunken man in smashing a sixteen-year-old girl's face in does not deflect, dissuade or in any way undermine the shared belonging of the businessman and the group of thugs. More than that, the businessman in his generalised 'we' speaks on behalf of (though not necessarily with the authority of) the rest of the crowd. Kay need not fear any repeat of her earlier shame, the matter that matters about her here (her skin's colour) is sufficient to ensure she will never be adopted by this 'we', this self-defined 'us'.

Kay's narrative cannot be simplified. It is not a narrative of despair, nor is it one of dewy-eyed optimism. It does not shrink away from her encounters with exclusion, belonging, adoption, and versions of originality and the real. It is funny, filled with pathos, love, optimism, tempered disquiet. And it is not proposing a philosophy of the unreal, or the assertion of the epistemic affect – my reading has drawn that out because I think it is the way her texts genuinely offer a critical engagement with assumed modes of identifying identity. But her memoir ends with a delightful and unambiguous assertion of the material, the earth, the ancestral, and the magical, the story-filled. She has been given pods from a moringa tree by one of her ancestral uncles (she has no legal-familial uncles or aunts) and decides to plant them. The insistence on the tree as metaphor in *The Adoption Papers* is replaced by an insistence on the tree as matter, as mattering here. Yet, even as roots and earth and the real are celebrated, and a relation of belonging that is more than simply ancestral or familial or national (which is perhaps geological) is implied, and the roots and fruits of Scottish culture are literalised through subterranean rhizomes and proud upstanding arboreal assertion: even amidst all of this there is magic.

Kay does not end with the real tree but with her own narrative of it, her imagining of it – a material future made immaterial in present conjecture. So, in addition to the real moringa in front of her terraced house in Manchester, there is also a 'magical moringa'. Endings, like identity, are not just one kind of thing – identity, nationality, belonging, adoption all are unstable, complicated, contradictory things and Kay's work refuses to simplify itself or her, or her reflections on Scotland, or England (to say nothing of sexuality, motherhood, class and so on). It is hard to make it real. Jackie Kay is an exceptional Scottish writer, and she challenges us to not know what that means.

## Notes

1  Jackie Kay, *The Adoption Papers* (Newcastle: Bloodaxe Books Ltd: 1991). Hereafter referred to as *AP* in the text.
2  Jackie Kay, 'So You Think I'm a Mule?', *Feminist Review* 17 (1984), p. 80.
3  Peter Clandfield, '"What is in my blood?": Contemporary Black Scottishness and the work of Jackie Kay', in Teresa Hubal and Neil Brooks (eds), *Literature and Racial Ambiguity* (Amsterdam: Rodopi, 2002), pp. 1–25 (2).
4  See Alastair Niven, 'Making her Way', *Poetry Review* 80.4 (Winter 1990–91), pp. 16–17, and Sean O'Brien, *The Deregulated Muse* (Newcastle: Bloodaxe, 1998).
5  Anne Varty, 'Poets in the theatre: Ure, Kay, Conn, Morgan', in Ian Brown (ed.), *The Edinburgh Companion to Scottish Drama* (Edinburgh: Edinburgh University Press, 2011), pp. 140–53 (143).
6  Jackie Kay, *Red Dust Road* (London: Picador, 2011).
7  C. L. Innes, 'Accent and identity: women poets of many parts', in James Acheson and Romana Huk (eds), *Contemporary British Poetry: Essays in Theory and Criticism* (Albany: SUNY University Press, 1996), pp. 315–41 (322).
8  Matthew Brown, 'In/Outside Scotland: Race and Citizenship in the Work of Jackie Kay', in Berthold Schoene (ed.), *The Edinburgh Companion to Contemporary Scottish Literature* (Edinburgh: Edinburgh University Press, 2007), pp. 219–27 (222).
9  Nancy K. Gish, 'Adoption, Identity and Voice: Jackie Kay's Invention of Self', in Marianne Novy (ed.), *Imagining Adoption: Essays on Literature and Culture* (Michigan: Michigan University Press, 2004), pp. 171–93 (180).
10  Matthew Brown, p. 221.
11  Matthew Brown, p. 224.
12  Paul Robbins and Alistair Fraser, 'A Forest of Contradictions: Producing the Landscapes of the Scottish Highlands', *Antipode* 35.1, pp. 95–118 (107).
13  Ibid., p. 101.
14  Ibid., p. 113.
15  Ibid., pp. 95–118.
16  Clandfield, p. 7.
17  Bill Readings, 'Pagans, Perverts or Primitives? Experimental Justice in the Empire of Capital', in Andrew Benjamin (ed.), *Judging Lyotard* (London: Routledge, 1992), pp. 168–91 (176).

# 7: The Kailyard's ghost: community in modern Scottish fiction

SCOTT LYALL

Community is important in twentieth-century Scottish fiction. From George Douglas Brown's *The House with the Green Shutters* (1901) to Jackie Kay's *Trumpet*, published at the end of the century (1998), community in one form or another is a core theme, often by its very absence. Many twentieth-century Scottish novels feature failed or failing communities, and an implicit yearning, nostalgia even, for better or real communities. Also central to many of these novels is the cultural legacy of the Kailyard.

The Kailyard is vital to any understanding of community in modern Scottish literature. Kailyard means cabbage-patch. It was a term first used in the April 1895 edition of *The New Review* by the historian of law and literature John Hepburn Millar, who continued his criticism of the Kailyard novelists in his *A Literary History of Scotland* (1903). Millar set the tone: 'Kailyard' has since normally been used in a derogatory sense. The traditional view is that Kailyard literature was written by J. M. Barrie early in his career, and Samuel Rutherford Crockett and Ian Maclaren, both Free Church of Scotland ministers. According to George Blake, the Kailyard novelists 'all wrote [...] of life as seen through the windows of the Free Kirk manse'.[1] For Blake the Kailyard was in some measure a reaction against Scotland's too rapid industrialisation, as well as the cultural consequence of the over-influence of the Presbyterian Church.[2] The Kailyard depicts a small-town Scotland where community is unified, Christian, untainted by industrialism and the urban working class, and where there is little or no immigration, which at that stage would have meant primarily Irish Catholic immigration. The Kailyard is a kind of prelapsarian Scotland, before the fall into industrialism, a country of small communities untroubled by the world outside. Thomas D. Knowles offers a succinct definition:

> In its 'classic' form, the Kailyard is characterised by the sentimental
> and nostalgic treatment of parochial Scottish scenes, often centred

on the church community, often on individual careers which move from childhood innocence to urban awakening (and contamination), and back again to the comfort and security of the native hearth.[3]

*The House with the Green Shutters*, the seminal modern Scottish novel, features the small town of Barbie, which is Brown's nightmarish inversion of the Kailyard. Francis Russell Hart argues that the 'anti-Kailyardism' of *The House with the Green Shutters* is not only an attack on the maudlin, cosy and conservative form of Kailyard novels, but also on the theological underpinning to the Kailyard: 'the denial of evil' in an almost paradisal community setting.[4] In contrast, 'Barbie is a grotesquely hellish vision, a view of human degradation, alienation, and malignity.'[5] Brown's attack on the Kailyard perhaps undermines the artistic integrity of his novel. He writes to his Oxford friend Ernest Barker, shortly after the novel's publication:

> Well, I suppose you have read the *Green Shutters* by this time. 'Tis a brutal and a bloody work [...]. There is too much black for the white in it. Even so it is more complimentary to Scotland, I think, than the sentimental slop of Barrie, and Crockett, and Maclaren. It was antagonism to their method that made me embitter the blackness; like old Gourlay I was going 'to show the dogs what I thought of them.' Which was a gross blunder, of course. A novelist should never have an axe of his own to grind. If he allows a personal animus to obtrude ever so slightly it knocks his work out of balance. He should be an aloof individual, if possible, stating all sides and taking none.[6]

The Kailyard has somewhat dogged modern Scottish literature, and in many ways the very self-conscious modernism of Hugh MacDiarmid during the interwar Scottish literary revival was a way of counteracting what the poet perceived as the retrograde and reactionary nature of the Kailyard and its effects on Scottish literary culture. MacDiarmid was the Kailyard's main opponent in the modernist camp in Scotland, and he wrote a poem, 'Frae Anither Window in Thrums', lamenting his own Kailyard-like position in Montrose as a journalist for the *Montrose Review* – so name-checking Barrie's 1889 novel *A Window in Thrums*.[7] For the ultra-modernist MacDiarmid, the Kailyard, which included not just Barrie and the Kailyard novelists

Crockett and Maclaren, but the likes of the novelist Neil Munro, the poet Charles Murray, the prolific writer Annie S. Swan, and the Burns cult, represented a whole literary mode in Scotland that had sidetracked the culture from internationalist modernity. MacDiarmid aimed to re-masculinise a national community that he regarded as being not only colonised by anglicisation, but weakened internally by what Robert Crawford calls the 'feminine genre' of the populist Kailyard.[8] MacDiarmid thought the Kailyard fostered a false sense of local and national community in what was actually an advanced capitalist, class-riven industrialised nation: 'There is little relationship between Thrums and Clydebank.'[9] His thesis was taken up by Blake, author of the Clydeside-set novel *The Shipbuilders* (1935), for whom the Kailyard represented a 'betrayal of national dignity'.[10]

Contemporary critics, such as Andrew Nash, are more accepting of the Kailyard. Nash argues for the superior artistic merits of Barrie's work, as well as its place in the development of the regional novel, which has a specifically Scottish genesis in the work of Walter Scott. More broadly, Nash points to the way in which the Kailyard has been used to denude the whole Victorian period in Scotland of literary worth; and the raising of the term's status to that of myth, one often used to attack so-called Scottish provincialism. However, as Nash comments:

> the word which was probably first intended as a joke became the context from which much of the study of Scottish culture was shaped in the twentieth century. From literature and light entertainment, through political history, film, sociology and the Scottish Parliament, Kailyard remains an essential term of reference.[11]

Most countries, no doubt, have their Kailyard, whether it is perceived as such or not, and, as Ian Campbell argues, 'To reject the kailyard is to reject much that is central to any attempt to define "Scottishness".'[12] The Kailyard remains, for better or worse, fundamental to our understanding of community in modern Scottish fiction, but it also shows distinct limits as to what community might mean. It is something Scottish novelists, such as Brown, have reacted against; but it continues to haunt the Scottish imagination because it portrays an idea of community that is both nostalgic and ultimately unrealisable, especially in urban modernity, and against which contemporary representations of community can only seem fractured and failed. As Jean-Luc Nancy writes:

> The lost, or broken, community can be exemplified in all kinds of ways, by all kinds of paradigms [... but] always it is a matter of a lost age in which community was woven of tight, harmonious, and infrangible bonds and in which above all it played back to itself [...] the representation [...] of its own immanent unity, intimacy, and autonomy.[13]

Community is a contentious, heavily debated term, perhaps wishy-washy, and certainly not easily definable. The influential nature of Benedict Anderson's highly evocative phrase 'imagined communities' has meant that, if previously we were not, we are now highly attuned to seeing community as a narrative, a work of the imagination, every bit as much as, and also influenced by, narratives of the literary imagination. Often, and in particular in a pre-devolution stateless Scotland, literary representation has been mapped directly onto out-there-in-the-world action, as if there is a straight and relatively unproblematic relationship between culture and politics. This is perhaps a professional pitfall of literary critics, but we might be wise to be a little wary of such supposed causalities, as they may warp a more nuanced understanding of how 'unacknowledged legislation' may (or may not) operate. However, with this proviso in mind, there is no doubt that in Scotland, especially throughout the twentieth century, culture, particularly literary and critical work, attempted to fill the gaps, plug the holes in an absent national community, and that, indeed, culture has preceded and informed politics, in the broadest sense of that term, on what the practice of that community might actually look like.

I will not only be examining national community in this chapter. But the national community, or communities, will be the shadow of my discussion of social and interpersonal communities in the novels discussed here. This chapter will necessarily be a historical survey, mapping changes in the representation of community in three key periods throughout the twentieth century: pre-1979 devolution referendum; post-1979; and then during the devolutionary 1990s. In the pre-1979 period it will look at *The House with the Green Shutters* (1901) and Lewis Grassic Gibbon's *A Scots Quair*, first published as a trilogy in 1946, but which appeared as single volumes in the early 1930s; then, later, Muriel Spark's *The Prime of Miss Jean Brodie* (1961), and *Docherty* (1975) by William McIlvanney. From post-1979: *The Trick is to Keep Breathing* (1989) by Janice Galloway, and Alan Warner's *Morvern Callar* (1995). Then post-devolution it will end by discussing Jackie Kay's *Trumpet*, which was published in 1998, between the vote for devolution in 1997 and the reconvening of the Scottish Parliament in 1999.

This chapter will identify themes that recur and pertinent motifs that cannot be ignored. Structured around the timeframe of devolution, it will not, however, provide a happy nationalist ending in the manner of Cairns Craig's examination of community in *The Modern Scottish Novel*. Craig's analysis of 'Character, Community and the Scottish Imagination' proposes that the fearful selves inhabiting and inhibiting Scottish community with an 'ethics of fear' arise from the repressive influence of Calvinism.[14] Craig, who also identifies the founding importance of the Kailyard on ideas of community in modern Scottish fiction, concludes his argument on the fearful selves of Scottish community by saying that, in the 1979 referendum:

> The Scottish people were too afraid to take control of their own destiny: fear-stricken when confronted by a choice which might allow them to stop being afraid. In the following two decades narratives of mutually destructive fearful selves burgeoned in Scottish writing. In 1997 the Scottish people voted finally and determinedly for their own parliament – perhaps in part because the Scottish novel had plumbed the depth of their fears.[15]

Actually, the Scottish people, and no doubt other non-Scots resident in Scotland, voted 'Yes' in 1979: fear was not the issue, but rather the unionist managerialism of a fearful centralised British state. What this chapter suggests is that in many of the novels it discusses, it is not an absent national community – meaning independent state control – that is the issue; the lack is, rather, a social, even socialist, communalism, mythic perhaps, but threatened or eradicated by market individualism. Another key theme is the recurrent ghost of the Kailyard.

The implosion of community in *The House with the Green Shutters* is not only Brown throwing a bomb into the Kailyard. The novel also signals the destruction of the myth of the Scot as communalist, a myth the Kailyard – paradoxically, a deeply conservative literary form – helped to propagate and through which Kailyard authors profited massively. According to Brown's narrator:

> For many reasons intimate to the Scots character, envious scandal is rampant in petty towns like Barbie. To go back to the beginning, the Scot, as pundits will tell you, is an individualist. His religion alone is enough to make him so. For it is a scheme of personal salvation significantly described once by the Reverend Mr Struthers of Barbie. 'At the Day of Judgement, my frehnds,' said Mr Struthers; 'at the Day of Judgement every herring must hang by his own tail!' Self-dependence was never more luridly expressed. History, climate, social conditions, and the national beverage have all combined (the pundits go on) to make the Scot an individualist, fighting for his own hand. The better for him if it be so; from that he gets the grit that tells.[16]

Protestantism and the spirit of capitalist competition promote the individualism of the Scot in Brown's novel. The voice of the community – the body of the community – comes through the 'bodies': mainly 'nesty bodies' in the 'nippy locality' of Barbie.[17] For Brown 'the Scot is largely endowed with the commercial imagination', an imaginative faculty of the lower order and one that will never be sufficient to imagine or reimagine the community into being as it is fundamentally individualist.[18] As such, the national imagination in *The House with the Green Shutters* is diseased in the case of young Gourlay, or blockheaded in the case of his father. Education provides no escape – and this will be a recurring theme in later novels, and signify the shattering of another Scottish myth. In Edinburgh young John joins a community of affected poseurs every bit as mordant as the nesty bodies of Barbie. In Barbie only one voice offers a positive valence of what community might be: the 'Burnsomaniac' baker.[19] As he quotes poetry, he is duly ignored.

Lewis Grassic Gibbon, especially in *Sunset Song* (1932), inherits the same literary and ethical problems, and the same audience expectations, that Brown was dealing with in relation to the Kailyard. Gibbon's response is subtler, and more successful. Walking us through Kinraddie in *Sunset Song*, the narrative voice says:

> So that was Kinraddie that bleak winter of nineteen eleven and the new minister, him they chose early next year, he was to say it was the Scots countryside itself, fathered between a kailyard and a bonny brier bush in the lee of a house with green shutters. And what he meant by that you could guess at yourself if you'd a mind for puzzles and dirt, there wasn't a house with green shutters in the whole of Kinraddie.[20]

As in Brown's novel, the community in *Sunset Song*, and in the other two novels of the *Quair, Cloud Howe* (1933) and *Grey Granite* (1934), is founded on and founders on gossip. Again, like Brown's novel when the railway comes to Barbie, it is the outside world that punctures the inverted Kailyard of *Sunset Song*, in this case, through the community-shattering impact of World War One. Once more, educational advancement is stymied: Chris Guthrie refuses the individualistic route of training as a teacher to stay in the local community, arguably a tragic choice as the community she is rooted in is dying. We witness the dissipation of community in Chris's journey: from Kinraddie in *Sunset Song*, to Segget in *Cloud Howe*, and on to the alienation, political strife and poverty of the city of Duncairn during the Depression in *Grey Granite*. In the elusive ending to the *Quair*, Gibbon spells out the difference that has persisted between Chris's worldview and the idealism of that of the men in her life. Her son, Ewan the communist leader, says: 'There will always be you and I, I think, Mother. It's the old fight that maybe will never have a finish, whatever the names we give to it – the fight in the end between FREEDOM and GOD.'[21] Chris's self-reliance signifies freedom, while Ewan's communism is a new religion. Yet even Ewan's communalism is hardly that. His is an elite vision, nourished in a manse by the clouds of his stepfather Robert's Christian socialism, and he is never a 'keelie' (Scots for a rough, urban male) like the other workers. His communism is not of the community, but above it, beyond it; it comes not as the saviour of community, but signals instead community's very death throes in the face of capitalist atomisation.

Chris goes back to where she came from at the end of the *Quair*, and dies alone, while Ewan marches on into the future, leading a particular class, not fostering a whole community. No solution is found in the *Quair* to community's disintegration. As such, one of the major literary inheritors of Gibbon's trilogy, William McIlvanney's *Docherty*, can only look back with an almost Kailyard-like nostalgia from its vantage point of publication in 1975 to an early twentieth century when community was still, at least in McIlvanney's novel, tangible. Yet, even *Docherty* opens with a symbol of community's demise: Miss Gilfillan, the spinster, believing her apartness to be a sign of her gentility, is actually simply isolated. When a peeping Tom looks at Miss Gilfillan through her window, this represents a perversion of the idea of looking in on the neighbours in a thriving community; a healthy neighbourliness, a real concern with the welfare of others, has gone wrong and descended into voyeurism. Tam Docherty's defence of Miss Gilfillan is not only a robust defence of an old-fashioned community ethos. That Miss Gilfillan's 'impression of Mr Docherty was not of one man but of several' does little to change the sense that Tam's action is a desperate and violent bid to stave off the encroachment of community breakdown, a dissolution that has already occurred, as Tam is the only one in the neighbourhood to come to her aid.[22]

*Docherty* is a novel about history. But this is a history that happens elsewhere, a working-class community under pressure of events it does not control. The High Street of Graithnock was 'a mere distant province of the truth'.[23] Like *The House with the Green Shutters*, *Docherty* infuses the ordinary with the classical – Angus, for instance, is said to be a 'Greek God in a semmet an' drawers [vest and underpants]'.[24] It is a novel that, like *The Prime of Miss Jean Brodie*, attempts to transfigure the commonplace. Yet McIlvanney is nostalgic for a Red Clydeside masculinity, as well as for the idea of a progressive history – history as hope – that by 1975 was severely depleted.[25] The novel posits several contending options of what a community might look like, notably all through the guise of male characters: the 'us and them' socialist humanism of Tam; the 'me versus the world' capitalist individualism of Angus; and the revolutionary socialism of the war-wounded Mick, who joins the Communist Party. The youngest, Conn, has to decide between these various routes. However, Conn's ability to decide is somewhat blocked by an education system that, as in *Sunset Song*, creates not a whole person and a vibrant community, but a divided personality and an individual set against the community from which they come. Like the 'two Chrisses' of Gibbon's novel, Conn is split between the Scots vernacular community of his family and the English language individualism of school.[26] The educational system promotes a systematic denial of the cultural self-worth of working-class communities. Tam understands that there is an 'us and them' social system, yet still reveres the educational system upon which the class disparities of competitive capitalism develop. The working-class community is deformed by this system, the injured Mick being a living symbol of such deformation. If the educational system does not help the community to understand its situation, but merely functions as a means of social control, then, like Mick, reader of Robert Tressell's 1914 novel *The Ragged Trousered Philanthropists*, one must seek to understand the systematic policing of a community through one's own autodidactic education.

Muriel Spark's *The Prime of Miss Jean Brodie* is the most famous novel written by a Scot about education, and, as with the other novels discussed so far, education is central to the functioning, or rather non-functioning, of community in this novel. In her 1992 autobiography *Curriculum Vitae*, Spark explains the views on education of her own teacher at Gillespie's, Christina Kay, the prototype for Jean Brodie:

> In *The Prime of Miss Jean Brodie* I said that Miss Brodie pointed out to us (as Miss Kay so often did) that 'educate' derives from the Latin *e* (out) and *duco* (I lead). She had strong views on education. She believed it was a 'leading out' of what was there already (I believe this is basically an Aristotelian theory) rather than a 'putting in'.[27]

Although Brodie conceives of education as an Aristotelian leading out, actually she inculcates, she puts in: '"Who is the greatest Italian painter?" "Leonardo da Vinci, Miss Brodie." "That is incorrect. The answer is Giotto, he is my favourite."'[28] Brodie's idiosyncratic educational generalism and her solipsistic individualism undermine the education of her girls. Brodie is only interested in the acculturation of her set to her own tastes. Yet the 'Brodie set', the so-called 'crème de la crème', are nothing of the sort.[29] They represent the failure of Brodie's individualism, becoming in her mind mere types, and the failure of her conception of an elite community. The dual nature of Calvinist Edinburgh – New Town and Old Town, rich and poor – is another community that fails to cohere.

Alasdair Gray's *Lanark*, first published in 1981, and arguably the greatest modern Scottish novel in the tradition of duality witnessed in *The Prime*, is *the* pivotal post-1979 Scottish novel. Influenced by, amongst other works, Brown's *The House with the Green Shutters*, it is another novel that rebels against state education. Gray's novel illustrates the dystopian nature of the capitalist Leviathan Anglo-British state, and the representational crisis in Scotland during the 1970s and on into the Thatcherite 1980s.

If *Lanark* is about consumption ('man is the pie that bakes and eats itself, and the recipe is separation'),[30] about community being consumed by capitalist individualism, then Janice Galloway's *The Trick is to Keep Breathing* is about a female teacher who has stopped consuming, stopped eating, and a novel about the Thatcherite 'no such thing as society' 1980s. Ironically, the then UK Prime Minister, later Lady Thatcher, claimed 'there is no such thing as society. There are individual men and women' in a 1987 interview with *Woman's Own*,[31] one of the type of populist women's magazines that Joy Stone finds herself reading, and hating herself for reading, in Galloway's novel. Joy, who claims 'I didn't need to eat', also says: 'I have to stop reading these fucking magazines', which are full of horoscopes and agony aunts and 'thin women doing exercises and smiling all the time. They make me guilty.[32] Joy has a problematic relationship with her sister Myra, and says that she 'Just couldn't get my mouth round *sister*.[33] There is not only no familial bond, but, in this patriarchal and post-feminist culture, there is no political bond, no community of women, no real fellow sisters – only competition marketed by and through women's magazines.

Community between women is not the only form of community under threat here. Community per se has disappeared, to be replaced by state intermediation, care in the community. Joy lives on a housing scheme, a place where 'Every fourth house in this estate is empty.[34] She says, 'Nobody knows anybody round here. We keep ourselves to ourselves for our various reasons.[35] The housing estate, sited on the outskirts of town, with few amenities, an artificial community with no real community ethos, is described by Joy as 'an annexe of nowhere'.[36] Her only visitor is a state health visitor, and even that relationship is seen by Joy as a 'fucking game'.[37]

For company Joy goes to supermarkets, post-community communities: Tesco, the British hypermarket, is seen as a refuge, and with knowing irony, Joy walks past a church to reach Marks & Spencer. Strangely, perhaps, given that she is a teacher, Joy apportions some of the blame for her alienation onto the Scottish education system on whose behalf she works. 'SEPARATE YOURSELVES', Joy and Paul, her first boyfriend, are told by a schoolteacher.[38] And separation, not just between the sexes, but more generally between individuals and any sense of community, is central to what is wrong with Joy's society.

The characters in Alan Warner's *Morvern Callar* attempt to escape this atomised separateness of traditional community-gone-wrong through the alternative community of rave culture. The Port of the novel, suggestive of Warner's hometown of Oban in the Western Scottish Highlands, is a Kailyard hell. Warner's narrator is aware of the Port's Kailyard legacy: 'On Hogmanay I was early at the Kale Onion Hotel. It's really called The Caledonian Hotel, but the "D" fell off the big sign and they never bothered to fix it.'[39] In the realism of *Morvern Callar* we go from romantic Caledonia to Kailyard dystopia, a Scotland in decline. The Port is characterised by cold and snow, and frozen emotions, betrayal, and brutal gender relations, particularly male violence towards women. The women are characterised in sexist terms as either 'Boots' or 'Rides'; there is a club called the Mantrap; and in the Complex, another housing scheme, 'one young husband owned a camcorder so his four married brothers and him swapped porno videos of the unknowing wives'.[40] The beach resort where Morvern goes on holiday is a mirror community of the Port, only with better weather, where humiliating sex games are organised by the tour operator: 'This is like living hell on earth', says Morvern.[41]

Leaving this hell to move down the coast, Morvern finds the rave community. Rave emerged in the late 1980s, and in tandem with the use of club drugs such as ecstasy, became an important working-class subculture in Britain, that also found a home in Ibiza. Key aspects of rave were unification, non-violence and non-sexualised dancing – dancing was largely in a group, not pairing off in couples. One phrase used at this time was the 'Second Summer of Love', suggesting a 1960s, hippy progenitor to the rave movement, although this may be to misconstrue rave's more working-class origins. Another aspect to rave was the attempt, through drugs, but also through trance music, to transcend the individual self and achieve a kind of communal love: to be 'loved-up'. This search for transcendence has clear religious connotations that *Morvern Callar* does not shy away from, which also involve a loss of self: in rave, says Morvern, 'You didn't really have your body as your own, it was part of the dance, the music, the rave.'[42] In Warner's novel there is anonymity and loss of self, or transcendence of self, in others and music; not the self in relation to others in traditional working-class (socialistic) community as in *Docherty*, or self in competition with others in capitalist community as in *The House with the Green Shutters*. In *Morvern Callar* we see the postmodern fragmentation of authentic selfhood, the failure or rejection of traditional community, and the rise of alternative community.

*Morvern Callar* is a theoretically savvy book where the death of the author happens before the novel begins. Jackie Kay's *Trumpet* has a similar postmodern theoretical nous, exemplifying, perhaps a little too neatly, Judith Butler's theory of gender as performative in the figure of the cross-dressing jazz musician Joss Moody.[43] This is a novel that problematises identity: gender identity, black identity and Scottish national identity. It is also a novel that, at the end of the twentieth century, resurrects a never entirely dead Kailyard into Scottish literary fiction. The Scottish community of Torr, where Joss's wife Millie returns after his death to escape the media attention in London, is a place that she first brought Joss to in 1956 – before the so-called sexual revolution of the 1960s. 'Torr is off the beaten track', as Millie says.[44] It is a rural retreat from the madness and intrusion of the metropolis. According to Millie, 'The people are kinder here and, strangely enough, more real'.[45] This is a place of refuge for Millie because little changes, time stands still:

> The harbour has stayed the same since I was a girl and came up from England on holidays here with my family. The chippie is the same chippie. The photography shop here that was established in 1886 is still standing – F. Futcher and Son. The Family Butcher, B. Savage, has been here since I was a girl. His son runs the shop now. He's also called Bruce, like his father. They both have butcher's red cheeks and hands. There's a little Italian café run by the Dalsassos that does the best ice-cream for miles around and sells sweets in those big plastic jars. Sweets that so inhabited my childhood holidays here, it makes

me laugh to see that they are still in existence. Soor plooms. Tablet. Sherbet Fountains. Cinnamon balls. Aniseed balls. Lemon bon bons. Coconut mushrooms. Peppermint creams. The Italian café does a good breakfast too. On impulse I go and sit down. Mrs Dalsasso is pleased to see me. 'The usual?'[46]

'The usual' is a near-timeless Kailyard community, where the past and the future are one. When Joss's father arrived in Scotland at the turn of the twentieth century he saw it as a 'Ghost country', and the Scots a 'Shadow people',

people [who] looked as if they would never find who they were waiting for; the fallen and the lost, blowing on their hands to try to bring themselves to life. They had been standing there waiting for ever with their bloodless cheeks in their secretive weather. Those people, my father used to joke, *were* the last century.[47]

As the twentieth century turned into a new century, Kay gave us a novel that is a story of diaspora, the exile of identity and the merging of identities; a novel, too, that, without forgetting the ghosts of the past, may allow us to view community in Scotland in the twenty-first century in a more open, diverse light. I began by suggesting that community is important in twentieth-century Scottish fiction. I would argue that it remains so, but that the concept of 'community' became more and more varied, complex and problematic in Scottish fiction as the twenty-first century and its new political settlement approached.

## Notes

1   George Blake, *Barrie and the Kailyard School* (London: Arthur Baker, 1951), p. 42.
2   Trevor Royle sees the Kailyard as a child of the Common Sense School of Scottish philosophy, with its emphasis on emotions, and cites the importance of Henry Mackenzie's sentimental novel *The Man of Feeling* (1771), a favourite of Robert Burns. See Royle, *The Mainstream Companion to Scottish Literature* (Edinburgh and London: Mainstream, 1993), p. 166.
3   Thomas D. Knowles, *Ideology, Art and Commerce: Aspects of Literary Sociology in the Late Victorian Scottish Kailyard* (Göteborg: Acta Universitatis Gothoburgensis, 1983), p. 13.
4   Francis Russell Hart, *The Scottish Novel: From Smollett to Spark* (Cambridge, Massachusetts: Harvard University Press, 1978), p. 131.

5   Hart, *The Scottish Novel*, p. 137.

6   G. D. Brown, letter of 24 October 1901; quoted in James Veitch, *George Douglas Brown* (London: Herbert Jenkins, 1952), p. 153.

7   See my *Hugh MacDiarmid's Poetry and Politics of Place: Imagining a Scottish Republic* (Edinburgh: Edinburgh University Press, 2006), Chapter 3.

8   Robert Crawford, *Scotland's Books: The Penguin History of Scottish Literature* (London: Penguin, 2007), p. 487.

9   C. M. Grieve, 'Leaves from a London Scottish Diary', *The Scots Pictorial*, 19 May 1923; reprinted in Angus Calder, Glen Murray and Alan Riach (eds), *Hugh MacDiarmid, the Raucle Tongue: Hitherto Uncollected Prose, Volume I: 1911–1926*, p. 48.

10  Blake, *Barrie and the Kailyard School*, p. 75.

11  Andrew Nash, *Kailyard and Scottish Literature* (Amsterdam and New York: Rodopi, 2007), p. 249.

12  Ian Campbell, *Kailyard: A New Assessment* (Edinburgh: Ramsay Head Press, 1981), p. 16. The British television schedules for Sunday evening continue to be the traditional home of an English Kailyard (or, rose garden); see, for instance, Julia Raeside, 'Is *Call the Midwife* perfect Sunday night television?', *Guardian* Online, 26 January 2012.

13  Jean-Luc Nancy, *The Inoperative Community*, trans. Peter Connor et al. (Minneapolis: University of Minnesota Press, 1991), p. 9.

14  Cairns Craig, *The Modern Scottish Novel: Narrative and the National Imagination* (Edinburgh: Edinburgh University Press, 1999), p. 58.

15  Craig, *The Modern Scottish Novel*, p. 74.

16  George Douglas Brown, *The House with the Green Shutters* (Edinburgh: Polygon, 2005), p. 74.

17  Brown, *The House with the Green Shutters*, p. 107.

18  Brown, *The House with the Green Shutters*, p. 114.

19  Brown, *The House with the Green Shutters*, p. 70.

20  Lewis Grassic Gibbon, *A Scots Quair* (Edinburgh: Canongate, 2008), p. 24.

21  Gibbon, *A Scots Quair*, p. 202.

22  William McIlvanney, *Docherty* (London: Sceptre, 2007), p. 5.

23  McIlvanney, *Docherty*, p. 139.

24  McIlvanney, *Docherty*, p. 298.

25  See Beth Dickson, 'Class and Being in the Novels of William McIlvanney', in Randall Stevenson and Gavin Wallace (eds), *The Scottish Novel since the Seventies: New Visions, Old Dreams* (Edinburgh: Edinburgh University Press, 1993), pp. 54–70, for a questioning of McIlvanney's traditional representations of male violence and female experience.

26  Gibbon, *A Scots Quair*, p. 32.

27  Muriel Spark, *Curriculum Vitae: A Volume of Autobiography* (London: Penguin, 1993), p. 61.

28  Muriel Spark, *The Prime of Miss Jean Brodie* (London: Penguin, 2000), p. 11.

29  Spark, *The Prime of Miss Jean Brodie*, pp. 9, 8.

30  Alasdair Gray, *Lanark: A Life in 4 Books* (London: Picador, 1985), p. 411.

31  'I think we have gone through a period when too many children and people have been given to understand "I have a problem, it is the Government's job to cope with it!" or "I have a problem, I will go and get a grant to cope with it!" "I am homeless, the Government must house me!" and so they are casting their problems on society and who is society?

There is no such thing! There are individual men and women and there are families and no government can do anything except through people and people look to themselves first.' Margaret Thatcher, interviewed by Douglas Keay, 23 September 1987; an edited version of the interview was published in *Woman's Own*, 31 October 1987, entitled 'Aids, education and the year 2000.' Full transcript on the Margaret Thatcher Foundation website: www.margaretthatcher.org/document/106689, accessed 25 July 2012.

32  Janice Galloway, *The Trick is to Keep Breathing* (London: Vintage, 1999), pp. 38, 223, 37.

33  Galloway, *The Trick is to Keep Breathing*, p. 72.

34  Galloway, *The Trick is to Keep Breathing*, p. 18.

35  Galloway, *The Trick is to Keep Breathing*, p. 26.

36  Galloway, *The Trick is to Keep Breathing*, p. 37.

37  Galloway, *The Trick is to Keep Breathing*, p. 22.

38  Galloway, *The Trick is to Keep Breathing*, p. 41.

39  Alan Warner, *Morvern Callar* (London: Vintage, 1996), p. 57.

40  Warner, *Morvern Callar*, pp. 76, 43.

41  Warner, *Morvern Callar*, p. 142.

42  Warner, *Morvern Callar*, p. 203. Morvern's thoughts here can be seen as politically reactionary. See Maria Pini, *Club Cultures and Female Subjectivity: The Move from Home to House* (Basingstoke: Palgrave, 2001) for the view that club culture has not been liberating for women.

43  'If one thinks that one sees a man dressed as a woman or a woman dressed as a man, then one takes the first term of each of those perceptions as the "reality" of gender: the gender that is introduced through the simile lacks "reality", and is taken to constitute an illusory appearance. In such perceptions in which an ostensible reality is coupled with unreality, we think we know what the reality is, and take the secondary appearance of gender to be mere artifice, play, falsehood, and illusion. But what is the sense of "gender reality" that founds this perception in this way? Perhaps we think we know what the anatomy of the person is (sometimes we do not, and we certainly have not appreciated the variation that exists at the level of anatomical description). Or we derive that knowledge from the clothes that the person wears, or how the clothes are worn. This is naturalized knowledge, even though it is based on a series of cultural inferences, some of which are highly erroneous. [...] The moment in which one's staid and usual cultural perceptions fail, when one cannot with surety read the body that one sees, is precisely the moment when one is no longer sure whether the body encountered is that of a man or a woman. The vacillation between the categories itself constitutes the experience of the body in question.' Judith Butler, *Gender Trouble: Feminism and the Subversion of Identity* (1990; London and New York: Routledge, 2007), pp. xxiii–xxiv.

44  Jackie Kay, *Trumpet* (London: Picador, 1999), p. 5.

45  Kay, *Trumpet*, p. 22.

46  Kay, *Trumpet*, p. 24.

47  Kay, *Trumpet*, p. 273.

# 8: Historicity, narration and myths in Karin Altenberg's *Island of Wings*[1]

## PHILIPPE LAPLACE

> I shall for the present close my journal, and that in the words of Dr MacCulloch, with some little deviation, *viz*: if St Kilda is not the Eutopia so long sought, where will it be found? Where is the land which has neither arms, money, care, physic, politics, nor taxes? That land is St Kilda. [...] Well may the pampered native of happy *Hirt* [St Kilda] refuse to change his situation – his slumbers are late – his labours are light – his occupation his amusement. Government he has not – law he feels not – physic he wants not – politics he heeds not – money he sees not – of war he hears not. His state is his city – his city his social circle – he has the liberty of his thoughts, his actions, and his kingdom and all the world are his equals. His climate is mild, and his island green, and the stranger who might corrupt him shuns his shores. If happiness is not a dweller in St Kilda, where shall it be sought?[2]

One of the most conspicuous features when researching Scottish literature – whether one talks about literary classics, modern or even sometimes contemporary productions – is the collusion of history and myths. Mythopoeia is indeed a classic occurrence throughout the literature of Scotland. After all, as many scholars have convincingly argued before, history and myths are natural constituents of sentiments of nationhood. It is therefore not surprising to see them used by writers who wish to express feelings of identity or of belonging. The Highlands and the islands of Scotland have more particularly lent themselves to such ideological and rhetorical use.

This chapter considers history and myths in *Island of Wings*, Karin Altenberg's first novel which takes place on the remote isle of St Kilda. As it is demonstrated in the epigraph to this chapter, St Kilda and the St Kildans have repeatedly been subjected to myth-making; this chapter will also consider Altenberg's deliberate respect for authentic sources, that is to say the extent of her novel's historicity, and the paradoxical angle she has adopted towards developing her own fiction.

Because of its distance from the mainland, rough sea crossings and total isolation, the isle of St Kilda – or to be more accurate Hirta, as St Kilda is the name given to the archipelago – was a favourite subject for travel writers throughout the seventeenth, eighteenth and nineteenth centuries. One of the first narrations, and probably the one which is responsible for a mythicised vision and a fascination for this island, is Martin Martin's 1698 *A Late Voyage to St Kilda*. Martin presents an island where contemporary worries and concerns are unknown to a population whose main occupation and means of existence is fowling. Contacts with the outside world are by all means scarce and limited to the yearly visit of the taxman, to occasional shipwrecks and to the rare visitors who venture the rough crossing from South Uist. According to Martin, trips to the island and the visit to its hundred or so inhabitants were sadly undervalued adventures which offered the exoticism which many were keen to find abroad.[3] Martin, in a way, succeeded in promoting journeys to the Scottish isles: Samuel Johnson, for instance, acknowledges that it is one of Martin's later books which triggered his decision to visit the Western Islands of Scotland.[4]

In *A Late Voyage to St Kilda*, Martin describes a peaceful community where bartering is the only means of acquiring anything, where crime and violence are virtually unheard of, and where islanders frugally live off what nature provides. Rousseau's theories of the noble savage, Herder's considerations on primitive authenticity, quests for the sublime, the flurry of travels and travel writings to the Highlands and Islands of Scotland and the beginning of the age of tourism in the second half of the nineteenth century were later to amplify this vision of a peaceful idyllic world existing outside time. The decision by the few remaining St Kildan families to finally abandon the island in 1930 paradoxically reinforced these myths. All these legends gave way to what the archaeologist Andrew Fleming derogatorily calls the 'Hardrock consensus', from the name given to the 1957 military operation on St Kilda. It symbolises what Fleming sees as the extension of myths about idyllic life on the island, that is to say the outsiders' first impression that St Kilda was the last repository of ancient traditions and that the islanders lived in a Golden Age which came to an abrupt end because of tourism and the lure of emigration. The 'Hardrock consensus' propounds that rather than a mere decision based on the difficulties of life on St Kilda, the regular shortage of food and the desire to improve their conditions, only basic external forces, that is the irruption of Victorian and Edwardian values, led its inhabitants eventually to prefer self-exile.[5] For instance, in a 2011 revised edition of an earlier book devoted to St Kilda one reads: 'Like many Celts, they were dreamers rather than men of action. [...] As contact with the mainland increased [...] the St Kildans were incapable of adapting to a more complex set of rules of behaviour and became introverted'.[6]

Observers with better knowledge of Highland culture had on the contrary praised the St Kildans' adaptability. For instance in the notes left by Rev. Neil Mackenzie, who is, by the way, the protagonist of Altenberg's novel, the St Kildans are described as crafty and calculating. For instance:

> Encouraged by the amazing credulity of the ordinary tourist, the natives have got to be very successful in imposing upon them. The tourist comes with a certain idea in his mind as to what the native is like, and would be disappointed if they did not find him like that; this the natives have been shrewd enough to discover and turn to their own profit.[7]

Rev. Mackenzie then describes how the St Kildans would, in Gaelic, comment on the tourists' naivety and on their own acting skills. As far as the benign atmosphere of St Kilda is concerned, Rev. Mackenzie also downplays the apparent peaceful serenity of the island. He gives two instances of acts of revenge – punishments condoned by the villagers – committed in the 1830s by groups of St Kildans on fellow islanders guilty of having betrayed their community.[8]

St Kilda – now owned by the National Trust of Scotland, a military base and a UNESCO World Heritage Site – has continued to exert a certain fascination. The island has inspired many works and research, a craze that the already cited Andrew Fleming names as 'Hirtophilia'.[9] The St Kildans' simple way of life and society have also been at the heart of a somewhat incongruous fascination. The poet Douglas Dunn, for example, used one of the key features of St Kilda's social organisation – what was known as the 'Parliament' – and the famous 1886 photograph as a metaphor for the lost dream of sovereignty following the 1979 abortive referendum on devolution.[10]

Karin Altenberg's *Island of Wings* is the very latest element in this popular fancy for St Kilda, but its goal is utterly different and it does away with most of the varnish St Kilda and its inhabitants had been embellished with. Published in April 2011, it describes St Kilda and life on the island during the middle of the nineteenth century. Writing a novel about St Kilda is a daunting challenge as one has to wrestle with mythicised representations, emotional accounts and distorted historical facts. Karin Altenberg complicates her task by writing a biographical fiction about one of the most significant outsiders having lived on the island; somebody responsible – and probably guilty according to the 'Hardrock' consensus – for having had a profound influence on the islanders' way of life, an achievement that the same Andrew Fleming describes in a very positive way as 'phenomenal'.[11] However, Altenberg's protagonist has become a tragic hero, his professional success creating collateral damage at the expense of his wife and family.

Altenberg's novel depicts the thirteen years spent on St Kilda by the envoy of the Society for the Propagation of Christian Knowledge (SPCK), the Church of Scotland minister Reverend Neil Mackenzie and his wife, from their arrival in July 1830 to their departure in May 1843, shortly after Rev. Mackenzie's refusal to walk out from the General Assembly to join the dissenting Free Church ministers led by Chalmers. (I will use the names 'Neil Mackenzie' and 'Elizabeth Mackenzie' when talking about Altenberg's characters and 'Rev. Mackenzie' and 'Mrs Mackenzie' when talking about the non-fictional couple who lived on St Kilda.) Although Altenberg heavily relies on the few documentary sources and historical data available, a fact she acknowledges in a postface to the novel,[12] such as Rev. Mackenzie's notes, travellers' accounts or scientific studies, she also stresses that Neil and Elizabeth Mackenzie's personal lives, turmoils and sentiments as they are presented in the novel are utterly fictional. The fact that she felt the need to provide the reader with a paratext shows the thin line between history and fiction in the novel and, more generally, when talking about St Kilda. It is indeed worth mentioning that Rev. Mackenzie, in the notes he left which were later published by one of his sons, rarely refers to his wife or to his children. The main focus of his attention was the island itself. It included, of course, the islanders' spiritual redemption, but also their physical well-being and improvement, the former being the reason why he had been dispatched to the island by the SPCK and the latter having been his greatest achievement. His passion for the island and its inhabitants comes at the detriment of his family. This is also a key feature of the novel, to the extent that Altenberg, when they are about to leave to return to the mainland once his duties for the SPCK are accomplished, makes his wife say: 'Your mission was always most important, was it not? More important than me and the children. [...] I think at times that perhaps you were never really brave enough to love us' (297). This serves as the main chorus to the novel: the story of St Kilda is told from two viewpoints in *Island of Wings*: Neil Mackenzie's nearly scientific observations of the island and its inhabitants, and Elizabeth Mackenzie's personal sentiments towards the island, her relationships with the inhabitants and her feelings towards her husband and his involvement in his evangelical mission. Authenticity is a clear concern for Altenberg, and she has managed the seemingly impossible task of scrupulously respecting historical documents concerning the island while managing to write a fictional biography of the Mackenzie family.

*Island of Wings* therefore allows us to glimpse into narratological issues: Altenberg gives us access to Neil Mackenzie's subjectivity. Despite having lived and transformed life on St Kilda, Neil Mackenzie is a fictional character whose thoughts and secrets are imagined by the author. Biographical fiction, or biopics in cinematographical parlance, is a genre which has nearly always been ignored by literary critics and, apart from the first hagiographers, by academia as a whole. Michel Foucault once considered the editing of the archives of the Hôpital Général and the Bastille into a fictional form in order to tell these people's stories, what he calls 'an anthology of existences'. However, Foucault never pursued this idea much further and concluded very harshly on the genre:

> I began by saying that these texts might be read as so many 'short stories'. That was saying too much, no doubt; none of them will ever measure up to the least tale by Chekhov, Maupassant or James. Neither 'quasi-' nor 'subliterature', they are not even the first sketch of a genre; they are the action, in disorder, noise, and pain, of power on lives, and the discourse that comes of it.[13]

Altenberg has crafted her novel by putting together a mosaic of accounts. By referring to archives and documented data not only regarding Mackenzie's achievements but also about life on St Kilda, she keeps confusing the reader and, in a way, clouding the issue: is this a fictional work based on Rev. Mackenzie's life or a very detailed – quasi-historical – document about life on the island and Rev. Mackenzie's achievements? And this is very much what could be held against Altenberg's book: the presence – or the absence – of fictional elements is difficult to assess. As Lukàcs had noted, 'it is inevitable that biography should appear as the specific form of the modern historical novel'.[14] However, by adding purely fictional elements, Altenberg makes it more difficult for anyone who does not know what has already been published about St Kilda and Rev. Mackenzie to distinguish between history and fiction. The only clue is her hint in the postface that 'the account is accurate in most historical details' (310), from which we can infer that all personal elements are purely fictional.

Altenberg faithfully follows the main points of Reverend Mackenzie's years on St Kilda as he and visitors recorded them. The second chapter, entitled 'May 1831–A Visit', for instance, records George Clayton Atkinson's expedition to St Kilda which he related in an article published in 1838.[15] Altenberg carefully mixes Atkinson's scientific observations and descriptions of the few weeks he spent on the island with fictional episodes. She quotes from the article and makes it appear as an extract from Atkinson's notebook (87), a narrative device she acknowledges in her postface; but she also deliberately paraphrases or uses passages of Atkinson's article at various instances without using italics or quotation marks, therefore weaving together authentic details in order to create a rich tapestry to illustrate one of the island's crucial developments, as in the following example where textual similarities are highlighted in **bold**:

*Atkinson:*

We were **much struck with the good looks of the inhabitants as they turned out**, men, women, and children, to receive us. They are of **rather short** stature, but **present neat compact specimens of the human form**, set off by lively **intelligent countenances**, adorned almost always with beautifully **white teeth**. […] The women wear a gown of the same blue woollen material of which the men's coats are made, drawn in at the waist, but as they **are not generally, I think, so good-looking as the men, this negligence is not becoming**.[16]

*Altenberg:*

'I was **struck**,' said Mr George Atkinson, '**by the good looks of the inhabitants as they turned out** to meet us on the landing rocks'.

'Yes', agreed the minister enthusiastically, 'although they are **rather short** they **present neat** and **compact specimens of the human form**.'

'I have never seen **teeth as white** as theirs; did you not notice their teeth?' asked Mrs Mackenzie of no one in particular as if the thought had just occurred to her.

'Oh yes, I did indeed', said the other Mr Atkinson [G. C. Atkinson's brother]. 'However, I was mainly impressed by the **air of intelligence** which they conveyed. […] Although I think, […] that the women **are not generally so good-looking as the men. The negligence in their dress is not becoming!**'[17]

This is quite recurrent throughout the novel. I have managed to find large extracts from Mackenzie's notes which have become part of the plot or are developed as a subplot: concerning the island, the islanders' accommodation, local traditions such as weddings or various incidents such as the stealing of a rug in Mackenzie's manse, or Mackenzie giving a hand in the building of new accommodation and surprising the islanders by his strength and ingenuity.[18] She also sometimes puts someone else's words into another character's mouth; for example, part of the epigraph to this article is ascribed to Atkinson instead of Lachlan Maclean (61–62). Altenberg also gives us an insight into Neil Mackenzie's notebook, and the passages, this time highlighted in italics in the novel, faithfully correspond to the notes left by Rev. Mackenzie.[19] Authenticity, and the desire to be as close as possible to the true history and life of the St Kildans, is at the core of the novel, to such an extent that official documents and reports are disseminated throughout the novel.[20]

However, *Island of Wings* is definitely not a hagiography: Neil Mackenzie does appear, in spite of – or maybe because of – his Church of Scotland mantle, as a very weak and frail man in front of the awesome St Kildan traditions, myths and rites. A fight for power and domination lies at the heart of the novel: Neil Mackenzie was sent by the SPCK to establish God's power on this forsaken land and to turn paganism into Christianity. On leaving the island he reflects on his own achievements:

> There was a time when they were like puppets in my hands,
> impressionable and naive – I wanted to protect them from their
> misdemeanours and show them the purifying properties of the
> heart's sorrow. I moved their world when they did not think it
> possible; I waged war upon the ghosts of their minds and chased
> away the witches of their imagination; I have ridden the storm and
> relaxed in the eye of the wind. This was my art. I was strong once,
> and then weakness overcame me. (304)

Neil Mackenzie, like a Prospero exercising his art, clearly sees his role as
that of the patriarch, wielding control and domination over the subjugated
islanders. However, as demonstrated by the islanders' refusal to knock
over the idols which have assumed the form of immemorial traditions, the
spirit of St Kilda lives on in spite of his struggles and he will eventually
come to the conclusion that nothing can erase the St Kildans' collective
unconscious and their attachment to the land. Neil Mackenzie, whose
analytical approach relegates sentimental concerns to the sideline, concludes:
'I have watched them as closely as a scientist looks at insects under a
glass. I have been able to touch them, to heal them, to encourage them, to
instruct them – but I still do not understand them' (296). His logical
reasoning and analysis however drove him to radically improve their
lives by convincing them to destroy their antiquated and unhygienic
accommodation and to build modern houses.

All visitors to St Kilda, prior to Rev. Mackenzie, had indeed lamented
the poor quality of accommodation. Living in dirty hovels, hygiene was not
a consideration for St Kildans who were affected by what they called the
'8-day sickness', namely the frequent death of newborn babies within eight
days of their birth.[21] Their accommodation is described at length by Rev.
Mackenzie in his notes and Altenberg extensively uses his descriptions in
the novel. The trigger of the minister's resolution to change this situation
is the visit of Sir Thomas Acland and his wife in 1834, an episode also faithfully described in the novel. Appalled at the islanders' living conditions,
Acland donates money to encourage people to build new homes. The St
Kildans, at first reluctant, finally accept Rev. Mackenzie's plans in 1838.
Within four years a new village springs out with brand new houses and
furniture donated by subscriptions on the mainland. At that time many

observers remarked that the St Kildans' accommodation was the most pleasant and comfortable that could be found in the Hebrides. This is clearly due to Mackenzie's stubborn achievement. However, he was not able to uproot old traditions and pagan rites: a subsequent shortage of food is attributed to the new village structure by the islanders (266–75).

Despite being a book written about one of the most influential men who ever lived on St Kilda, the novel's point of view is clearly from his wife's stance. Elizabeth is the one who takes us through Neil's private conflicts and personal turmoil. Altenberg makes use of a whole range of symbolic images in *Island of Wings* and birds indeed play a key part in the novel. Birds after all were crucial to St Kildans' culture and fowling was the main source of food. They also often play a symbolic part in Neil and Elizabeth's lives and fate. In 1830, when approaching St Kilda by boat, Elizabeth, pregnant with her first child, notices the shape of a cross drawn by an albatross hovering over the ship (7). This is of course highly significant of what the newly-wed Elizabeth Mackenzie is going to endure on St Kilda. Her dreams of marrying a minister of the Church of Scotland, of living the life of a missionary's wife, will be shattered by the rough existence on the island and the total lack of communication between her and the natives, this being further exacerbated by the breakdown in communication with her husband. Their thirteen years on the island resemble more an ordeal than a voluntary exile or an evangelistic mission. Altenberg repeats the same Christian image of the cross when the couple leaves St Kilda: Elizabeth hurts herself with splinters when stroking her hand over the wooden crates where they have deposited their belongings (305). Her suffering is probably not over yet despite their leaving the island. After all, the man she married confesses on several occasions to having been changed by life on St Kilda: 'This island changes us – it eats into you and won't leave you alone' (235). Neil Mackenzie is oblivious to his own family in order to succeed in his evangelising tasks and to turn the St Kildans into obedient subjects of the Presbyterian Church. 'Is this the man for whom I left everything?' asks Elizabeth Mackenzie as she ponders her husband's rigid and uncompromising attitudes only two years after their arrival on the island (59). Love between them slowly but surely fades away.

The turning point between Elizabeth and Neil in the novel is the discovery of a foreign sailor marooned on St Kilda after a shipwreck. This is purely fictional as no shipwreck is recorded between 1830 and 1843. The survivor is found seriously injured, and Elizabeth takes care of him despite her husband's reluctance. Of Spanish or Portuguese origins, nobody manages to understand him or to talk to him. The islanders, used to sheltering castaways and shipwrecked sailors, do not pay much attention to him. However, relationships and sentiments between Elizabeth and Neil – which had started to break up – definitely fall apart because of his presence. She decides to call this man Nathaniel, in memory of the first child she lost on the island, and this foreshadows their impossible relationship. She decides to shelter him in the manse, to feed him properly and to look after him. With a mixture of pure jealousy and Presbyterian suspicion, Neil Mackenzie resents this intrusion and eventually forbids his wife from taking care of him. This mysterious man indeed reawakens sentiments of love, physical desire and a passion in the young woman. Neil's reaction to the sailor, apart from basic male jealousy, is full of prejudice. Writing to the laird, the minister says: 'I cannot say whether he wants salvation or whether his mouth, which speaks so coarsely in a foreign tongue, is still greedy for wrong. As far as I can tell, his character will take no goodness' (197). It is only when this man leaves the island, in the care of the tacksman, that he reveals his real name to Elizabeth: he is called Solano, a name conjuring up the image of the sunshine he briefly brought to her life. This man marks the watershed point in the novel. Not only does he awaken physical desire in Elizabeth's life but he also opens up the concealed wound Neil Mackenzie meant to forget. At the heart of his decision to become a minister of the Church and then later to go to St Kilda was the drowning of one of his friends.[22] This element, an obsessive psalmody in the novel, is also a true biographical feature, as Rev. Mackenzie's son tells us.[23]

Rev. Mackenzie's family, from Glen Sannox in Sutherland, had been forced to move to the coast during the Highland Clearances and Rev. Mackenzie probably saw many companions emigrate to North America. Gaelic being his mother tongue, he was therefore very well equipped to preach in St Kilda. Altenberg also uses the memory of the Clearances in order to stress the fact that Neil Mackenzie was prone to seeking to transform life on St Kilda. Improvement, in a different sense than what was meant by landlords and factors who used the term to justify the Clearances, was a necessary development in order to provide the inhabitants with means of existence and to avoid further clearances, as Neil Mackenzie tells Atkinson. However, the death of his companion in a fishing incident still haunts him and, in the novel, not only does he feel responsible but he is presented as having been responsible. He did not save his drowning companion. Neil Mackenzie managed to keep his balance thanks to the Presbyterian concept of predestination. Once in St Kilda – and this time this is a purely fictional element – Neil Mackenzie watches a young boy drown and merely stands aside. This of course reawakens and reinforces his previous guilt and suffering and throws him into the angst of a personal and a deep religious crisis:

> But in his darkest moments, when his faith and his confidence were failing him, a thought might occur to him: what if I was not chosen? What if I survived merely because I was stronger, because I saved my life and left Will to die? What if there is no afterlife, no heaven for the young dead? What if I have deceived myself? (238)

When confronted with such a memory, Neil Mackenzie's defence is to brush aside all feelings of guilt and to remind his wife that she lost her first child. The lack of communication is characteristic of life in St Kilda. There are clearly two sides, and, as he is a native Gaelic speaker, this is not only linguistic, related to Gaelic. His wife, who does not speak a word of Gaelic, sides with the St Kildan women, sharing their grief and their fate on this inhospitable island (125–26). Referring to Gaelic, the language spoken by the inhabitants, George Atkinson wrote (and this is an extract from his article not quoted in the novel): 'Mrs Mackenzie, a Glasgow lady, does not speak it, and therefore, was, I am inclined to think, very glad to see us, as it must have been six months since she exchanged a sentiment with any one but her husband.'[24] This lack of communication is after all Elizabeth's predicament on the island.

The novel ends with the same image as at the beginning: the couple on a boat, but this time – thirteen years after their arrival – they are now leaving St Kilda. There is a clear sense of failure: Neil Mackenzie feels he has let down the islanders and the SPCK in his evangelising task and, apart from a considerable improvement as far as the islanders' conditions of life are concerned, his mission has been tragically unsuccessful.[25] He lacked the nerve to join the 1843 Disruption and he is clearly aware that his marriage has reached a point of no return. Neil Mackenzie's last action is much more than a mere token gesture: offering his bible as a sacrifice to the sea sums up his sense of failure at redeeming the islanders and at coming to terms with the guilt feelings afflicting him and the religious crisis he has experienced on the island.[26]

> As the island subsided into the vanishing skies behind him he took out of his coat his Gaelic bible and opened it to the title page where his name had once been inscribed. For a moment he looked at the browning ink that spelled out his past before he closed the book and, leaning over the bulwarks, dropped it into the silencing sea. (308)

The strong and tragic image chosen by Altenberg also forecasts the fate of St Kilda and of its society. Altenberg's use of the bible is a clever adaptation and a reversal of history: those who witnessed the 1930 abandonment of the island say that the St Kildans left a bible on the table of their houses, and one of them had it open on the Book of Exodus.[27]

What actually followed the Mackenzies' departure was a long period of cultural oblivion for the St Kildans. Charles Maclean referred to a 'vacuum' left after Rev. Neil Mackenzie's return to the mainland.[28] Rev. Mackenzie, a Highlander himself, despite his opposition to the island's traditions and culture, had been careful not to prohibit them. He even collected poems and songs from St Kilda which were later edited in the *Celtic Review*.[29] The Kirk elders who replaced him imposed a very strict ideological censorship until a Free Church minister was eventually sent in 1865. Many visitors described the natives as having discarded and then forgotten their own music, poetry, traditions and dancing. St Kildans started emigrating and this, with the outbreak of disease and long periods of food shortage that severely threatened life itself on the island in the 1920s, eventually led to the abandonment of the island by its last thirty-six inhabitants in 1930. At the end of the nineteenth century, when tourist expeditions to St Kilda were valued by the Scottish gentry, the *Glasgow Herald* special correspondent to St Kilda had already remarked:

> Writers like Martin and Macaulay saw only the most delightful romance in this simple primitive people leading a life of all but

complete isolation on their lonely rock [...] The romance is gone; it could not by any possibility survive the stern fact of repeated periods of destitution imperilling the very existence of the community. It is these recurring seasons of scarcity that have forced the problem of the future of St Kilda upon the attention of the public, and have led many sensible people to think that the only way of solving it satisfactorily is to abandon the island.[30]

Sentimental stories had indeed flourished about the island and its inhabitants and had led to many romantic tales blurring the grim and difficult life of the St Kildans. Karin Altenberg's novel does justice to Rev. Mackenzie's achievement and, through her patient compilation of first-hand reports and official data, restores the islanders' history. She is, after all, an archaeologist who works on the field of cultural heritage. Her fictional biography, presenting Neil Mackenzie's mission and achievements and his wife's shattered dreams and subsequent distress, is also an invaluable historical document on a key moment in the tragic history of Hirta.

## Notes

1    K. Altenberg, *Island of Wings* (London: Quercus, 2011). All references to this edition will appear in the text between brackets.
2    Lachlan Maclean, *Sketches on the Island of St Kilda* (Glasgow: McPhun, 1838). Quoted in Francis Thompson, *St Kilda and Other Hebridean Outliers,* new edition (London: David & Charles, 1988), pp. 111–12. The original reference, by MacCulloch, reads: 'The pampered native of St Kilda may with reason refuse to change his situation; finding his amusement where his chief occupation lies, in the pursuit of sea fowl, that constitute at the same time his game, his luxury, and a considerable part of his wealth. Free from the reputed evils of law, physic, politics, and taxes; living under a patriarchal government, among a social circle of his relations; in a mild climate, without knowledge of a higher state of things; if he thinks not his island an Utopia, the pursuit of happiness is indeed a dream.' John MacCulloch, *A Description of the Western Islands, including the Isle of Man,* vol. II (London: Archibald Constable, 1819), pp. 29–30.
3    Martin Martin reported having seen above one hundred and eighty people, which is one of the largest figures recorded for St Kilda: Martin Martin, *A Late Voyage to St Kilda, the remotest of all the Hebrides, or Western Isles of Scotland* (London: D. Brown & T. Goodwin, 1698), p. 51. See also: Mary Harman, *An Isle Called Hirte: A History and Culture of St Kilda to 1930* (Waternish: Maclean Press, 1997), pp. 124–42. In his preface, Martin wrote: 'It is a piece of weakness and folly merely to value things because of their distance from the place where we are born: thus men have travelled far enough in the search of foreign plants and animals, and yet continue strangers to those produced in their own climate.'

4   As recorded by Boswell in the very first paragraph of his *Journal of a Tour to the Hebrides with Samuel Johnson.*
5   See: A. Fleming, *St Kilda and the Wider World: Tales of an Iconic Island* (Macclesfield: Windgather Press, 2005), pp. 1–13.
6   T. Steel, *The Life and Death of St Kilda: The Moving Story of a Vanished Island Community* (London: Harper Press, 2011), pp. 51–53. Quoted by Fleming, p. 6.
7   J. B. Mackenzie, *Episode in the Life of the Rev. Neil Mackenzie at St Kilda from 1829 to 1843,* edited by his son the Rev. J. B. Mackenzie Minister at Kenmore (1911), p. 28. Rev. Neil Mackenzie's first visit to St Kilda was in 1829, accompanied by John MacDonald (known as 'the Apostle of the North'). Rev. Neil Mackenzie came back with his wife in July 1830.
8   J. B. Mackenzie, p. 30.
9   A. Fleming, p. 5.
10  D. Dunn, 'St Kilda's Parliament: 1879–1979. The photographer revisits his picture', in *St Kilda's Parliament* (London: Faber & Faber, 1981), pp. 13–15.
11  A. Fleming, p. 131.
12  'It builds largely on documentary sources […] and published research […] Students of these texts will realise that I have taken a number of liberties regarding the individual characters and their personalities, but the account is accurate in most historical details.' (Altenberg, p. 310).
13  M. Foucault, 'Lives of Infamous Men', in *Power: Essential Works of Foucault, 1954–84,* edited by James D. Faubion, translated by Robert Hurley and others, vol. III (New York: The New Press, 2001), pp. 157–75 (p. 174).
14  G. Lukàcs, *The Historical Novel,* translated from the German by Hannah and Stanley Mitchell (London: Merlin Press, 1962), p. 301.
15  G. C. Atkinson, 'Notice of the island of St Kilda, on the North-West coast of Scotland', *Transactions of the Natural History Society, of Northumberland, Durham, and Newcastle upon Tyne,* II (1838), pp. 215–25.
16  G. C. Atkinson, p. 217.
17  K. Altenberg, pp. 56–57.
18  Altenberg, (the rug incident) p. 13; (Mackenzie's ingenuity) p. 16; (description of houses) pp. 18–22.
19  Altenberg, pp. 28–30.
20  Altenberg also introduces Lachlan Maclean as a visitor to the island (247). He comments: 'A land where everything is held in common, where crime and war are unknown and where there is an abundance of food to feed my people and no one would have to work too hard'. Maclean was beaming. […] "Did you ever imagine paradise such as this?" Maclean cried in exultation.' (258).
21  Medical science later explained that the precise cause of the '8-day sickness' was due to a local tradition of cleaning the umbilical cord with a mixture of oil from birds, some babies developing a form of tetanus. Moreover, problems of house hygiene should certainly not be dismissed: 'Two weeks later Mrs Mackenzie gave birth to twin girls. It all happened as it should. The old crone from the village was called to cut the umbilical cord from the tiny bodies and smear the stumps with bird grease. […] The old woman wrapped the girls in linen towels, but rather poorly as there was only enough linen for one baby. Lizzie was concerned that the girls were not washed before being wrapped but was too exhausted to do anything about it just then.' (Altenberg, p. 97).

22  J. B. Mackenzie, p. 3.

23  'The drowning of a companion by the capsizing of a new fishing wherry which they were trying, and his own narrow escape from the same fate, caused him to make up his mind to become a preacher of the Gospel and to go somewhere as a missionary.' (J. B. Mackenzie, p. 3).

24  G. C. Atkinson, p. 219.

25  In his notes, Rev. Mackenzie commented: 'It appears to me that my work here is now finished, and that I would be more useful somewhere else. I have therefore made up my mind, as there is an opportunity, to leave the island for a time, and it may be for ever. The labours and anxieties of the past two years have told heavily, both on my bodily health and mental vigour, and I need a time of rest and mental refreshment.' (J. B. Mackenzie, p. 38).

26  'But in his darkest moments, when his faith and his confidence were failing him, a thought might occur to him: what if I was not chosen? What if I survived merely because I was stronger, because I saved my life and left Will to die? What if there is no afterlife, no heaven for the young dead? What if I have deceived myself?' (Altenberg, p. 238).

27  Tom Steel, p. 21.

28  Charles Maclean, St Kilda: Island on the Edge of the World. Afterwords by Margaret Buchanan (Edinburgh: Canongate Classics, 1998), p. 126.

29  Neil Mackenzie, 'Bardachd Irteach', Celtic Review, 2 (1906), pp. 328–42. 'Antiquities and Old Customs of St Kilda, compiled from notes by the Rev. Neil Mackenzie', Proceedings of the Society of Antiquaries of Scotland, 38 (1904), pp. 397–402.

30  Robert Connell, St Kilda and the St Kildians (London & Glasgow: Hamilton, Adams & Co. and Thomas D. Morison, 1887), p. 158.

# 9: James Robertson's angle on Scottish society and politics in *And the Land Lay Still*

## MORAG J. MUNRO-LANDI

James Robertson initially outlined his root intentions for *And the Land Lay Still*,[1] which was awarded the 2010 Saltire Scottish Book of the Year, as follows: 'to write a novel charting the big political, social and cultural changes that have occurred in Scotland from 1945 to 1999, the year our Parliament was re-established after a gap of nearly 300 years. [...] To be honest, at this point, I've no idea what's going to emerge.'[2] Born in 1958, Robertson felt he had himself to reach a point in time from which he was able to 'look both far enough back and far enough forward' after his own participation in the 1980s and 1990s lead-up to that watershed event: 'Life on either side of that vantage point seems more complete now, it makes more sense. In fiction it's called resolution.'[3] His technique involves a particular angle on Scotland similar to the 'Angus Angle' adopted by Michael Pendreich's Cartier-Bresson-influenced photographer of a father, an angle that focuses via off-centre bystanders or onlookers rather than on central figures or objects, creating off-centre and sometimes asymmetrical visual narratives.[4] Robertson, too, swings his lens over to the edge, and takes in ordinary Scots in small-town Scotland. This chapter's discussion will concern three main areas. The first – '*And the Land Lay Still* as a multi-part song of Scotland' – considers the overall configuration and the multilevel, multi-voiced interconnected narratives as a challenge for writer and reader. The second – 'Charting the changes' – considers representations of social and political identities and their evolution over the decades depicted. The third – 'From fringe to mainstream: Robertson's affirmative gender agenda' – considers Robertson's approach to gender issues, and the way in which homosexuality is central to the novel and an integral part of twenty-first-century Scotland as Robertson sees it.

## 1. *And the Land Lay Still* as a multi-part song of Scotland

Before any further discussion, it is necessary to come to grips with the composition of this multilayered and multi-voiced novel. Its most visible and identifiable structural elements are its six parts, each bearing a title which, although enigmatic at first sight, of course means more once the book has been read. Part One, 'The Mouth in the Box', may refer to story-teller Jean Barbour in her flat and to the embedded eponymous tale she tells (59–63); it could also refer to Angus Pendreich's photographic discourse. Part Two, 'The Persistence of Memory', may express one of the messages of the novel: the past is still with us in the present, in particular for some war-worn characters. Part Three, 'The Original Mr Bond', has a rather tongue-in-cheek title: it includes the story of the 'first' spy of the name of James Bond, rather than of the famous 1952 Ian Fleming character – Robertson's fictional character is represented as a 'real' person, Peter Bond, who preceded Fleming's fictional character, James. Part Four, 'Scenes from Olden Days', announces a return once more to earlier times. Part Five, 'Questions of Loyalties', hints at the complexities and dilemmas within interconnecting personal relationships and political allegiances. Part Six, 'The Gift of the Moment', alludes, among other things, to the final gathering at the exhibition of Angus Pendreich's photographs and to all that it brings to the characters and foreshadows for the days to come.

Robertson's own *narrative* approach is reflected well in the final *sceno-graphic* approach in the photograph archive display. As one visitor remarks: 'The photographs are not chronological, at least not consistently so. He thought he was working his way forward in time but now he seems to be going back' (665). Similarly, the novel is made up of sequels and prequels – in that order. Parts One and Six are a framing narrative set in 2008 around Michael Pendreich's preparation for, and then holding of, the exhibition of a selection of his father's photographs, three years after his death. The first, 'The Mouth in the Box', opens with Michael Pendreich's third-person narrative. This includes, besides the few months of 2008 leading up to and after his visit to Edinburgh and his new relationship with Murdo, fragmentary flashbacks relating to his own past life, specifically until 1979 and the failed devolution referendum. In this section, various important characters are introduced or briefly mentioned (for example, Murdo, Angus and Isabel Pendreich, Jean Barbour, Freddy and David Eddlestane, Catriona MacDonald, Adam Shaw), most of whose own life stories are to be told in other sections (often from childhood onwards). The second part, 'The Persistence of Memory', involves a retrospective on Scotland from the 1950s onwards, in particular through the eyes and mindset of Don Lennie in the Central Lowlands village and small-town contexts of Wharryburn and Drumkirk, respectively. Through him we meet Jack Gordon and his wife Sarah and daughter Barbara. Both Lennie and Gordon are World War Two veterans, trying to move on.

The third section, 'The Original Mr Bond' ('the pre-Connery, pre-Roger Moore, pre-Timothy Dalton, pre-Daniel fucking Craig version' (667)), is pivotal, moving forward again to the initial time coordinate of 2008. It opens with the immediate recognition by Peter Bond of Michael Pendreich in a café: 'He placed the guy in the café at once. Pendreich, Michael. Photographer. Did some of the covers of *Root & Branch*. Devoporn' (233). He recurs throughout the novel. He is spotted by Michael in the early 1970s, first, as an enigmatic figure in a pub, 'Dufflecoat' (51–52), then at Jean Barbour's, with the 'same calculating look' (64); he is already described at the time by Jean Barbour as a '"spook, a spy"' (78–89). Bond also appears in Part Two, as Jimmy, Jack Gordon's young nephew whom Don and Billy Lennie meet by chance while out for a walk. He also gatecrashes the exhibition preview in Part Six. Here, in Part Three, there is a striking shift in narrative and linguistic mode, as well as a switch to unjustified, ragged-looking text (this layout will reappear with the character in other parts of the novel, for example: 607–10; 666–68). Bond is the central consciousness throughout. His self-definition is eloquent: 'you're a pensioned-off drunk in a stinking flat in a run-down street that you, you shaky auld cunt [...], should be afraid to go out in at night.' The second-person, self-reflexive narrative is composed of introspective retrospection and hindsight, in which imagined dramatic scenes of dialogue are inserted, the character talking to himself or supposedly to the ghosts that haunt his own past: 'All these fucking conversations in your head. Single-sided, a lot of them. One-versations' (231). The configuration of this whole section is arguably yet another contemporary Scottish variation/hypertext of James Hogg's *Private Memoirs and Confessions of a Justified Sinner* (1824).[5] It also, however, reminds us of passages of Robertson's own *The Fanatic*, in which the main character regularly talks to himself/his second self who expresses himself in similar register, in a mirror in his flat.[6] Bond's own past, but also that of Scottish political life, is viewed through his alcohol-soaked imagination (another drunk man looking at a thistle?). Were we to consider him a reliable narrator, Bond's account might be seen to shed new (if sometimes somewhat hazy) light on key political events (Scottish and British) narrated elsewhere in the novel from other angles, and on the nature of Michael Pendreich's political activism: to him, Pendreich is 'a soft-left, soft-left nationalist' (233), among other things.

'Scenes from Olden Days', the fourth section, moves back once again to Scotland in the 1950s before moving forward again at random. Events are partially seen from the female perspective of the Imlachs (Mary, then daughter Ellen) in the former mining town of Borlanslogie, 'just over the Fife border' (106). The Shaw twin cousins, Adam and Gavin, come to live with Ellen and her mother. There is also a return to the increasingly diverging lives and world views of Don Lennie and his sons Billy and Charlie, and in particular to Liz Lennie's sphere, as well as to the Eddlestanes, in particular David and dropout Lucy. The narrative threads cross for better or worse, the rape scene involving Charlie Lennie and Ellen Imlach, and its aftermath, appearing towards the close. In the fifth section, 'A Question of Loyalties', the lives of all the characters are picked up and again put down further along their way at different moments and in different places during the 1980s and 1990s. Robertson, wandering through the different time-space dimensions – central and peripheral – of his novel, seems to be following this logic, that of his recurrent wandering figure:

> You kept a pocket full of stones. The stones had no purpose, they were just a story. You kept the story going. That was what you had to do. You picked up the stones where you found them and you took them on, and every so often you laid them down again. You were making a pattern, but you didn't know what the pattern was. You didn't know where you were in the pattern or where it would end. (145)

Eventually, the final section, 'The Gift of the Moment', in a process of conjunction, draws all the initially separate, then connecting and/or intertwining, narrative threads together, on the occasion of Michael Pendreich's exhibition preview. Nearly all the characters are present either physically or in the photographs on display or in conversation. Some new, unexpected connections resulting from this gathering emerge or are discovered which, in turn, herald further new relationships:

> But the connections, more of them even than he can know or imagine
> at this moment – with Catriona and Billy and beyond, with the wife
> and daughter that Jack had – the connections will be made, and he
> understands that it has fallen to him to make them. (671)

The expression 'visible and identifiable' used of the novel's structural
elements in the second sentence of this chapter section is deliberately chosen:
there is a further, less visible and, altogether, less clearly identifiable dimension
to *And the Land Lay Still*, a further dimension that is structural, narrative,
lyrical and ideological. The reference here is to the texts – like the one
quoted in the previous paragraph – outwith the six parts, passages set apart,
in italics, on the margin of the main text, but which will turn out to be of
vital import to the comprehension and meaning of the whole. Both the
self-reflexive narrative voice and the insightful vision of these opening, and
then interstitial, passages are initially disembodied and unidentified, those
of some wandering, troubled soul who has sought solitude for his own
survival, who has evidently withdrawn from society in a gesture of self-
effacement. This mysterious figure, who has left the society of men to be
able to 'breathe more easily', appears sporadically, almost ghostlike, to
characters in the main sections as an anonymous wanderer. He is also an
onlooker. He appears to Michael Pendreich in Part One, 'A man who
happened to be walking along the road at the time' (9), to Ellen Imlach in
Part Four, 'a strange, unreal figure was coming down the street towards her,
a man' (401). He gives Michael a pebble from his pocket (11) to keep, although
Michael eventually loses it; he '*made an offering to* [Ellen] *from the pocket
of stones*', laying it down for her to go and get (227). We realise that the
skeleton with pebbles lying within it, found by Murdo on a remote, 'unfor-
giving' beach at Sandwood Bay on Sutherland's furthest north-west coast,
must be the same person (140). It corresponds to the self-description in the
final interstitial passage of the wanderer's lying down to rest (635–636):

> *You settled on a bank of sand under a low cliff.* […] *Your fading hand
> reached into the pocket where the stones were. There were hardly any
> left.* […] *You swallowed them slowly, one after another.* […] *You ate
> the stones, and the sea faded, and the land faded.*

Vital counterbalance to the political debate(s) within the main narrative is provided by this solitary man's angle on the evolution of Scotland through the decades, not least the arrival of new populations: *'you became aware of new people around you as you travelled.* [...] *bus drivers in turbans* [...] *a group of quiet, brown wary-looking men drinking tea outside* [...] *clusters of black-haired boys'* (521), and by his recognition of the final futility of simple nationalism and party politics given man's destruction of the environment and the inexorable supremacy of money: *'It wasn't the age of small nations as you'd thought, it was the age of money and waste and garbage and pollution and destruction and it was all going to get worse'* (228).

The careful reader should therefore be able to link up the exocentric narrative passages with elements in Part Two, Part Three and Part Four that will allow him/her to identify this voice and this vision of changing Scotland as being those of Jack Gordon. He is actually recognised, a few years before the courts declare him dead, by Liz Lennie, as she admits to Don many years later in Part Four:

> 'I didna ken if it was really him. [...] I was gaun intae Drumkirk and the bus had stopped at the lights and I looked oot and there he was, gaun in the other direction. [...] But I saw his face, and it was him. [...] I thought,' she said, 'if it was him, it was his ghost.' (416)

This, then, is Don Lennie's war veteran friend. Having been through horrendous experiences in a Japanese POW camp, including his witnessing the beheading of one of his fellow Scots, a Burns enthusiast, Gordon has been unable, in the period of reconstruction after the war, to rebuild his own life around his job, his wife and his daughter. He is suffering from what we would now call 'post-traumatic stress disorder'. He has planned his own disappearance, as is revealed in 'The Original Mr Bond' by that other almost invisible ghostlike figure, also cut off from society, his nephew, Jimmy/Peter Bond, 'Jack in miniature' (211), as Don Lennie describes him. A climactic moment is reached in the novel when Don, haunted as he has been by the memory of Jack Gordon all through his life, suddenly recognises the man in the Dounreay archive photograph (669), as has Peter Bond: 'Mad Uncle Jack' (667). This single photograph marks close to both the beginning (11) and the end (two pages before the conclusion on 671) of the novel: it has triggered remembrance and the whole narrative; it subsequently brings – albeit relative – closure.

Together with the multiple, interconnecting narrative levels, this multi-voiced novel recounts its personal histories within the history of Scotland itself over its timescale. The characters, past and present, are a continuum and they participate actively in a communal effort towards the making of history. Various key socio-political and cultural events that seem to have marked collective Scottish memory are told and retold. Robertson's choices may be somewhat influenced, for example, by Louise Yeoman's *Reportage Scotland*: in her 1947–1999 chapter 'The Road to Home Rule', out of the ten topics dealt with, eight are featured in the novel, including 'The Hamilton Bye-Election', 'Referendum – 1979', 'The Miners' Strike', 'Piper Alpha', 'The Poll Tax', and two topics are also related to photographs taken by Angus Pendreich, 'Stealing the Stone' and 'Elvis at Prestwick'.[7] The Elvis photograph as described in the novel also bears striking resemblance to one featured in the *Herald*'s 2001 *Decades* 'Pictorial series celebrating Scottish life, culture and events'.[8] What of Robertson's angles on politics?

As the versions of events vary in the novel, so do political sentiments: as Jean Barbour says, '"Stories aren't static, Mike. That's what we were talking about earlier. They grow, they shrink, they change with the retelling"' (101). Indeed, the slants given by different characters to landmark events like the SNP successes in Hamilton in 1967 or in Govan in 1974, the first devolution referendum's 1979 failure, Margaret Thatcher's arrival in 10 Downing Street, the 1997 referendum or the setting up of the new parliament depend on their various angles of vision. For example, Margo MacDonald's SNP Govan victory over Labour is not viewed in the same way by soft-left-wing devolutionist Michael Pendreich as by intelligence informer Jimmy/James/Peter Bond. Obviously, socialist union shop-steward Don Lennie will not apprehend Margaret Thatcher's electoral victories or her intransigence in the same way as Tory David Eddlestane. Subjectivity invades history in *And the Land Lay Still*; historical truth becomes relative.

## 2. Charting the changes

As part of the exploration of such subjectivities, *And the Land Lay Still* represents socio-economic and political evolution through time, concentrating on two particular areas: firstly, the relationship between social background and occupation and, secondly, the relationship between social background and political alignment. Overall, the trend seems to be to represent the shifting and the blurring of traditional boundaries.

With regard to the novel's representation of the relationship between social background and occupation, David McCrone has observed that Scottish society from the 1950s and 1960s onwards became less class-conscious, with Scots differentiating themselves thus from persistent attitudes across the border. Post-war class consciousness is shown briefly through Don and Liz Lennie – through Don's relationship with the more moneyed Jack (152), and through Liz's reverence towards the Cotters' 'big house' in which she finds work (430, 554–555), as well as her parents' hostility to her marriage to Don (161). Nonetheless, in McCrone's terminology, uninhibited 'intergenerational social mobility'[9] is ultimately the predominant trend portrayed. McCrone continues:

> Such has been the rate of occupational and social change in Britain, especially since the war, that social classes are fluid and open insofar as, in the words of Payne, 'at all levels of society a majority of sons enter other classes, and in all classes, the incomers outnumber those whose fathers were in the same class'. The implication of these findings [...] is far-reaching, namely that Scotland's middle classes have not only grown in size, but have become more diverse in terms of social origins [...].

In the working families represented over two or three generations – the Lennies, the Imlachs and the Shaws – some members of the second generation bear witness to this fluidity and upward mobility. Don Lennie is a blue-collar worker, a skilled mechanic in a Drumkirk family haulage firm, whose first son, Billy, leaves and trains to be a history teacher in Glasgow. His second son, Charlie, on the other hand, becomes a gang-leader and drug-dealer and ends up joining the army to escape possible prosecution for the rape he commits. He is killed in an accident. Jack Gordon is a white-collar office supervisor in an engineering firm in Drumkirk; his daughter leaves and trains to be a mathematics teacher in Glasgow. From the Borlanslogie mining community originally, Jock Imlach, who has already refused to follow his father's mining footsteps, is seen by some as a 'dodger': he is supposedly away on hydroelectric civil engineering construction sites around Scotland. His daughter, Ellen, leaves to become a reporter in Dundee and then all over the UK: 'She certainly did not want [motherhood] as the wife of a miner [...]. The wide world was changing and she wanted a different place in it' (500). Although influenced by her father's wanting to work 'out in the light' (500), rather than down the mines, her impetus to get on is certainly shown to emanate also from her mother, Mary. She, contrary to social convention, manages to keep her job as a tracer at the pit when she marries Jock and even when she has Ellen. Ellen's cousins, the Shaw twins, who are also from a mining family, their father having perished in a mining disaster in Borlanslogie, get on in a different way, one becoming a white-collar hospital clerical officer and the other a university politics lecturer. New Asian-Scots are also seen to benefit from upward mobility. Saleem Khan, the Pakistani who opens a general store in the mid-1960s, has a daughter Nasreen, who becomes a biochemist, making him '[the] last of the Khan bloody shopkeepers' (563).

About the relationship, seen in the novel, between social/occupational background, political alignment and the Scottish question, McCrone again makes an interesting comment on the effects of changes in occupation: 'Far less than before are we able to read off the politics of class interests from occupational position.'[10] The older generations tend initially to show traditional political alignment according to their socio-economic background. In *And the Land Lay Still*, there are initially very clear-cut boundaries between, say, Sir Malcolm Eddlestane, a wealthy – therefore Conservative – MP and his family, and Don Lennie, who, from a deprived background, embraces socialism, actively supports the Labour Party and is a union member and, later, militant shop steward. Sir Malcolm's elder son, David, will eventually follow his father's political footsteps, and Lennie's son Billy will remain Marxist-influenced and become a CND activist (422). These differences take place against the background of the divide between those from the Borlanslogie mining community, traditionally advocating strong leftist beliefs, and the very Conservative Isobel Pendreich from a relatively wealthy background in nearby Perthshire. Although Borlanslogie is not far from the Conservative-dominated Perthshire Glenallen constituency where Michael Pendreich's mother lives, the communities are, ideologically speaking, according to paradoxically pro-devolution Labour councillor Adam Shaw, 'aboot a million miles apart' (107).

Political debate takes place in various epochs in the novel, from varied angles and in a variety of surroundings, ranging from the Wharryburn Blackthorn Inn in the 1950s to Sandy Bell's in Edinburgh in the 1970s, or to Jean Barbour's flat over at least three decades, until devolution comes about. A striking representation of the historical opposition between Labour centralist, internationalist-oriented discourse and Scottish Nationalist fundamentalist discourse is to be found on the pages of 'The Persistence of Memory'. Don Lennie and Jack Gordon's discussions on a Saturday night during the 1950s at the Blackthorn Inn, when not about war memories, revolve around politics and the Scottish question. The heated argument they have comes to an end without either of them backing down (163–66). Yet, with time, both will be shown to see their political sentiments change. Don Lennie's orthodox Labour mindset, for example, will give way to the acceptance of the need for a new, specifically Scotland-oriented political agenda, Saleem Khan encouraging him in 1967 on the SNP victory in Hamilton actually to become a nationalist. By contrast, Jack Gordon's staunch belief in the age of small nations and Scotland's right to full independence in a post-imperial era will be swept away once he has moved off the pages of the main narrative into the marginal narrative space, leaving the world behind in his solitary wanderings around the country and finally northwards. Jack's original romantic nationalist stance will be replaced by a more environmentally oriented, alternative political perspective, fuelled by his developing sense that party politics are ultimately irrelevant in a world on the brink of ecological disaster. Adam Shaw expresses similar pessimism – or cynicism – in the mainstream narrative when the new devolved institutions have been put in place. His disillusionment is shown to originate from the fact that for him, now that the battle for devolution has been won, there is no longer any purpose in being a political activist. His solution, paralleling Jack Gordon's much earlier dropping out of society, is to 'go into exile', as he puts it, that is, leave Scotland to live abroad. In particular, he will miss Michael Pendreich's exhibition in 2008. Within this blurring of political boundaries and the shifting of political values, other protagonists will be brought to question their initial traditional loyalties, not least Sir Malcolm, and even David, Eddlestane. These dilemmas lead to disaffection and, in some cases, defection. The tricky position of the Conservative Party in Scotland

and its decline through the 1990s is clearly represented through the first-hand perspective of the Eddlestane family, father and son. They are pushed farther and farther to the edge of the Scottish political picture, as other political identities are shown to converge. These move towards a recentred, devolutionist, Scottish-oriented political identity, particularly when, among other things, Margaret Thatcher's ethos of the individual and private enterprise goes against the grain of Scottish political and social sentiment, fired much more, as it seemed to be, by desire for a caring, altruistic society.

### 3. From fringe to mainstream: Robertson's affirmative gender agenda

The question arises as to whether gender – or sexual identity – is an agenda in this novel. Are Robertson's characters identified by their sexual leanings as well as their political ones? Why is there such a concentration on Scottish males? Why is there once again, as in all Robertson's other novels, so little space in text or story granted to women? Arguably, indeed, *And the Land Lay Still* is essentially an androcentric novel and the implied reader male (perhaps male and homosexual). How indeed are female readers to relate to the explicit sex between Murdo and Michael Pendreich (143–44) or to the latter's 'wee fling' of mutual masturbation with David Eddlestane in a 'hidden yet magical space' in Edinburgh (91–92/487), and his reference to the club with 'more cocks on display than beers on the gantry' (89)? First, however, what space in the novel is actually given over to womankind and female central consciousness?

Actual female perspective is limited to a few pages in this novel. Certainly, the 'fascinating, witchlike, imperishable' (63) wise old doyenne, Jean Barbour, occupies a central ideological position. She was once Angus Pendreich's partner. Her Edinburgh Old Town house – 'otherworldly' (63), 'secretly misshapen' (64), 'it was as if you were also stepping out of the moment, going a long way back in time or maybe forward' (63) – is indeed a spiritual headquarters for left-wing pro-devolution politics and Scots and Gaelic storytelling and song from the 1970s until 1999. Yet, already, in 2005 conversations with Robertson, Isobel Murray had remarked upon the lack of significant female characters in his first two novels, *The Fanatic* and *Joseph Knight* (2003). Robertson acquiesced:

In the books I've written so far there hasn't been a really major female character partly because the male characters have been to the fore. I'm aware that actually it's a pattern. I'd like to think that in some of the books I plan to write in the future there are going to be big female characters.[11]

*And the Land Lay Still* is not one of those. Having said that, female characters whose narrative perspectives are recorded include Mary Murray/Imlach, an untypical Scottish working wife *and* mother in the 1950s (381–386), Ellen Imlach telling of her own childhood and family in Borlanslogie and the development of her leftist political awareness with her grandparents (390–397), her life from her adolescence to when she reaches thirty and the day she was raped (507) and her 'life after rape' (509–516), Liz Lennie, when looking for a job and during the special moments she spends working and resting at the big house, until she realises how ill she is (430, 554–559), and Marjorie Taylor, Don Lennie's English nurse, at the moment she meets him again after Liz's death (620–624).

Among these examples, Ellen Imlach is the only female character and female central consciousness that really stands out as significant in the novel. She appears in several narrative strands. In Michael Pendreich's sphere, she is linked to him both personally, as his partner Adam's cousin, and professionally, firstly as the journalist who asks him to come along as a photographer covering a feature on Borlanslogie and secondly as the person he asks to help prepare his exhibition catalogue's introduction. She attends the exhibition preview with her daughter, Kirsty. Strikingly, her narration of her own story is shown as a deliberate act. She sets out to write 'herself down as a story', so as to try and stand back a little: 'get some perspective put some distance between you and what's happened to you. Use your journalistic skills. Use the typewriter. This is not about you, this is about someone else' (499). She writes on her typewriter in the third person (the typographical presentation changes to that of old-fashioned typescript), starting off thus: 'As a teenager, Ellen was far too smart to fall for the patter of good-looking boys at the dancing ...' She goes on to describe her relationships with the opposite sex: 'The relationships usually foundered on the rocks of male egotism or her increasingly vociferous feminism. None of the men she shared a bed with objected to her being on the pill but most of them found it difficult to accept that in principle she was their intellectual equal, and in practice usually their superior' (504). She explains the professional reason she ends up in the town where she will eventually be brought into the presence of her rapist-to-be, that is, to research a piece on the Drumkirk 'protection rackets and gangs', and she mentions her meeting with Denny Hogg, her old neighbour from Borlanslogie. He is the one who introduces her to 'a tall, powerfully built young man called Charlie Lennie. [...] To her horror she found herself flirting with him' (507). The uncontrollable events go beyond her self-imposed copy limits, and she is dissatisfied with the result: 'what she'd written seemed pedestrian and false, she'd nowhere near finished the story [...] what was she trying to achieve?' (507). Certainly, we realise that Robertson has her write with ironic hindsight, rather than just in retrospective mode. She includes allusions and prolepses that can have little meaning to a reader unaware of what is coming. She does not reach the rape episode, breaks off her typing, and the original text narrative returns to her new life with her daughter (507–509). Although *she* agrees with Robin Piggot that she need not write down the rest, 'It was imprinted in her memory for ever' (509), *Robertson* is the one to take the reader straight back to the rape and to the shocked and depressed state Ellen was in afterwards (509–516). This is supposed to be a purely first-hand female account of the rape itself and of the destructive effect it had on her. Paradoxically, this representation of female perspective on such an event, rather than merely augmenting the actual horror, is, as we see it, also somehow designed by Robertson to deliberately emphasise Ellen's admission that the rape was the result of her own misjudgement of her relationship with Charlie Lennie and her lack of self-control:

> She was flushed from the heat and drunk on white wine, [...] she
> vaguely came to realise that he was sober; also that she was naked
> and her clothes scattered around the room yet he still had most of
> his on. Until this moment she had felt free and relaxed and *in* [sic]
> the moment. Now something jolted [...]' (511)

Robertson adopts a much too conventional male view of the 'weak(er)' sex. The question remains open as to whether the inclusion of a rape in the novel was absolutely necessary, some essential phase – getting back to brutal reality – for the writer after *The Testament of Gideon Mack* (2006) or merely sensationalist, or indirectly moralistic.

Parallel questions arise with regard to the representations of masculine identities. Before dealing specifically with Robertson's bringing of male homosexuality centre stage, what about male heterosexual experience? This seems to leave much to be desired. Don Lennie becomes a disenchanted yet faithful husband (415) in spite of being attracted to Marjory Taylor, the English nurse he meets at the maternity hospital where his second son Charles is born (arguably, altogether a rather contrived set-up). He also becomes a 'disowned' father; Charlie, eighteen, with whom Don has difficulties as a baby, eventually violently rejects him in public during a street argument (448–451). As a widower, much later in life, Don comes across the English nurse, and decides to set up home with her as his partner, or 'bidie-in', as he prefers to say. Initially, Don's moral viewpoint would have gone against sharing life with a common-law wife. He is shown to evolve as society does. Don's elder son, Billy, strikes up a relationship (rather too conveniently?) with Jack Gordon's daughter Barbara, who Robertson portrays as an overbearing feminist. Initially, Billy shares much with her in their Marxist activism and anti-nuclear protests and lets himself be influenced by her somewhat alien feminist practices:

> Billy and Barbara stripped sex back to their primal urges, then built it up again. [...] They analysed touch till they couldn't feel it any more. [...] Barbara tasted her menstrual blood. In an act of solidarity, sort of, he tasted his sperm. (473–74)

He eventually, 'after lengthy debate and thought', agrees with her affirmation that 'all men are potential rapists' (473). When he expresses his desire to have children, however, wishing to assert that particular aspect of his masculinity, their relationship breaks down (491–492). In the final resolution of the final section of the novel, 'The Gift of the Moment', Billy turns out to be the partner of Catriona MacDonald, Michael Pendreich's young student girlfriend in the 1970s, who opened his eyes to his homosexual identity. Billy's brother Charlie grows up into the Scots 'wee hard man' type – or else quite simply a universal hardman – who needs to dominate and be seen to dominate the males with whom he competes, his father and, then, his older brother Billy especially:

> it was Charlie who intimidated Billy. At two, five, seven, Charlie knew
> how to work his brother, trigger his sense of fairness or guilt or fear
> or generosity to get the toy, the food, the attention he wanted. (422)

What is more, Charlie's homophobia and domination of women go to the extreme. This is borne out when he goes for a drink with Billy and Barbara, accompanied by his battered, subservient girlfriend, in the subsequent electric confrontation with Barbara, who dares stand up to him (478–84). Ultimately, Charlie's violent hyper-virility is crystallised in the premeditated rape of Ellen Imlach. In complete contrast to Charlie Lennie, Robin Piggot is what we might define as a gentle (not a soft) man. He is characterised largely through Ellen Imlach's perspective, firstly when she makes his acquaintance – 'a mild, unassuming boy from Surrey' (503) – and then as he agrees without hesitation to become the carer/provider for Ellen until Ellen has recovered from her ordeal. He takes Ellen in very soon after the rape, and once she has had Charlie's child, their original 'firm but platonic friendship' moves onto another level. One wonders, however, whether it is really necessary for her to remind the reader that he is English – '[H]is sunny Englishness was quite alien to her' (508) – as she breaks with the dark Scottish 'wee hardman', Charlie Lennie. Does his national identity relate then to his masculine identity? A final male figure in this rich tableau is David Eddlestane. He becomes in public the up-and-coming Tory MP, happily married to the rich and lovely Melissa Braco, and is, in his own secret world, a shoe fetishist who searches out excitement and pleasure in London and then in Edinburgh. His attraction to Margaret Thatcher is shown to relate more to her legs and shoes than to her politics.

Both in representations and in discourse, it is on the theme of male homosexuality, however, that Robertson's gender agenda appears to focus. Had Michael Pendreich been heterosexual, this would not have been the same novel at all:

> Making his central character gay was also a crucial decision. 'He
> wasn't when I started,' Robertson says. 'Then one morning I woke

up and thought, of course, he's gay. I felt the man who was telling the story shouldn't be someone like me – a white, male, middle-class heterosexual Scot.'[12]

Robertson's angle definitely shows being Scottish and gay as an acceptably mainstream combination. From the vantage point of the first decade of the twenty-first century, Robertson portrays the predicament of homosexuals in the 1970s, social and familial homophobia, and the evolution of attitudes from homosexuality's being marginalised until 2008, by when it is shown as no longer 'a fringe issue'. Perhaps predictably, there is a wide palette of male gay figures. Nevertheless, Robertson's treatment of this issue of socio-political attitudes embodies a plea for the general acceptance in Scotland of settled homosexual relationships between consenting adult males, as opposed to the promiscuity and exhibitionist behaviour to be found as in the heterosexual sphere.

In this, Robertson focuses on Michael Pendreich and the realisation and consolidation of his sexual identity. In the opening passage of 'The Mouth in the Box', Michael, a middle-aged homosexual, is contemplating the promise of a new relationship with a man from the northern village, Murdo. He will then, as he chooses the photographs for the exhibition, look back on his childhood and adolescence, and on his *éducation sentimentale*. In the initial flashbacks, reference is made to what can be seen as schoolboy homosexuality in the private English-style boarding schools Michael goes to, outposts 'of an alien system'. In Bellcroft House, his prep school (23–24), he is full of indignation at the suggestion of his being a 'poof', yet wonders all the same. Freddy Eddlestane suggests his brother David is one, and they try and reassure each other about the difference between being 'weird' and being a 'poof'(35). It is then in a whisky-drenched conversation with Jean Barbour in 2008 that Michael actually goes back to the 1970s and describes his early relationship with the above-mentioned Catriona MacDonald, and how he experienced a sexual epiphany: 'I closed my eyes and it wasn't her I imagined being there with, even though I didn't have anybody in mind it wasn't a *her*. […] I walked out of her flat and I finally knew who I was' (77). In a flashback to 1974 Edinburgh, we are presented with Sam the Biker, an older, leather-clad man who is attracted to Mike (55–56); in another flashback moment, he is embarrassed as Sam the Biker makes a pass at him in public (74–75).

Michael fights him off: he is fully aware that that *'wasn't* what he wanted. Not like that. Not then and not there, and not with Sam'. In another passage in his retrospective narrative he finds himself wanting to catch up for lost time, and does so through what he sees as an interesting first-time experience with a homosexual lawyer, who was, however, not yet 'out': 'Most of the men he knew, professional men, weren't' (82). Michael has then to face up to his mother's prejudice on his coming out: '"Why would I have suspected *that*? You always seemed perfectly normal to me. [...] It's a sickness, that's what I think."' He is then mugged: 'there's a price, Michael Pendreich, for being gay in this country, and you just paid it' (88). In 1978, Jean Barbour introduces Michael to Adam Shaw, Ellen Imlach's cousin, and against the backdrop of the failure of the 1979 referendum, a serious relationship begins that will last twenty years. Michael reminds the reader even now that he and Sam the Biker are not out for the same thing at all: 'there was one club, you went in and there were more cocks on display than bottles on the gantry. Not Mike's scene. He wanted intimacy not excess. Sam said Mike was copping out, if you were gay, you had to flaunt it' (89). Obviously refusing any self-oppression, Sam, moving with the times, is all for living out in the open, showing his gay pride. The would-be flippant, but finally ominous, phrase appears here, 'The worst that could happen would be a dose of the clap'. A sense of doom is enhanced by the introduction of the fear of HIV in Edinburgh, the association being made with heroin and with gays. The narrative rather obviously returns to Sam, whose 'strutting, peacock', sex-loving style of homosexuality still holds no appeal for either Michael or Adam. Sam in turn makes fun of them out for a drink in a gay pub together as a couple: '"If you want to play mummies and daddies, why come here?"' (542). The reader is (all too) well prepared for what is to come, Sam's decline and eventual death through HIV, 'killed by devotion to his own desire. It was shocking and upsetting' (542). On a political level, both Mike and Adam are active, though their allegiances differ, and even if they often come together to take part in the widely followed campaign for devolution, Adam strangely refuses Mike's presence on his own home territory in Borlanslogie. Their relationship ultimately becomes strained through a political disagreement over the Poll Tax (576). It is not until 1999 that they finally break up over their differing visions of the new parliament and the opening up of a new era for Scotland (618–619). Adam feels part of the old Scotland; Michael, of the new.

## Conclusion

This chapter has concentrated on three main aspects of *And the Land Lay Still*: narratology, socio-political representations, and finally, gender and sexuality. This increasingly complex yet skilfully mastered novel keeps the reader in a state of 'imbalance or tension' as the narrative threads are 'chains of suspense and surprise'.[13] Having opted for oblique angles on Scotland, Scottish society and politics through ordinary Scots from a wide socio-political spectrum over the sixty-year time span, Robertson has endeavoured to bring what might have been on the edge into the centre. He constantly stresses the links between the local and the national, between personal (hi)stories and Scottish history. Robertson's piling up of historical data, or 'infodumping', as James Naughtie has called it,[14] is no doubt motivated by the desire to make ordinary Scots much more visible in the national, UK and wider world pictures as an integral part of these bigger pictures, a technique also used in *The Testament of Gideon Mack*. The reader may well be dissatisfied with the resulting unevenness of texture to be found in some passages of both these novels. Among these concluding remarks, it also seems important to point out that *And the Land Lay Still* comes across as a post-religious novel. 'We are living pretty much in a post-religious, post-Christian age, and you wonder what effect that it has on the way society conducts itself. Personally I would like to believe that we don't need religion, but I also worry sometimes that maybe we do,' says Robertson.[15] Has the Church in Scotland, be it Presbyterian or Catholic, gone into such extreme decline so as to justify the author's almost total exclusion of that particularly vital facet of Scottish society from a novel he claims to be an all-encompassing, panoramic view of Scotland from the 1950s onwards? Is this a logical follow-up, in reaction to the sometimes negative reception of *The Testament of Gideon Mack*? As for Robertson's angle on gender and sexual identities, even if the deliberate intention to shift male homosexuality from the edge into the centre in his depiction of mainstream twenty-first-century Scotland stems from a desire to see a broader-minded Scotland, the resulting vision is itself asymmetrical, rather overly 'one-gendered'. One has to wonder if Robertson has not somewhat forced the issue. His main purpose here, however, may have been to make an affirmative and purely literary 'gesture' so as to be able to state at last that 'to be gay and to be Scottish, it would seem, are [no longer] mutually exclusive conditions'.[16]

# Notes

1  London: Hamish Hamilton, 2010. Page references to this edition are given after quotations in the text.
2  Extract from an undated interview with James Robertson, www.scotgeog.com/interview.php [accessed 22 May 2011].
3  James Robertson, 'Six deaths, two funerals, a wedding and a divorce', in *Scotland into the New Era* (Edinburgh: Canongate Books, 2000), pp. 172–86, p. 186.
4  Gerard Carruthers, *Scottish Literature* (Edinburgh: EUP, 2009); chapter entitled 'Deconstructing Scottish Literature', p. 157.
5  See Gerard Genette, *Palimpsests: Literature in the Second Degree* (Nebraska: trans. by Nebraska University Press, 1997), p. 5.
6  London: Fourth Estate, 2000.
7  *Reportage Scotland: History in the Making* (Edinburgh: Luath Press, 2000); pp. 437–67.
8  *Decades* Part 1, 'The 60s', 11 September 2001, p. 15.
9  David McCrone, 'Towards a Principled Elite', in Tony Dickson and James H. Treble (eds), *People and Society in Scotland III 1914–1990* (Edinburgh: John Donald/The Economic and Social History of Scotland, 1992), pp. 193–94.
10  McCrone, p. 194.
11  Isobel Murray, *Scottish Writers Talking 4* (Glasgow: Kennedy and Boyd, 2008), p. 169.
12  Chitra Ramaswamy, *Scotland on Sunday*, 27 July 2010, scotlandonsunday.scotsman.com/features/Interview-James-Robertson-author-.6438775.jp [accessed 19 April 2011].
13  H. Porter Abbot, *The Cambridge Introduction to Narrative* (Cambridge: Cambridge University Press, 2008), p. 57.
14  Edinburgh Bookfest Event around launching of *And the Land Lay Still*, 14/08/2010; James Naughtie interviews James Robertson, www.edbookfest.co.uk/media-gallery/item/james-robertson-2010-event [accessed 20 April 2011].
15  Murray, p. 157.
16  With reference to an original quote, which reads 'To be gay and to be Scottish, it would seem, are still mutually exclusive conditions', from Christopher Whyte (ed.), *Gendering the Nation* (Edinburgh: Edinburgh University Press, 1995), p. xv.

# 10: 'Scotland', literature, history, home, and melancholy in Andrew Greig's novel *Romanno Bridge*

## JEAN BERTON

This chapter aims to explore what Umberto Eco calls 'intentio operis'[1] with a view to analysing what makes the substance of 'Scotland' that is sucked through the roots of Scottish history to nurture literary fruit in the shape of Andrew Greig's novel *Romanno Bridge* (2008). To futher this aim I shall leave aside all that serves to develop the thriller genre – taken as no more than a cover – of the novel and study its historical aspect. Then I shall visit extensions of it, before finally investigating various aspects embodying this so-called essence of Scotland.

Julian Meldon D'Arcy, in *Subversive Scott*,[2] states that 'The Waverley Novels have been an indispensable (if sometime hidden or unacknowledged) element of Scottish national consciousness over the last two centuries [...]'. We could add that, ever since Walter Scott set the trend, Scotland's history has fed the roots of fruitful Scottish literature. Andrew Greig's *Romanno Bridge*[3] is both a historical novel and a thriller, as well as the narrative of a quest for the essence of Scotland, metaphorically represented by the search for the real Stone of Destiny – not to be confused with the Stone of Westminster violently confiscated by Edward I in 1296, taken away on Christmas 1950, recovered on 11 April 1951, and solemnly handed back to Scotland in 1996. Instead, Greig is concerned with the stone that was eventually discovered by his heroes under a blanket of ivy and moss (306) in a privately owned garden in the middle of a moonlit night. This was when the champions symbolically seated the innocent child, Eve, on the stone (307) then to be left in its secret place. One must also keep in mind that *Romanno Bridge* is a sequel to Andrew Greig's *The Return of John Macnab* (1996).[4] This is a revised and updated version of the narrative of John Buchan's *John Macnab* (1925),[5] in which the character of Leithen reads Walter Scott's *Redgauntlet* (1824), which includes the timeless tale of 'Wandering Willie'. This may be understood to match Kirsty's restless run from her own ghosts in Greig's novel: Neil thinks 'she could [never quite control] being a bolter' (97).

## 1. A historical novel

Emulating Walter Scott who, according to Douglas Gifford,[6] built *Waverley* on history and psychology, Andrew Greig shapes his novel not on a particular historical background, but on the whole of the history of Scotland from Roman days up to the day before the Stone was given back to Scotland by John Major in 1996. More precisely, the Macnab gang's narrative is set in 1995, but the group of heroes are sent to travel through history as far back as the days of the Celts, on the trail of the Stone of Destiny. The John Macnab team in action in *The Return of John Macnab*, after the pattern of Dumas's three Musketeers, had to include a fourth member, Kirsty; in *Romanno Bridge*, the crew is increased by a Norwegian girl and a New Zealander of mixed race. Greig sees to it that each character has a distinct psychology, or rather a separate history. They share, however, a common melancholy. Their collective quest is spurred on by the challenge embodied by the villain, Adamson, and not by any higher political motive, as in *The Return of John Macnab* where the collective heroes challenge the property of their homeland. They compete to secure the real Coronation Stone and eventually beat their rival, Adamson, discovering the real Stone in a privately owned garden, but leaving it in its unknown hiding place before breaking up. They fool the self-proclaimed owner, HRH, by handing over a real fake stone. Their quest is successful, but they reject any form of triumphalism.

Like Scott, Greig uses real places in this narrative: Romanno Bridge, named in the title, is a village in the Borders – 'Neil Lindores […] walked up the road to Romanno Bridge' (102) – whose origins can be traced back to the first and second centuries AD. Then Dere Street was used to journey from York (*Eburacum*) to the Antonine Wall (*Veluniate*, or Carriden, or Bo'ness), via Corbridge (*Coria*). The narrative, however, starts in Dumfries, and the characters travel throughout Scotland: 'A thaw was on as they drove on the long and winding road out of the deep Borders into the Central Belt' (68). The reader follows Kirsty and Leo driving to Crieff, while others are visiting Islay, Dunstaffnage, Dunsinnan, Rothiemurchus Forest, and Oslo. Impending tragedy is clearly set in actual places: 'Baddingsgill, Kirsty thought. We've been through West Linton and now we're on that track to Baddingsgill Reservoir, South side of the Pentlands' (241). Realism is another feature of the historical novel: the scenes are set in either a ruined bothy, or a castle under repair, or a 'normal Fifties' pebbledash bungalow' (69).

The narrative ends in the wonderful garden of Dunsinnan Hall, allegedly belonging to an ignorant Englishman, in the dead of night. This ornamental garden is given the Greek name of 'Little Delphi', apt to confer a mytho-logical value to the narrative – to be upgraded to a Scottish legend?: 'Inside Little Delphi, ivy, rhododendron, fuchsia and hawthorn had run wild'. The narrator concludes the description with '*Et in Arcadia ego*' (305), invoking Virgil and painters of the early modern era, like Nicolas Poussin. (The name of the garden, Little Delphi, is most likely a reference to Ian Hamilton Finlay's garden, Little Sparta, in the Pentland Hills, which integrates literary, visual and horticultural arts and is on certain days open to the public. The quotation '*Et in Arcadia ego*' is to be found in that garden and Finlay was an admirer of the work of Poussin. This is a complex literary cross-reference, just as the novel itself constantly cross-refers to aspects of Scottish history and literature.)

The reader finds it logical to see Murray and Alasdair dispatched to inspect the Stone lying in Westminster Abbey. They are briefly seen in 'the Confessor's Chapel' where the coronation chair stands (121): those two characters are in a real place which is also a historical place. They convey the reader to London and remember King/Saint Edward the Confessor who lived in the eleventh century. Thus, the reader follows every member of 'the former Macnabs' (113) to distant places – and this cannot fail to remind them of the aptly named young Waverley. Journeying from Dumfries to the Borders, to Crieff, to Islay, to the Grampians, to Edinburgh, to Kirkintilloch, as well as to Norway – implying the Viking regions of Scotland – the collective John Macnab is delimiting an area with an actual soil into which to grow roots. Places are indeed connected with history through vestiges: Alasdair on his way to Dunstaffnage makes a detour to the hill of Dunadd, the place of appointment by standing in an incised footprint to the throne of the kings of the early-medieval proto-Scottish kingdom of Dalriata – 'A wee knoll, really, a mere few hundred feet of rock outcrop, but still one of the most significant sites in the formation of Scotland' (276). History is dependent, however, on points of view and interpretations that vary as generations go by. Historians have to struggle against erosion and oblivion, while novelists are free to adapt facts to fiction: Jim is about to reveal the supposed real hiding place of the Stone, and needs the support of his ancestors:

> He looked at the mountains of Mull while his mind went further
> West across the Minch. He thought on Skye, on Lewis, on Angus Og
> the *Ri Innse Gall*, and he tried to weigh his sense of what was right
> against what the Law required. (297)

The Stone has a history of its own connected with history. It is set within 'Billy Mackie's story', meaning that history is blended with fiction: the Stone was stolen from Westminster on Christmas Day 1950 (12), which is a fact, and brought to Billy's employer's stoneyard for three copies to be made (12–13), which is a parody of actual events, or realistic fiction. Facts about how the Stone reached Scone are lost and replaced by conjecture voiced by Kirsty informing her partner: 'It probably came from Ireland with the Scotti in the eighth century. [...] Possibly it had once been a Mithraic stone left by one of the Roman legions' (44).

Greig never pretends to be a historian. Rather, he is playing with history, warping facts to produce fiction. He even plays with truth and lies, calling the various stones his characters handle 'real fake' or 'fake fake': 'they got their real fake Westminster Stone back' (300). He takes care not to use a professional historian: 'I'm just an independent historian looking at sources and evidence [...]' (74), says P. B. Sidlaw, an amateur historian who has a pseudonym derived from Robert Louis Stevenson's work, Alan Breck Stewart (72). Greig turns history into a story, from the roots to the present outcome, as in the Dunstaffnage chapters, 37 to 39. Mixing reality and fiction, he creates realistic effects: Ailsa suggests engaging on a visit to the Western Isles: 'If I were looking for another interesting stone, I'd put my money, if I had any, on Finlaggan, in Islay. There have been rumours of something being moved before the recent archaeological dig' (86). The reference to Finlaggan, the seat from the thirteenth to the fifteenth centuries of the Lords of the Isles, shows Greig imbricating key historical locations in his narrative, as he does with the visit to Dunadd or his naming of the place the stone is found Dunsinnan, the modern spelling of Dunsinane, the location where Shakespeare placed the deposition and death of Macbeth. In this way Greig plays with historically important locations as he also plays with his characters: Sidlaw, whose surname is embedded in the geographical history of Scotland in eponymous Hills, is introduced as a fragile and modest researcher to be made more appealing – 'I was a young schoolmaster with romantic notions. I believed a story about twelfth century Scottish farming and ecclesiastical people would have widespread popular appeal [...]' (72). The characters serve the author's purpose at their own expense: 'Full of tea and shortbread and folk myths masquerading as rumours pretending to be history, it was time to leave Crieff' (76). After reading the postscript to the Dundas family story, Jim MacIver will know the hiding place of the Stone, but this is not the author's main point, for the narrator interrupts the dialogue: 'With Angus Og, founding father of the MacDonald clan, they had just stepped back into the great peat bog where myth and history ooze together' (268).

*Romanno Bridge* is enhanced by knowledge that serves the narrative. Yet, we may find it next to impossible to distinguish emulation from parody of Scott's novelistic technique in asides with a didactic tone: 'On that short exhilarating crossing to the next loch system (tarbet equals "place where boats are hauled over", thus several of them in Scotland), he thought of his dear Jane [...]' (272). We may also think that Greig is taunting his reader with hints at etymology: 'He was musing about Nes or Ness. River mouth or confluence of waters. As in Inverness, Blackness, Stromness [...]' (257). Whatever the actual intention of the author, we may find here what Philippe Lejeune calls the *pacte autobiographique*[7] linking authors and their readers, for they will share the same culture. It remains, however, to be demonstrated that history lessons can spark off some kind of emotion, such as in the scene when Alasdair walks to the top of Dunadd: '[Alasdair] removed his right boot, then the sock. He took a deep breath and fitted his bare foot into the imprint in the living rock, stood tall and stared out'. This action, replicating the ceremony of enthronement of Dalriatan kings, becomes an excuse for a history lesson: 'The Scotti had come from Ireland to land boats on these shores [...]' (277).

Greig offers his readers a narrative open to speculation and interpretation. John Macnab has been replaced with Adamson, a self-proclaimed Mr Nobody – a villain with an elusive name. Is he a symbolic 'Adam's son', a trading Cain intent on selling a prize he does not own at whatever cost, or Adam (Smith)'s son turned wild? Whether in those guises, or even others, Adamson's function is to create tension and spur the narrative onward. He is competing with John Macnab in a modern quest with a simple choice between saving the Stone and keeping it in Scotland (as if it were its hard disk or heart) or taking it to the market and selling it for money, after the archetypal pattern of Judas and the thirty pieces of silver: 'Collect twenty million dollars' (288) is Adamson's obsession. His only motive is money, as he explains to Inga (155–56). He causes terror for '[m]oney, of course' (163) and not out of passion, even though he reveals his perversion when saying: '[My vocation] is getting things for people, often from other people who don't want to give them up. It's … satisfying' (163). Greig does not express a moral viewpoint on the violent trader. He is playing with the character who says, 'I have a very wealthy and slightly mad client, a Scottish enthusiast […]' (288), but who will never lay his hands on the Stone. That, ironically enough, will remain sitting peacefully in the garden of some anonymous English owner.

## 2. A narrative encompassing Scottish literature

The John Macnab trio was born from the tale of Jim Tarras told by Archie in John Buchan's *John Macnab* (21). Andrew Greig transformed it into a trio of Scotsmen and added a female partner, Christine Fowler (does she foul the game?), in *The Return of John Macnab*, and eventually the single hero of Archie's tale developed into the John Macnab gang in *Romanno Bridge*, with the addition of the triple Moon Runners and various helpers. Thus the 1925 trio becoming a quartet in 1996, develops to a full choir rivalling a threefold villain (Adamson and his two henchmen) for the discovery of the real Stone. Andrew Greig declares the link with his *The Return of John Macnab* in the first chapter: 'Willie Kincaid said slowly, "About how the John Macnab caper was all just a security training exercise, and no deer was ever poached at Balmoral, and HRH had nothing to do with it. I'm sure I believe every word"' (6). The connection is confirmed on the following page: 'By the time they reached his pub she'd got the job and had stopped thinking on the Highlands, that eventful summer and the pals she'd left' (7). However, the initial triple quest of the animal emblems for Scotland – the salmon, the grouse, and the stag – are replaced with three rings, bearing misleading rune carvings, worn by three Moon Runners ('runners' being a twist from 'rune-ers' (84)). The John Macnab gang will eventually find the two copies of the – allegedly fake – Westminster Stone discovered at Romanno Bridge. The triple prize will prove spurious when the real Destiny Stone is uncovered in the garden of Dunsinnan Hall, where it will remain incognito. This is how the myth of the real Stone can be preserved.

The function of such a mythical stone is open to debate and readers of *Romanno Bridge* are invited to refer hypertextually to *The Return of John Macnab*. One sees this especially when, at Neil's place, Inga lays her hand on Neil's account of the previous quest: 'She took the file, took in the cover scrawl "John Macnab revisited", glanced inside' (264). On opening Greig's novel *The Return of John Macnab*, the prologue in the form of a poster, entitled 'To whom it concerns', concludes with a reference to John Buchan's novel. If the readers follow the instruction, they will read Buchan's *John Macnab*, in which one of the Macnab trio, Leithen, occupies his free time reading Walter Scott's *Redgauntlet* – several occurrences are made on pages 140, 142, et al. Such a detail in the narrative is meaningful because *Redgauntlet* includes Wandering Willie's tale and the tale within the tale can be taken as a regular feature of the Scottian novel. It operates a *mise en abyme*, bridging the gap between literature and tale-telling and, further, between past and present, as well as there and here. Along with random references to *The Return of John Macnab* and *John Macnab* cropping up in the narrative of *Romanno Bridge*, readers must take in the Dunsinnan tale, allegedly by R. T. Dundas's ancestor: 'One bright, chilly February forenoon in 1802, keen to get outside after a week of great rains, two lads followed the swollen Kennaty burn to the lower slopes of Dunsinnan Hill' (259–61). There remains little doubt about a hint to Scott's technique when the reader reaches page 119 and finds the only footnote in the novel, '[the penny] turned out to be worth considerably more. Just how much, Murray won't say', for it is ludicrously pointless. Indeed, for a character to find an old coin in an old staircase and refuse to let the reader know the actual value of it today is a show of humour through a parody of Walter Scott's habit of writing footnotes and endnotes in his novels. (One might bear in mind here that two hungry young Frenchmen, Auguste Callet and Javelin Pagnon, managed to publish a pastiche of Walter Scott's novels, in 1841: *Allan Caméron*. In their preface, they claimed that it was the translation into French of an old manuscript found in some dark attic. In the narrative one finds a single footnote (p. 268 of the new edition) which is a ludicrous comment on the name of a character; what is more, it shows a major error in translation, produced for an obvious self-debunking effect.[8]) Furthermore, in *Redgauntlet*, we meet a character called Benjie. Another Benjie, called 'fish Benjie', in Buchan's *John Macnab*, appears in a scene under the guise of a tinker (58). In *Romanno Bridge*, Greig introduces the character of Inga with a powerful connection with street buskers, and the author reveals Neil's biographical note (Chapter 29) on Inga, who ran away on the day she was eighteen to go back home to Norway: 'She left one autumn morning in Barcelona' (228). Further, possibly with a view to misleading the reader about the meaning of 'Romanno', there briefly appears on the stage a Romany – not in Scotland but Norway: 'Cisko Holland is a true Romany [...] A gypsy without a home, but at home everywhere' (214). All in all, Andrew Greig has scattered enough signs in this narrative for the reader to sense an option for deliberate hypertextuality.

When he wrote *The Return of John Macnab*, Greig could harp again on the hot theme of landowning: instead of a Scotsman, an American and an Englishman, Greig could update the owners to an Arab, a Dutch consortium manager (109), and His Royal Highness. The challengers were turned into self-proclaimed rebels against foreign ownership. In *Romanno Bridge*, the John Macnab gang act to preserve the nation's honour, and the leader, Kirsty, is magnified. Far from being turned into a Scottish Boadicea, the character of Kirsty is drawn as a restless wandering hero – less a female counterpart of Steenie Steenson, than a true Byronic heroine who 'tried to reform her hooligan ways' (7). Greig, then, is not telling the same story, nor even using the same pattern, even though one could say that Kirsty and her John Macnab crew went through hell to retrieve the Stone. Kirsty, with all her Byronic heroine aspects, is an appealing character: she answers Billie Mackie's question 'Are you a patriot, lass?' with an enigmatic 'No, I'm a refugee, [...] I'm not really from anywhere' (9). What could have concluded *The Return of John Macnab* with a happy ending – parodying Archie's marrying Janet in *John Macnab* – might have excluded the possibility of a follow-up:

> If anyone had asked, she'd have said she was cooling off. Hiding out, if you must. The moment Neil Lindores admitted he loved her, the panic had started in her blood. He didn't know what he was saying. Maybe he did, but he'd said it to the wrong person. (7)

Greig makes full use of oxymora. The generic nature of *Romanno Bridge* exemplifies this: readers will find enough violent actions in it to qualify the novel as a thriller, or a modern Gothic novel. As a Byronic heroine, Kirsty is beset by contradiction and paradoxes, if only for leaving the man she loved and was loved by. She is so much this that she operates as a running oxymoron. Greig has Kirsty say to Neil, 'We found the real fake' (254), and again, 'They got their real fake Westminster Stone back' (300). The reader will debate the humour or polemics in 'Abernethy says they may return the fake fake to Scotland, to please the natives' (300). After Adamson's motivations have been made clear, Kirsty says about Adamson's employer, 'Some collector. Maybe some ultra nationalist tax-exile with more money than morality' (204). Greig's handling of oxymora extends to the paradox of inversion within the structure of the narrative: the Prologue is entitled 'Closing' (1) and the epilogue 'Opening' (309). There, the last few words of the story display a softened oxymoron: '[Inga] takes up the banjo and airs an evolving Blues that is not so unhappy after all' (309). The song ending the novel amplifies the intended inversion – 'Deep inside my heart / Burns an inverted flame' (309) – and sounds like an invitation to read the story 'invertedly', that is with second levels of interpretation coming first.

Greig also makes use of symbols with an oxymoronic effect, connecting two items, like the Stone and autonomy, with a view to creating a forceful sensation. The number three commonly stands for perfection, exemplified by the holy trinity: Greig hires Buchan's triple hero under the collective name of John Macnab, then transforms it and opposes it to three Moon Runners and their three rings, three fake stones, and three villains. Readers will also note that the only prepubescent character in the narrative is called Eve: such a name stands as the counterpart of Adam, yet is the converse of Adamson. The innocent young girl who was not part of the search was nevertheless allowed to find the Stone:

> At the end of the garden furthest from the big house, Eve stood by an ivy-smothered Greek temple. Neil saw his goddaughter's hands flitter like albino bats in the moonlight as she silently, frantically, waved. (306)

The much-looked-for Scottish Stone of Destiny is sitting in a mock Greek temple. Although entirely invented, it is paradoxically made real by its description: 'Celtic knots … Pictish salmon, wolf, stag, plus some beast that never was … Norse galleys … and waterhorses' (306–07).

As already noted, Greig emulates Walter Scott's narrative technique, using tales within the tale; such a *mise en abyme* can be viewed as a large-scale oxymoron. The piece of fiction within fiction (56–58), which starts 'A damp afternoon in early August when the wind dies in the Southern Highlands is similarly cursed now as it was in 1296' (56), is meant to be taken as a historical document throwing light on fictional narrative. Waterhorses are legendary characters found in folklore, yet they are given some degree of reality because the carvings on the real Stone are copies of the strange carvings found on standing stones in north-east Scotland, such as the Aberlemno picture stone. *Romanno Bridge* blends facts and reported history, through Sidlaw, with fiction, hence the notion of expanded oxymoron. Greig's novel validates the notion of gap-bridging literature, linking its roots to its fruits.

## 3. An inquisitive piece of fiction ('Home' and melancholy)

Searching for the Stone is only an excuse to explore the notion of 'Home'. Kirsty asks the expert, Sidlaw, 'By the way, [...] where would you say "home" was for the Stone?' (76). Kirsty ironically suggested the answer when she mentions the Laird's house at Dunsinnan. In the last section of the narrative, Kirsty voices their actual quest: 'These runes might indicate Dunstaffnage, but that doesn't square with what Andrew Jamieson said, about it having been "sent back hame"' (257). What matters is the home of the Stone, rather than the object itself, for it stands as a metaphor of the substance that produces the essence of Scotland. Yet, a definition of Scotland seems an unattainable achievement, which accounts for endless questioning. Home is where roots grow: Leo asks, 'Where do you feel at home?', and Kirsty the wanderer answers, 'Home doesn't figure big with me, Leo. On good days it's wherever I happen to be' (69). While linking New Zealand, his fatherland, to Scotland, Leo illustrates the parable of roots and fruits: 'It's like this down the bottom end of South Island. Full of Scots too, only they ate better and got taller once they left home. Some even mated with the natives' (69). Thus the allies of the John Macnab gang enable the author to develop the fundamental issue of home. And the Samye Ling Buddhist temple in the Borders operates as a *mise en abyme*, especially as Kirsty 'dropped her bag on the floor and felt as near to home as she ever wanted to' (215). Ellen Stobo, the Canadian supporter of John Macnab, ponders 'How hard we work to build and maintain a corner of the world we can call Home, [...] Home is the place we navigate in the dark when we get up in the night [...]' (79). She harps on about the subject – 'This morning Ellen had talked of home' (275) – so much that Jim MacIver eventually entreats her, 'I mean to say, for goodness sake, *a ghràidh*, please take me home' (303). Later, Jim MacIver reveals to Kirsty, 'They [British power] made a desert of the Gaeltachd and now they want our Destiny Stone? I'd rather go and live in Canada' (305), suggesting that both Gaeldom and the Stone are vital substance to him. Gaeldom, even though no precise place-name is specifically indicated, is home to the Macnab team: '[...] that small Highland town [is] the centre of the world' (113).

In the last few pages of the novel, Leo, the New Zealander, and Inga, the Scandinavian, discuss the notion of home. Leo admits, 'I'm not ready to go home. If it is still home', and Inga answers, 'Here is not my home, but these people care about it so much it makes me curious' (304). Previously, Greig had used the technique of stream of consciousness to develop the theme of home and belonging, even highlighting it with an epanadiplosis:

> It wasn't her country, but it seemed to mean a lot to her friend. 'It's not so much my country, more that I am its,' [Neil] had said as they crossed Rannoch Moor. 'Independence is a mirage, but I believe in this.' Strange place, to inspire such belonging. Alasdair, Shonagh, even Murray, they had it too. How different it must be to have this feeling. To be part of. Maybe not a weakness but an inspiration. (286)

The conclusion to this development appears in Inga's answer to Leo, 'So we are part of this bunch now', 'What a strange thought, being part of something' (304). Yet, Greig carefully avoids clear-cut answers. If the Stone's home is ironically in the garden of Dunsinnan Hall, which the Dundas family sold to an anonymous Englishman who remains unaware of his possession – 'No reason to think they had a clue what was within' (304) – the owner of Balmoral castle, HRH, has been conned with a real fake. And the reader cannot overlook the historical fact that the Stone was handed back to Scotland on Saint Andrew's Day, 1996, that is, shortly after the end of the novel. Nevertheless, there remains Alasdair's symbolic act of belonging, if not owning, at the top of Dunadd: 'He removed his right boot, then the sock. He took a deep breath and fitted his bare foot into the imprint in the living rock, stood tall and stared out' (277). John Macnab's hunt for the Stone is an excuse for all members of the gang to leave home and meet in Scotland, but in no particular living place. If we are to try and find some offspring, we can only turn to young Eve sitting on the Stone: she is the only child from within the Macnab couples. Seating the prepubescent girl on the Stone reminds us of fertility rituals: she shall bear fruit.

However, we must observe that most couples in the novel are fruitless. Some are broken couples, like Leo and his wife who parted after the death of their daughter. Neil is a widower who can hardly recover from the death of his wife, even if Eve is his goddaughter. Eve's parents, Murray and Tricia, were about to part when Murray was nearly shot dead by Adamson's henchmen. They will not part eventually, but love has vanished. John MacIver is a widower who proposes to Ellen Stobo: they will leave for Canada and symbolically reactivate the special relationship between Scotland and Canada, but they will not start a family. Alasdair and Jane are a loving free couple with no known offspring. Shonagh, a lesbian, finds a partner, Ailsa Traquair, but no future as a couple is foretold for them. Ken and Isa appear briefly in the first part of the narrative – 'Kirsty walked with the long time happy couple Ken and Isa (apparently such do exist) down the High Street […]' (24) – only to serve as a foil to Kirsty's loneliness. Restless Kirsty, the wandering heroine – much like Adamson who is not surviving – highlights the fruitlessness of couples and pairs. The champion of freedom vaguely thinks of going to New Zealand with Leo, yet nothing is definite. Inga, the young Norwegian woman, is single; and there is a faint possibility of pairing off with Neil, or Leo. Greig shows couples with no clear commitment, and ambiguous or uncertain feelings.

*Romanno Bridge* shows, nonetheless, a large variety of couples and families, somehow mirroring the couples Walter Scott staged in his novels. Moreover, we can turn to John Arbuthnot's symbolic post-Union couple in his *History of John Bull* (1712) and ask how John Bull's sister, Peg, and Jack the Kirk can grow and multiply. The trio of John Bull, Peg and Jack serve to rouse polemics and arguably mirror several intimate relationships in Greig's novel. Surmising that all those Scottish characters correspond to as many facets of Scotland herself, we may, remembering that the time of the narrative is shortly before the referendum of 1997, wonder whether Scotland herself wants to be wedded, paired, or allowed to go free. The characters are adrift and the tone of the narrative in the concluding chapter, together with the epilogue, sounds dispirited.

We feel that the John Macnab gang are melancholy, as the story ends as we listen to Inga's song, the 'evolving Blues' (309):

> *I can hear the whistle*
> *But I can't see the train*
> *Deep inside my heart*
> *Burns an inverted flame*
> *Been a long time getting here*
> *Gonna be a long time gone.*

The betraying or self-sacrificing – it is hard to decide which – character of Dundas appears in the last part of the novel. Although he gives clues to Jim as to where the Stone lies, he emanates melancholy: '[Dundas] looked, Jim thought, like a grey setter in his refined gentleness, fine high cheekbones, the melancholy' (269). Throughout the narrative, Leo is tired, or beaten, or even sick, when being in a hospital reminds him of his daughter dying of leukaemia,

> Sleep-starved, half-concussed, he looks round the room now rancid with sweat, sorrow and fear. [...] None of us will be all right. Mountains, sunsets, good times, bad times, mates, children – nothing endures. Nothing. No exceptions. (249)

The whole of Chapter 32 produces a sour, sickly atmosphere. The story starts with the imminent death of Billie Mackie in a home and closes with Murray, the lively radical, lying in pain in hospital: 'For now Neil was forced to admit what they had all been denying, that for some time Murray's despair had run unvoiced and deep' (253). In between, even journeys through the Highlands fail to exhilarate: 'In the back seat Shonagh was humming as she watched the hills go by. *I've heard them lilting at the ewe-milking.* Laments, laments, is it all the Gaeltachd can do now?' (231). Greig keeps playing cheerless songs to highlight events: 'Mama died and left me restless, Papa died and left me wild ...' (191). The group of players end their concert with

'Night and day I weep and moan' (201). No doubt, such a show of pessimism will appeal to the French!

It is a prominent feature in the novel that all possible notes of optimism are continually toned down: 'Weaving up the B709 as it flirted with the White Esk through the heart of lonesome Ettrickdale in wintry first light, one might say they had a date with destiny. Which, however uncertain, beats having no further destiny at all' (225). However successful the John Macnab gang are, there is no final dramatic victory: they find the real Stone in a garden belonging to an Englishman, and they leave it there. The ending is symbolic – the Stone is no spoil to be exhibited like a stag's head, like 'MacPherson' in *The Return of John Macnab*.

## Afterword

Throughout the novel, the reader may wonder about Greig's choice of title. Why decide on Romanno Bridge, such an exotic place name among the many other villages visited by the characters? A possible answer may be found in what Shonagh thinks of Ailsa Traquair by the end of the narrative: 'She's straight from El Greco. Beautiful. Hasn't anyone noticed?' (302).

As already noted, the village of Romanno Bridge is situated on the route of Dere Street, the Roman road running from York to the east end of Antonine's Wall, via Corbridge. Yet, because of the reference to El Greco and even though they were not of the same generation within the Renaissance, the word "roman(n)o" cannot fail to remind one of Giulio Romano, a pseudonym, who painted the fresco of the *Battle of Milvian Bridge*. This can still be seen in the Vatican's Apostolic Palace and offers an interpretation of the battle of Pons Milvius where Constantine, although outnumbered, defeated Maxentius on 8 October 312, leading the Senate to make him an emperor. Giulio Romano also painted *The Donation of Constantine*, based on a decree allegedly attributed to emperor Constantine, shortly after he achieved power, establishing Pope Sylvester's religious authority over most of the empire. In this painting, we cannot fail to spot in the foreground, to the right, a character dressed differently from all the others: he is not taking part in the ceremony, but is looking at the viewer. This character, a young man most likely representing the artist, or his sponsor, is wearing what might today be mistaken for a kilt. Whether the decree is a fake matters little to us at this point. The emperor Constantine's name, however, reminds the reader that a namesake, Constantine II, who ruled the Kingdom of Alba from 900 to 943, met with Bishop Cellach at the Hill of Belief, near Scone, in 906 to establish the authority of the Church in his kingdom. Later he signed a charter on 13 September 934, at the court of the King of Wessex, alleged to acknowledge Æthelstan's overlordship.

Some four centuries later, Edward I managed to confiscate the coronation stone in 1296 in order to symbolise England's claimed supremacy over Scotland. However, contrary to Constantine II, Robert the Bruce definitely rejected English kings' claim to supremacy, particularly after the battle of Bannockburn in 1314. Further, doubts were rumoured about the authenticity of the stone lying at Westminster. Andrew Greig distils such facts, viewpoints and rumours into a fiction whose intention, according to Umberto Eco's phrase, is open to debate. It frees us to allow the ghosts of King Constantine, Bishop Cellach, Emperor Constantine, Pope Sylvester, Giulio Romano, and El Greco to loom in the background of Little Delphi and watch Eve seated on the Stone of Destiny.

## Notes

1    Umberto Eco, *Les limites de l'interprétation* (Paris: Bernard Grasset, 1990).

2    Julian M. D'Arcy, *Subversive Scott* (Reykjavik: University of Iceland Press, 2005), p. 28.

3    Andrew Greig, *Romanno Bridge* (London: Quercus, 2008). All the following references to the text are taken from the paperback edition and only the page will be indicated after the quotation.

4    Andrew Greig, *The Return of John Macnab* (London: Faber & Faber, 2002 [1996]). All references will be from the 2002 paperback. We may note that on the cover page, the title is followed by 'by the author of *That Summer*', which reminds us of the phrase 'by the author of *Waverley*'. Following the annual SAES Conference at Avignon in 2007, my paper entitled 'John Macnab et l'envers du décor dans *John Macnab* de J. Buchan et *The Return of John Macnab* d'Andrew Greig' was published in *Etudes Ecossaises* 12, 2009. *Etudes Ecossaises* is a publication by Ellug, Université de Grenoble III.

5    John Buchan, *John Macnab* (Harmondsworth: Penguin, 1956 [1925]). All references will be from the 1962 reprint of the 1956 Penguin edition.

6    Douglas Gifford, *Scottish Literature* (Edinburgh: Edinburgh University Press, 2002), p. 236.

7    Philippe Lejeune, *Le Pacte autobiographique* (Paris: Le Seuil, 1975).

8    The full text, edited by Jean Berton, was published by Presses Universitaires de Saint-Etienne, in 2007.

# 11: Investigating the body politic: dystopian visions of a new Scotland in Paul Johnston's Quintilian Dalrymple novels

### DAVID CLARK

Scottish literature has never, it might be said, been too big on the future. The past is usually glorious, the present miserable, but the future? In the few occasions it is shown, it is generally every bit as wretched, if not more so than the present. Dystopian fiction is, we could suggest, a perfectly valid literary format for modern Scotland in that it compresses the traditional pessimism often attributed to the Scottish character into a neat package where moral warnings and the pessimism generally perceived within the ethos of Calvinism are bound tightly together with an often witty and generally acerbic attack on the potential failings of political and social institutions.

The term 'dystopian' was first coined, incidentally, by John Stewart Mill, a London-born Scot. He preferred the term – from the Greek 'bad or negative place' – to that used by his friend and mentor, Jeremy Bentham, 'cacotopia', meaning 'the worst place'. In literary terms, however, the term dystopian has generally been preferred. It is used to refer to a type of narrative which reached its zenith in the interwar years of the twentieth century and moved comfortably from the generic confines of science fiction to the school textbook acceptance of works by the likes of Orwell and Huxley. Helga Nowotny, writing – quite aptly – in the year 1984, suggested that dystopia can be seen as a 'dysfunctional version of science and technology having fallen victim to the surplus of order and control that we have seen inherent in utopian thought',[1] and this explanation would seem to justify the claim made by Gordin, Tilly and Prakash that dystopia is 'utopia's twentieth-century doppelgänger',[2] though it could well be argued that James Hogg's *The Private Memoirs and Confessions of a Justified Sinner* can be seen as a forerunner of the Scottish form of this novel. Gordin et al. also insist that, in spite of its name, dystopia is not simply the opposite of utopia; this, they claim, would be a society that is 'either completely unplanned or is planned to be deliberately terrifying and awful'.[3] In short, they argue, dystopia is always 'a utopia that has gone wrong, or a utopia that functions only for a particular segment of society'.[4]

Dystopian fiction can generally be seen to contain a series of recurring tropes, some or all of which are present in all examples of the genre. In these narratives, for example, there is a habitual emphasis on the power of the state, and the coercive powers of this state in obliging citizens to follow the objectives of the ruling class. This ruling class is generally recruited from a political elite drawn out of a strict caste system from a hierarchical society. The state also generates negative feelings of hatred, fear, revulsion and disgust towards any country or form of social organisation outwith the dystopian state. The citizens within this state share a high level of conformity to the existing state of affairs, although this conformity is often brought about by means of some form of brainwashing or some type of ethically dubious form of education or re-education. This education of the citizens is supported by a strong use of police and legal machinery to invigilate, control and otherwise avoid any hint of activity which might be deemed subversive or contrary to the specified aims of the society in question. Imprisonment and all forms of physical and/or mental torture are used to prevent subversion. Lastly, citizens are encouraged to reveal any deviance from the accepted social norms that may be undertaken by their peers and fellow citizens.

The dystopian state, in such narratives, generally reinvents or embellishes its own history, especially with regard to supposed foundational myths and the perceived 'duty' of the dystopian government in righting the alleged wrongs of a pre-dystopian past. In this, it is believed, corruption and or moral laxity had been responsible for bringing the state to a condition of collapse or emergency. Thus, the ruling elite in dystopian fiction inevitably sees itself as being a saviour of sorts, and this role is believed to have been forced onto the governing class by the misgovernment of a past regime or a past political or social system. The new regime generally rejects and/or despises earlier traditions or values and, in many examples of this type of literature, exalts new technological advances which also help the new state to function. Finally, but of great importance to the dystopian fiction, are the figures of hero and anti-hero which typically arise from the narrative. While the latter is generally a charismatic leader who generates a personality cult, the hero is usually the protagonist of the fiction, a non-conformer who questions and opposes the values and activities of the dystopian society.[5]

Not all of these elements are always featured, but many of them regularly appear in dystopian novels. The dystopian narrative is largely a twentieth-century invention, although a number of older texts, including, for example, parts of *Gulliver's Travels*, can be seen as proto-dystopian in their approach. It is, however, perhaps important to place the dystopian novel within the framework of post-religious secularity. Dystopian fiction is, according to Erika Gottlieb, 'a post-Christian genre'[6] and as such has become the central form of drama of our modern secular age in which 'salvation is represented by a just society governed by worthy representatives chosen by an enlightened people'. There, damnation is represented by 'an unjust society, a degraded mob led by a power-crazed elite'.[7] Although the concepts of Heaven and Hell still exist in dystopian fiction, these are translated into secular terms. Thus, in a society in which religion ceases to hold the significance it once had, dystopian narrative models exist as a means of objectifying human fears and dreads, transforming actual models of social organisation into horrifying nightmares. Dystopian fiction is regularly used for the effect of political satire – at least as one of its principal aims – and it is important to remember that

> each dystopian society contains within it seeds of a utopian dream [which is generally] articulated by the ruling elite's original promise when its new system was implemented, a promise which is always either 'miscarried', 'betrayed' or 'fulfilled in ways that show up the unexpected shortcomings of the dream'.[8]

Western dystopian fiction reached its high point between the two world wars when the political systems of fascism and Stalinism were perceived as potential threats to the western liberal democracies. Aldous Huxley's *Brave New World* (1932) and George Orwell's later *Nineteen Eighty-Four* (1949) represent the two best known and most studied examples of the genre. Interestingly, perhaps, Eric Blair, writing under his pen-name of George Orwell, wrote his dystopian masterpiece on the Isle of Jura in Scotland 'having moved there to escape the sudden, blistering fame that followed the publication of *Animal Farm*', an anecdote which for Scottish crime writer Denise Mina 'somehow makes it a Scottish book'.[9] *Nineteen Eighty-Four* is considered by Keith Booker to be 'one of the central defining texts of the genre of dystopian fiction, dealing in important ways with almost all of the central motifs associated with the genre'[10] and by Erika Gottlieb as 'the prototype of the genre'.[11] Neil M. Gunn's much underrated *The Green Isle of the Great Deep* (1944) is probably the great Scottish example of the dystopian model, juxtaposing as it does Gunn's appreciation of what he believed to be the core values of the traditional Highland community with those of imported totalitarianism.[12]

Paul Johnston, therefore, when he came to write his 'Quintilian Dalrymple' novels, had some sort of Scottish precedent for his work. The novels, published between 1997 and 2001, appeared at a moment of rare and stimulating self-confidence in Scotland, in a period in which a large amount of good quality popular crime novels, set in Scotland and with Scottish affairs in their centre, were being published. That this rise in self-confident popular fiction should coincide with the reopening of the Parliament was not, of course, coincidental, and the political situation of the period is covertly or overtly present in many novels of the period. Paul Johnston's five dystopian novels set in the Edinburgh of the 2020s are no exception, and represent fine examples of political satire based on the Edinburgh of the immediate pre- and post-devolution period.

The novels, *Body Politic* (1997), *The Bone Yard* (1998), *Water of Death* (1999), *The Blood Tree* (2000) and *House of Dust* (2001), are set in a post-devolution Edinburgh. After the failure of the devolution project in the early twenty-first century, a series of drug wars help bring about the disintegration of the United Kingdom. The state is divided into a number of city-states with little or no communication between one other, each being divided from other city-states by no-go areas of violent anarchy. Edinburgh has been saved by a totalitarian political group, the 'Enlightenment' party, which attempts to impose its own ethical codes on the city. These codes, flawed interpretations of eighteenth-century Enlightenment thought, are coyly familiar as a kind of political interpretation of Edinburgh's perceived moral hypocrisy, and as such the New Edinburgh is largely revealed as an exaggerated version of the city in the 1990s.

The city is run by a group of Enlightenment party officials, the 'Council of City Guardians', who act as the political elite, while policing is undertaken by the 'auxiliaries', the 'eyes and ears' (*BP*, 29) of the state, which is completed by the long-suffering 'citizens'. The Guardians have become corrupt over the years, and the city has been cut off from the rest of the world with the exception of a strong but declining tourist industry, the only means of income the city has. Citizens are controlled by the state in a number of ways. Marital relationships, for example, are discouraged, and citizens are obliged to engage in anonymous weekly sex sessions with other citizens. A curfew is enforced, and cars, cigarettes, popular entertainment – television, film, and so on – are banned. The obsession with American blues music, also banned by the Council, is shared by numerous key characters, and provides a musical soundtrack to the series. Coal is once again the main fuel, and the buildings of the city have reverted to the dark-hued smoke-stained image that gave Edinburgh the name of 'Auld Reekie'. The original ideals of the Guardians have long been abandoned as the city-state has sunk into moral and political decay, with gangs of disenchanted youths wandering the streets and corrupt officials reaping the few material benefits available. All items of luxury – which in this dystopian Edinburgh include water for a shower – are reserved for the money-generating tourists and the higher echelons of the enforced social scale.

The novels' main protagonist is Quintilian – 'Quint' – Dalrymple. The son of two founding members of the Enlightenment party, Quint was initially a sharp-witted auxiliary who was demoted and forced to find employment as a private detective, although he is constantly sought by the Council to help solve the various murders taking place in the degenerate city-state. Johnston admits that, with the figure of Quint, the writer 'wanted him to symbolize the individual standing up to faceless bureaucracy'.[13] The growth of dissidents to the regime worries the ruling elite, and Quint, 'Edinburgh's knight in a shiny donkey jacket' (*HD*, 84), is often caught in the political crossfire generated by dissident activity. 'In the perfect city', it appears, 'the only way to express free will was to commit murder' (*BP*, 332).

The Enlightenment has, we are told, provided 'stability, work and housing for everybody' (*BP*, 6), but citizens have no freedom. Photographs are controlled – and first name usage has been replaced by the use of numbers, in an attempt to 'get rid of the cult of the individual which had supposedly destroyed the United Kingdom's social fabric in the years around the millennium' (*BY*, 257). The decrepit state of Edinburgh is symbolised by the Scott

Monument, now renamed the Enlightenment Monument, whose broken spire 'rose up into the darkness, like a vandalized roadsign pointing to a utopia that no one believes in any more' (*BY*, 268).

If we examine the elements which we have above suggested are the essential features of dystopian narrative, based on the ideas of critics like Baccolini and Moylan, Booker, Gordin, Gottlieb, Jameson, Seed and Sion, we can see that these can easily be applied to the Quint Dalrymple series. The first of these is the existence of a strong caste system, artificially strengthened by the ruling class. Johnston's Edinburgh is just such a system, with a ruling elite which, 'in its relentless search for the utopian state' (*BY*, 171), has created a hierarchy in which the ordinary citizens are at the lowest rung of the ladder and all production is geared towards the smooth operation of the tourist industry. Secondly, citizens are coerced into following the aims of the ruling class by an educational system which promotes only the false benefits of the system and conformity and acceptance of the status quo through a number of communal activities culminating in the cult around the state lottery. Signs of individuality are, as we have seen, actively persecuted and, in caustic criticism of linguistic manipulation, citizens are actively discouraged from using 'the local accents that the Council proscribed years ago' (*BT*, 11): the first Council had 'banned all dialects and accents in an attempt to do away with socially divisive factors' (*BT*, 77).

The hatred and fear of the world outside the dystopian city-state of Edinburgh is apparent throughout the five novels in the series. Although the area that inspires greatest degrees of fear and disgust is the wasteland immediately surrounding the city, infested with drug dealers and dissidents, other states are also hated. England is regarded as 'a wasteland harbouring hundreds of drug gangs in search of new markets', while 'democratic' Glasgow, which sees itself as a 'thriving modern state, not a decrepit tourist trap like Edinburgh' (*BT*, 99), is considered to be degenerate, dangerous and uncouth. New Oxford, the most 'advanced' English city-state, which features in the fifth and final volume of the series, is basically a penal state in which terror and technology convert the lives of ordinary citizens into a horror which surpasses even that of Edinburgh. In 'its relentless search for the utopian state' the Council has tried to 'appeal to people's desire for knowledge and self-advancement, but all it's ended up doing is pandering to their animal appetites' (*BY*, 171); it had only achieved turning people into 'even more self-reliant, emotionally illiterate citizens' (*BY*, 257). In both Edinburgh and New Oxford, forms of brainwashing and 're-education' are used liberally, while the police and penal services of both states take up a vast proportion of the annual budget. Edinburgh's initial contact with New Oxford comes when the former contracts a vast new penal complex from the latter, and the half-robotic 'Grendels' provide a frightening development from Edinburgh's 'auxiliaries' corps.

Dystopian states within dystopian narratives are generally brought about by traumatic events, sometimes relating to natural catastrophes, but, more often than not, these events are perceived to have been 'forced onto' the ruling class by catastrophic and devastating past political events. These often relate to prior misgovernment within a previous social/political system. This is the case in Johnston's novels, in which the break-up of the old UK is linked to the rioting which followed the coronation of the last Crown Prince in 2002, engaged to a Colombian drug heiress. The problems were not restricted to the UK. France, for example, had been reduced 'to a collection of bankrupt city-states by Muslim fundamentalists' (*BP*, 286). Following the failure of a devolved Scottish government, Edinburgh had become an independent city-state. The notion of a nation called 'Scotland' seems to have been lost, and even the seemingly nationalist Macbeth cult which seeks the reunification of Scotland 'using the example of Macbeth as a talisman, an inspiration, a destiny' (*BT*, 256) is in fact just a cover for a genetic engineering scam. Baccolini and Moylan note that language is 'a key weapon for the reigning dystopian power structure',[14] and it is interesting to note that the language spoken by the characters is standard English, as both Scots and Gaelic have been oppressed by the Council. Although Dalrymple praises Ian Rankin's *Black and Blue* as 'a state of the nation novel, no less' (*WD*, 34), in the dystopian world of these novels the concept of Scotland as a nation no longer exists.

Enlightenment Edinburgh is officially an atheist state, although religion is 'tolerated' (*BP*, 79). As in many examples of the genre, traditional religions are replaced by a cult focused on the ruling powers. Interestingly, however, in Johnston's novels of dystopian Edinburgh, the cult of the individual leader is all but absent. Collective responsibility is shared by the senior members of the Council, and when an individual Council member appears to be becoming too powerful, the system (or murder) steps in to return things to the relative anonymity of Council rule.

In the early novels advanced technology plays a relatively small part in the workings of the dystopian state. Indeed, Johnston's Edinburgh is initially Luddite in its rejection of technological innovation. Nuclear power has been abandoned after the loss of the nuclear power station at Torness, and coal is once again the main source of fuel. Computers are rejected as being 'socially divisive and educationally sterile' (*BY*, 151). In the last two novels of the series, however, technology is applied to consolidate the weakening grip of the Council on control of the city. Scotland's history of genetic engineering – most notably, the cloning of Dolly the sheep – is exploited to bring about the cloning of human beings in *The Blood Tree*, and the technological advances of New Oxford are one of the main reasons why the Council is captivated by the English city-state.

At the centre of the novels, of course, is Quint Dalrymple, an archetypal nonconformist hero of the kind common in dystopian fiction. Although echoing many of the characteristics of the American 'hard-boiled' private detective figure, Quint's intricate relationship with the power structures of Enlightenment Edinburgh gives him the opportunity to act as a filter through which the reader can perceive the corrupt practices of the system. Quint's mother and father were both leading Enlightenment intellectuals, and their fall into corruption, on the part of the mother, and sad, resigned cynicism, on the part of the father, echo the fall into degeneration of the Enlightenment regime. Alongside his murder investigations, his love affairs – with Caro (like him, an eager young auxiliary who quickly becomes disillusioned with the Enlightenment), Sofia (the 'Ice Queen' and Medical – and one-time Senior – Guardian) and Katherine (the bitter dissident) – provide a background for Johnston's artistic creation of a future Edinburgh. Through this, he can criticise the Scotland of the turn of the millennium.

Johnston can do so because, of course, his novels are more than simply entertaining crime novels set in the near future; they are political satires which depict a Scotland that might be. Gottlieb insists on the importance of recognising the existence of two time frames within all dystopian fiction. Although set in an implied future, dystopian novels must constantly refer to a 'present time', shared ideally by author and reader. For Gottlieb, these two time planes are 'inherent in the structure of the genre',[15] and it is central to the effect of this type of fiction that the reader recognises that the protagonist's fate is 'in the conditional mood'.[16] That is to say, the future portrayed is a possible future and the characters who interact are possible characters, whose existence is conditioned upon a series of undesirable changes taking place. For this reason, dystopian fiction has very much the character of the cautionary tale in which the writer warns the reader that, given the predominance of a series of undesirable factors, unless certain behavioural patterns are corrected, the future could resemble the objectionable future as shown in the novel.

As such, dystopian fiction tends to reveal a version of the present that contains exaggerated features of that present. Again, in Gottlieb's words, 'it is crucial not only that we identify the difference between his time and ours but also that we recognize that these two time-planes are joined in a cause-effect relationship'.[17] Thus, the vision of the UK, of Scotland and of Edinburgh in Paul Johnston's Quintilian Dalrymple novels is rooted as much in a sense of guilt and trepidation about the past as in a sense of uncertainty about the future.

## Notes

1   Everett Mendelsohn and Helga Nowotny (eds), *Nineteen Eighty-Four: Science between Utopia and Dystopia. Sociology of the Sciences: A Yearbook, Vol. VIII* (Dordrecht, Netherlands: Kluwer, 1984), p. 15.

2   Michael Gordin, Helen Tilly and Gyan Prakash (eds), *Utopia/Dystopia: Conditions of Historical Possibility* (Princeton, NJ: Princeton University Press, 2010), p. 1.

3   Ibid.

4   Ibid.

5   Raffaella Baccolini and Tom Moylan (eds), *Dark Horizons: Science Fiction and the Dystopian Imagination* (London: Routledge, 2003), pp. 3–11; Michael Gordin, Helen Tilly and Gyan Prakash (eds) *Utopia/Dystopia: Conditions of Historical Possibility* (Princeton, NJ: Princeton University Press, 2010), pp. 1–17; Frederic Jameson, 'Utopia as Method: or the Uses of the Future', in Gordin, Tilly and Prakash (eds), pp. 21–43; David Seed, 'Cyberpunk and Dystopia: Pat Cadigan's Networks', in Baccolini and Moylan (eds), pp. 69–90; Ronald T. Sion, *Aldous Huxley and a Search for Meaning: A Study of the Eleven Novels* (Jefferson, CL: McFarland, 2009), pp. 125–68.

6   Erika Gottlieb, *Dystopian Fiction East and West: Universe of Terror and Trial* (Quebec: McGill-Queen's University Press, 2001), p. 3.

7   Ibid., p. 3.

8   Ibid., p. 8.

9   Willy Maley and Brian Donaldson, *100 Best Scottish Books of All Time* (Edinburgh: Scottish Book Trust, 2005), p. 36.

10  M. Keith Booker, *The Dystopian Impulse in Modern Literature: Fiction as Social Criticism* (Westport, CT: Greenwood Press, 1994), p. 208.

11  Erika Gottlieb, *The Orwell Conundrum: A Cry of Despair or Faith in the 'Spirit of Man?'* (Don Mills, Ontario: Carleton University Press, 1992), p. 4.

12  David M. Clark, 'Caledonian Dystopia: *The Green Island of the Great Deep*', *Grove: Working papers on English Studies* 7 (2000), pp. 33–52, 34.

13  Paul Johnson: www.paul-johnston.co.uk/pages/books/body_politic/body_politic_authors_introduction.htm, 2012, n.p., accessed 12 September 2012.

14  Baccolini and Moylan (eds), p. 5.

15  Erika Gottlieb, *Dystopian Fiction East and West*, p. 15.

16  Ibid.

17  Ibid.

# Notes on contributors

**Jean Berton** is currently professor at Toulouse II University and vice-president of the French Society for Scottish Studies. Most of his research has been on the literature of Scotland from Sir Walter Scott to post-devolution days. He is now working on the indigenous languages of modern Scotland to highlight the role of plurilingual literature.

**Ian Brown** is a playwright, poet, Professor of Drama at Kingston University and visiting professor (Honorary Senior Research Fellow) in Scottish Literature at Glasgow University. He has published widely on aspects of cultural policy and on Scottish culture, literature and theatre, most recently *Scottish Theatre: Diversity, Language, Continuity* (2013).

**David Clark** is Senior Lecturer in English Studies at the University of A Coruña, Galicia, Spain. He has held executive positions in both national and international Associations for Irish Studies and has published widely on contemporary Irish and Scottish writing.

**Karyn Wilson Costa** teaches English in France at the Lycée Thiers in Marseilles, and Aix-Marseille Université in Aix-en-Provence. She has published various articles on the reception and the cultural legacy of Robert Burns. Her book *Robert Burns: le poète et ses doubles* is due to be published in 2014.

**Philippe Laplace** lectures in English at the Université de Franche-Comté (Besançon). He wrote *Les Hautes-Terres, l'histoire et la mémoire dans les romans de Gunn* (2006) and co-edited *Cities on the Margin; On the Margin of Cities: Representation of Urban Space in Contemporary Irish and British Fiction* (2003) and *The Irish Celebrating: Festive and Tragic Overtones* (2008).

**Scott Lyall** is Lecturer in Modern Literature and Programme Leader for English at Edinburgh Napier University. He is author of *Hugh MacDiarmid's Poetry and Politics of Place* (2006), co-editor with Margery Palmer McCulloch of *The Edinburgh Companion to Hugh MacDiarmid* (2011) and editor of forthcoming volumes on Lewis Grassic Gibbon and Community in Modern Scottish Literature.

**Margery Palmer McCulloch**'s books include *Modernism and Nationalism* (2004), *Scottish Modernism and its Contexts* (2009), and, as co-editor, *The Edinburgh Companion to Hugh MacDiarmid* and *Scottish and International Modernisms* (both 2011). She is Leverhulme Emerita Fellow at Glasgow University, researching Edwin and Willa Muir and their Scottish and International contexts.

**Camille Manfredi** lectures in Scottish Studies at the University of Brest, France, where she teaches Scottish literature and history. Published widely in English and French in the areas of Scottish contemporary literature and visual arts, her works include a monograph, *Alasdair Gray: Le Faiseur d'Ecosse* (2012).

**Morag J. Munro-Landi** is Senior Lecturer in British Studies in the Applied Modern Languages Department of the University of Pau, France. Her research has included her doctoral thesis, and articles on the novels of Neil M. Gunn and, more recently, special focus on the novels of James Robertson.

**Matthew Pateman** is Head of Humanities at Sheffield Hallam University. He has published widely on literature, philosophy, film and television.

**Trish Reid** is Associate Professor and Director of Learning and Teaching in the School of Performance and Screen Studies at Kingston University. Author of *Theatre & Scotland* (2013) and many chapters and articles on contemporary Scottish theatre, she is currently working on a longer monograph for Palgrave and a critical companion to Anthony Neilson for Methuen.

Lightning Source UK Ltd.
Milton Keynes UK
UKOW07f2111191114

241836UK00008B/196/P